Dictionary of Gastronomy

For the translation and explanation of menus in five languages

Elisabeth Neiger

2nd Edition

Book Number 05433

Author:
Elisabeth Neiger, 39100 Bozen (Italy)

in collaboration with:
Ada Neiger, 39100 Bozen (Italy)

2nd Edition 2006

Impression 5 4 3 2 1

ISBN-10 3-8057-0543-3
ISBN-13 978-3-8057-0543-1

All rights reserved. This book is protected by copyright. Any commercial use beyond the legally specified uses requires written approval from the publisher.

© 2006 by Fachbuchverlag Pfanneberg GmbH & Co. KG, 42781 Haan
http://www.pfanneberg.de
Typesetting: Goar Engeländer, 33175 Bad Lippspringe
Print: Media-Print Informationstechnologie GmbH, 33100 Paderborn

FOREWORD

The increased demand for this booklet has called for an English edition, which is still available in the handy pocket-book format.

The booklet is of inestimable help for anybody in the catering business who has to make out menus. Furthermore, it offers a choice of tasty and widely-known dishes. With tourism becoming increasingly international, this booklet can also help foreign guests. Finally, it might also be of use to teachers in catering schools.

The editor would appreciate any suggestions as to how the book might be improved.

The editor, summer 2006

Abbreviations:

m = masculine	n = neuter	m. = mit	w. = with	Am. = American
f = feminine	pl = plural	u. = und	& = and	Vd. = usted

CONTENTS

Sauces 7	Vegetables 92	Non-alcoholic drinks 151
Butters 16	Potatoes 103	Breakfast 154
Hors-d'œvres 18	Farinaceous dishes 108	Culinary and service terms 159
Soups 27	Salads 112	Glossary and historical comments 192
Eggs 36	Cheese 116	
Fish and shell-fish . 40	Sweets & ice-creams 118	Appendix:
Meat 56	Fruit 136	
Meat dishes 57	Bread and pizzas 141	Dishes prepared at the guest's table 199
Poultry 77	Spices & condiments 144	Glossary of drinks 205
Game 84	Alcoholic drinks 147	Cocktails 207

Sauces

Sauces English	Saucen German	Sauces French	Salse Italian	Salsas Spanish
aïoli sauce (garlic mayonnaise)	Aïoli-Sauce (Knoblauch-Mayonnaise)	sauce aïoli[1] (mayonnaise au coulis d'ail)	salsa aioli (maionese all'aglio)	salsa alioli (mayonesa al ajo)
anchovy sauce	Sardellensauce	~ aux anchois	~ d'acciughe	~ de anchoas
Andalusian sauce (tomato-based mayonnaise)	Andalusische Sauce (tomatierte Mayonnaise)	~ andalouse (mayonnaise à la tomate)	~ andalusa (maionese al pomodoro)	~ andaluza (mayonesa al tomate)
apple sauce	Apfelmus	purée de pommes	~ di mele	~ de manzanas
béarnaise sauce (hollandaise sauce with tarragon)	Bérner Sauce; Sauce Béarnaise (Hollandaise mit Estragon)	sauce béarnaise (sauce hollandaise à l'estragon)	~ bearnese (salsa olandese al dragoncello)	~ bearnesa (salsa holandesa con estragón)
béchamel sauce[2]	Béchamelsauce	~ béchamel	~ besciamella	~ bechamel; ~ besamela
beer sauce	Biersauce	~ à la bière	~ alla birra	~ de cerveza
beetroot sauce	Rote-Bete-Sauce	~ de betterave	~ di barbabietole	~ de remolacha
Bercy sauce (butter, shallots, white wine)	Bercy-Sauce (Butter, Schalotten, Weißwein)	~ Bercy (beurre, échalotes, vin blanc)	~ Bercy (scalogno, burro e vino bianco)	~ Bercy (mantequilla, vino blanco, escaloñas)
bigarade sauce (flavoured with bitter oranges)	Bigarade-Sauce (mit Saft von Bitterorangen)	~ bigarade (avec oranges amères)	~ bigarade (a base di arance amare)	~ bigarade (salsa de naranjas amargas)
bordelaise sauce (wine sauce with beef marrow)	Sauce Bordelaise (Weinsauce mit Rindermark)	~ bordelaise (sauce au vin avec moelle de bœuf)	~ bordolese (salsa di vino con midollo di bue)	~ bordelesa (salsa de vino con tuétano)
brandy sauce	Weinbrandsauce	~ à l'eau de vie	~ al brandy	~ de aguardiente
bread sauce	Brotsauce	~ au pain	~ di pane	~ de pan
brown sauce	Braune Sauce	~ brune; ~ espagnole	~ bruna	~ española
Burgundy sauce (red wine sauce)	Burgunder Sauce (Rotweinsauce)	~ bourguignonne (sauce au vin rouge)	~ alla borgognona (salsa di vino rosso)	~ borgoñona (salsa de vino tinto)
butter sauce	Buttersauce	~ au beurre	~ al burro	~ de mantequilla
caper sauce	Kapernsauce	~ aux câpres	~ di capperi	~ de alcaparras
cardinal sauce (béchamel & lobster butter)	Kardinalsauce (Béchamel u. Hummerbutter)	~ cardinal (béchamel et beurre de homard)	~ cardinale (besciamella e burro d'astice)	~ cardenal (bechamel y mantequilla de langosta)
carrot sauce	Möhrensauce	~ aux carottes	~ di carote	~ de zanahorias

---

1) ou sauce ailloli - 2) also white sauce

Sauces

Sauces English	Saucen German	Sauces French	Salse Italian	Salsas Spanish
caviar sauce	Kaviarsauce	sauce au caviar	salsa al caviale	salsa de caviar
champagne sauce	Champagnersauce	~ au champagne	~ allo champagne	~ de champán
Champignon sauce	Champignonsauce	~ aux champignons de Paris	~ di champignon	~ de champiñones
chanterelle sauce	Pfifferlingsauce	~ aux girolles	~ di finferli	~ de rebozuelos
Chantilly sauce	Chantilly-Sauce	~ Chantilly	~ Chantilly	~ Chantilly
Chateaubriand sauce (meat glaze enriched with butter & parsley)	Chateaubriand-Sauce (Fleischglace, Butter, Petersilie)	~ Chateaubriand (glace de viande beurrée et petersillée)	~ Chateaubriand (gelatina di carne, burro e prezzemolo)	~ Chateaubriand (glasa de carne, mantequilla y perejil)
cheese sauce; Mornay sauce	Käsesauce; Mornaysauce (Béchamel mit Käse)	~ Mornay (béchamel au fromage)	~ Mornay (besciamella al formaggio)	~ Mornay (bechamel con queso)
chilli sauce	Chilisauce	~ au piment rouge	~ al peperoncino	~ de chile
chive sauce	Schnittlauchsauce	~ ciboulette	~ all'erba cipollina	~ de cebollino
Choron sauce (Béarnaise sauce with tomato purée)	Choron-Sauce (Sauce Béarnaise mit Tomatenmark)	~ Choron (sauce béarnaise tomatée)	~ Choron (salsa bearnese al pomodoro)	~ Choron (salsa bearnesa con tomate)
coconut sauce	Kokossauce	~ à la noix de coco	~ al cocco	~ de coco
Colbert sauce (maître d'hôtel butter blended with meat jelly)	Colbert-Sauce (Kräuterbutter mit Fleischsülze vermischt)	~ Colbert (beurre maître d'hôtel additionné de gelée de viande)	~ Colbert (burro maître d'hôtel con aggiunta di gelatina di carne)	~ Colbert (mantequilla maître d'hôtel con gelatina de carne)
coriander sauce	Koriandersauce	~ à la coriandre	~ al coriandolo	~ de cilantro
cranberry sauce	Preiselbeersauce	~ aux airelles	~ di mirtilli rossi	~ de arándanos
crayfish sauce	Krebssauce	~ aux écrevisses	~ di gamberi	~ de cangrejos
cream sauce	Sahnesauce; Rahmsauce	~ à la crème	~ alla panna; ~ alla crema	~ de crema
creole sauce	Kreolensauce	~ créole	~ creola	~ criolla
cucumber sauce	Gurkensauce	~ aux concombres	~ al cetriolo	~ de pepino

Sauces

Sauces English	**Saucen** German	**Sauces** French	**Salse** Italian	**Salsas** Spanish
Cumberland sauce (redcurrant jelly, mustard, orange juice and port)	Cumberlandsauce (Johannisbeergelee, Senf, Orangensaft, Portwein)	sauce Cumberland (gelée de groseilles, moutarde, jus d'orange, porto)	salsa Cumberland (gelatina di ribes, senape, succo d'arancia, porto)	salsa Cumberland (jalea de grosellas, mostaza, zumo de naranja, oporto)
curry sauce	indische Sauce; Currysauce	~ à l'indienne; ~ au curry	~ indiana; ~ al curry	~ india; ~ al curry
deviled sauce (demi-glace, white wine or vinegar, cayenne)	Teufelssauce (Demiglace, Weißwein oder Essig, Cayennepfeffer)	~ diable (demi-glace, vin blanc ou vinaigre, poivre de Cayenne)	~ alla diavola (demi-glace, aceto o vino bianco, pepe di Caienna)	~ a la diabla (salsa española con vinagre y pimienta de Cayena)
dill sauce	Dillsauce	~ à l'aneth	~ all'aneto	~ de eneldo
egg sauce	Eiersauce	~ aux œufs	~ d'uovo	~ de huevos
elderberry sauce	Holundersauce	~ au sureau	~ al sambuco	~ de saúco
fennel sauce	Fenchelsauce	~ au fenouil	~ al finocchio	~ de hinojo
fish sauce	Fischsauce	~ de poisson	~ di pesce	~ de pescado
garlic mayonnaise	Knoblauchmayonnaise	~ aïoli	maionese all'aglio	mayonesa al ajo
~ sauce	Knoblauchsauce	~ à l'ail	salsa all'aglio	salsa de ajo
genevoise sauce (red wine sauce with anchovy butter)	Genfer Sauce[1] (Rotwein mit Sardellenbutter)	~ genevoise (vin rouge et beurre d'anchois)	~ alla ginevrina (vino rosso con burro d'acciughe)	~ ginebrina (salsa de pescado, vino tinto, mantequilla de anchoas)
gentian sauce	Enziansauce	~ à la gentiane	~ alla genziana	~ de genciana
ginger sauce	Ingwersauce	~ au gingembre	~ allo zenzero	~ de jengibre
gooseberry sauce	Stachelbeersauce	~ aux groseilles à maquereau	~ di uva spina	~ de uva espina
green mayonnaise (with purée of herbs)	grüne Mayonnaise (mit Kräuterpüree)	mayonnaise verte (mayonnaise à la purée d'herbes)	maionese verde (con passato di erbe)	mayonesa verde (mayonesa con puré de hierbas)
~ sauce	~ Sauce	sauce verte	salsa verde	salsa verde
gribiche sauce (tartare sauce with capers)	Gribiche-Sauce (Tatarensauce mit Kapern)	~ gribiche (sauce tartare aux câpres)	~ gribiche (salsa tartara con capperi)	~ gribiche (salsa tártara con alcaparras)
herb sauce	Kräutersauce	~ aux herbes	~ alle erbe	~ de hierbas

[1] von Carême einst „génoise" (genuesische) genannt

Sauces

Sauces English	**Saucen** German	**Sauces** French	**Salse** Italian	**Salsas** Spanish
hollandaise sauce (yolks of egg, melted butter, lemon juice)	Hollandaise (Eigelb, geschmolzene Butter, Zitronensaft); holländische Sauce	sauce hollandaise (émulsion de beurre et de jaunes d'œufs, jus de citron)	salsa olandese (tuorli d'uovo, burro fuso, succo di limone)	salsa holandesa (yemas de huevo, mantequilla fundida, zumo de limón)
horseradish sauce	Meerrettichsauce	~ au raifort	~ di rafano	~ de rábano picante
Joinville sauce (fish sauce with shrimp butter)	Joinville-Sauce (Fischsauce mit Garnelenbutter)	~ Joinville (sauce de poisson avec beurre de crevettes)	~ Joinville (salsa di pesce con burro di gamberetti)	~ Joinville (salsa de pescado con mantequilla de cangrejos)
juniper berry sauce	Wacholdersauce	~ au genièvre	~ al ginepro	~ de enebro
leek sauce	Lauchsauce	~ aux poireaux	~ di porri	~ de puerros
lemon sauce	Zitronensauce	~ au citron	~ al limone	~ de limón
lemongrass sauce	Zitronengrassauce	~ à la citronnelle	~ di citronella	~ de citronela
lime sauce	Limettensauce	~ au citron vert	~ alla limetta	~ de lima
lobster sauce	Hummersauce	~ homard	~ d'astice	~ de langosta
lyonnaise sauce (onion sauce)	Lyoner Sauce (Zwiebelsauce)	~ lyonnaise (sauce à l'oignon)	~ lionese (salsa di cipolle)	~ lionesa (salsa de cebollas)
madeira sauce	Madeirasauce	~ madère	~ al madera	~ madera
maître d'hôtel sauce (butter, parsley and lemon juice)	Maître d'hôtel-Sauce (Butter, Petersilie und Zitronensaft)	~ maître d'hôtel (beurre, persil et jus de citron)	~ alla maître d'hôtel (burro, prezzemolo, succo di limone)	~ mayordoma (mantequilla, perejil, zumo de limón)
maltese sauce (hollandaise with orange juice)	Malteser Sauce (Hollandaise mit Orangensaft)	~ maltaise (sauce hollandaise à l'orange)	~ maltese (salsa olandese con succo di arancia sanguinella)	~ maltesa (salsa holandesa a la naranja)
marrow sauce	Marksauce	~ moelle	~ al midollo	~ de tuétano
matelote sauce	Matrosensauce	~ matelote	~ alla marinara	~ marinera
mayonnaise	Mayonnaise	~ mayonnaise	~ maionese	~ mayonesa; ~ mahonesa
mint sauce	Minzsauce	~ menthe	~ di menta	~ de menta
morel sauce	Morchelsauce	~ aux morilles	~ di spugnole	~ de colmenillas

Sauces

Sauces English	Saucen German	Sauces French	Salse Italian	Salsas Spanish
Mornay sauce; cheese sauce	Käsesauce; Mornaysauce (Béchamel mit Käse)	sauce Mornay (béchamel au fromage)	salsa Mornay (besciamella al formaggio)	salsa Mornay (bechamel con queso)
mousseline sauce (Hollandaise sauce with whipped cream)	Mousseline-Sauce (Hollandaise mit geschlagener Sahne)	~ mousseline (sauce hollandaise additionnée de créme fouettée)	~ mousseline (salsa olandese mescolata con panna montata)	~ muselina (salsa holandesa adicionada de nata batida)
mushroom sauce	Pilzsauce	~ aux champignons	~ di funghi	~ de setas
mustard sauce	Senfsauce	~ moutarde	~ di senape	~ de mostaza
Nantua sauce (béchamel with crayfish butter)	Nantua-Sauce (Béchamel mit Krebsbutter)	~ Nantua (béchamel et beurre d'écrevisses)	~ Nantua (besciamella e burro di gamberi)	~ Nantua (bechamel y mantequilla de cangrejos)
nut sauce; walnut sauce	Walnusssauce	~ aux noix	~ di noci	~ de nueces
onion sauce	Zwiebelsauce	~ à l'oignon	~ di cipolle	~ de cebolla
orange sauce	Orangensauce	~ à l'orange	~ all'arancia	~ de naranja
oyster sauce	Austernsauce	~ aux huîtres	~ di ostriche	~ de ostras
paprika sauce; sweet pepper sauce	Paprikasauce	~ au paprika; ~ aux poivrons	~ alla paprica; ~ di peperoni	~ de paprika; ~ de pimientos
parsley sauce	Petersiliensauce	~ persil	~ al prezzemolo	~ de perejil
peanut sauce	Erdnusssauce	~ aux cacahuètes	~ di arachidi	~ de cacahuetes
pepper sauce; poivrade sauce (with vinegar & pepper)	Pfeffersauce (mit Essig und Pfefferkörnern)	~ poivrade (avec vinaigre et poivre)	~ poivrade (con aceto e pepe); ~ al pepe	~ poivrade (con vinagre y pimienta); ~ de pimienta
pesto sauce (basil paste in olive oil)	Pesto-Sauce (Basilikumpaste in Olivenöl)	~ au pistou (basilic pilé à l'huile d'olive)	~ al pesto (pesto di basilico intriso d'olio)	~ de pesto (pasta de albahaca en aceite de oliva)
pine nut sauce	Pinienkernsauce	~ aux pignons	~ di pinoli	~ de piñones
piquant sauce (with vinegar, gherkins, parsley)	pikante Sauce (mit Essig, Petersilie, Essiggurken)	~ piquante (avec vinaigre, cornichons, persil)	~ piccante (con aceto, cetriolini, prezzemolo)	~ picante (con vinagre, pepinillos, perejil)
poivrade sauce (with vinegar & pepper); pepper sauce	Pfeffersauce (mit Essig und Pfefferkörnern)	~ poivrade (avec vinaigre et poivre)	~ poivrade (con aceto e pepe); ~ al pepe	~ poivrade (con vinagre y pimienta); ~ de pimienta
pomegranate sauce	Granatapfelsauce	~ à la grenade	~ di melagrana	~ de granada

Sauces

Sauces English	Saucen German	Sauces French	Salse Italian	Salsas Spanish
port wine sauce	Portweinsauce	sauce au porto	salsa al porto	salsa de vino de Oporto
Portuguese sauce	portugiesische Sauce	~ portugaise	~ portoghese	~ portuguesa
provençal sauce	provenzalische Sauce	~ provençal	~ provenzale	~ provenzal
radicchio sauce	Radicchiosauce	~ à la trévise	~ di radicchio	~ de achicoria
ravigote sauce (vinaigrette with capers and fine herbs)	Ravigote-Sauce (Vinaigrette mit Kapern und feinen Kräutern)	~ ravigote (vinaigrette avec câpres et fines herbes)	~ ravigote (vinaigrette con capperi e un trito di erbe)	~ ravigote (vinagreta con alcaparras y finas hierbas)
raw tomato sauce	rohe Tomatensauce	~ tomate crue	~ di pomodori crudi	~ de tomates crudos
red wine sauce	Rotweinsauce	~ vin rouge	~ di vino rosso	~ de vino tinto
redcurrant sauce	Johannisbeersauce	~ aux groseilles rouges	~ di ribes	~ de grosellas
rémoulade sauce (mayonnaise with mustard, capers & gherkins)	Remouladensauce[1] (Mayonnaise mit Senf, Kapern, Essiggurken)	~ rémoulade (mayonnaise à la moutarde, câpres et cornichons)	~ rémoulade (maionese con senape, capperi e cetriolini)	~ remolada (mayonesa con mostaza, alcaparras, pepinillos)
Robert sauce (onion, white wine, mustard)	Robert-Sauce (Zwiebel, Weißwein, Senf)	~ Robert (oignon, vin blanc, moutarde)	~ Roberto (cipolla, vino bianco, senape)	~ Robert (cebolla, vino blanco, mostaza)
rocket pesto	Raukepesto	pistou de roquette	pesto di rucola	~ de oruga
roquefort sauce	Roquefortsauce	sauce au roquefort	salsa al roquefort	~ de roquefort
rosemary sauce	Rosmarinsauce	~ au romarin	~ di rosmarino	~ de romero
saffron sauce	Safransauce	~ au safran	~ allo zafferano	~ de azafrán
sage sauce	Salbeisauce	~ à la sauge	~ alla salvia	~ de salvia
sauce chasseur (mushrooms, white wine, tomato sauce)	Jägersauce (Champignons, Weißwein, Tomatensauce)	~ chasseur (champignons, vin blanc, sauce tomate)	~ alla cacciatora (funghi, vino bianco, salsa di pomodoro)	~ a la cazadora (champiñones, vino blanco, salsa de tomate)
~ financière (Madeira sauce flavoured with truffle)	Finanzmannsauce (Madeirasauce mit Trüffelfond)	~ financière (sauce madère à l'essence de truffes)	~ alla finanziera (salsa al madera con essenza di tartufi)	~ financiera (salsa madera aromatizada con trufas)

---

[1] auch Remoulade

Sauces

Sauces English	**Saucen** German	**Sauces** French	**Salse** Italian	**Salsas** Spanish
sauce grand-veneur (poivrade sauce with game extract and redcurrant jelly); venison sauce	Grand veneur-Sauce (Pfeffersauce mit Wildextrakt und Johannisbeergelee); Wildsauce	sauce grand-veneur (sauce poivrade avec extrait de gibier et gelée de groseilles); ~ venaison	salsa grand-veneur (salsa poivrade con estratto di selvaggina e gelatina di ribes); ~ di cacciagione	salsa grand-veneur (salsa poivrade con extracto de caza y alea de grosellas); ~ de venado
~ normande (white wine sauce with fishstock)	normannische Sauce (Weißweinsauce mit Fischfond)	~ normande (sauce vin blanc au fumet de poisson)	~ normanna (salsa di vino bianco con essenza di pesce)	~ normanda (salsa de vino blanco aromatizada con pescado)
~ poulette (white sauce with egg yolk)	Poulette-Sauce (weiße Sauce mit Eigelb)	~ poulette (sauce blanche aux jaunes d'œufs)	~ poulette (salsa bianca al rosso d'uovo)	~ poulette (salsa blanca con yema)
~ suprême (chicken-stock with cream)	Suprême-Sauce (Geflügelrahmsauce)	~ suprême (velouté de volaille à la crème)	~ suprême (vellutata di pollo con panna)	~ suprema (salsa de ave con crema)
seafood sauce	Meeresfrüchtesauce	~ aux fruits de mer	~ ai frutti di mare	~ de mariscos
sesame sauce	Sesamsauce	~ au sésame	~ di sesamo	~ de sésamo
shallot sauce	Schalottensauce	~ Bercy (à l'échalote)	~ allo scalogno	~ de chalote
shellfish sauce	Krustentiersauce	~ aux crustacés	~ di crostacei	~ de crustacéos
sherry sauce	Sherrysauce	~ au xérès	~ allo sherry	~ de jerez
shrimp sauce	Garnelensauce	~ aux crevettes	~ di gamberetti	~ de camarones
smitane sauce; sour cream sauce	Sauerrahmsauce; Smitane	~ smitane (à la crème aigre)	~ smitane (con panna acida)	~ smitane (salsa de crema agria)
sorrel sauce	Sauerampfersauce	~ à l'oseille	~ di acetosella	~ de acederas
Soubise sauce (onion purée with béchamel)	Soubise-Sauce (Zwiebelpüree mit Béchamel)	~ Soubise (coulis d'oignons)	~ Soubise (purè di cipolle con besciamella)	~ Soubise (bechamel con puré de cebollas)
sour cream sauce; smitane sauce	Sauerrahmsauce; Smitane	~ smitane (à la crème aigre)	~ smitane (con panna acida)	~ smitane (salsa de crema agria)
soy sauce	Sojasauce	~ de soja	~ di soia	~ de soja
sweet-and-sour sauce	süßsaure Sauce	~ aigre-douce	~ agrodolce	~ agridulce

Sauces

Sauces English	**Saucen** German	**Sauces** French	**Salse** Italian	**Salsas** Spanish
sweet pepper sauce; paprika sauce	Paprikasauce	sauce au paprika; ~ aux poivrons	salsa alla paprica; ~ di peperoni	salsa de paprika; ~ de pimientos
tarragon sauce	Estragonsauce	~ à l'estragon	~ al dragoncello	~ de estragón
tartare sauce (mayonnaise with chopped pickles)	Tatarensauce (Mayonnaise aus hart gekochtem Eigelb mit Schnittlauch)	~ tartare (mayonnaise aux jaunes d'œufs durs)	~ tartara (maionese di uova sode con erba cipollina)	~ tártara (mayonesa de yemas de huevos duros con cebollino)
thyme sauce	Thymiansauce	~ au thym	~ al timo	~ de tomillo
tomato sauce	Tomatensauce	~ tomate	~ di pomodoro	~ de tomate
truffle sauce	Périgueux-Sauce; Trüffelsauce	~ Périgueux (aux truffes)	~ Périgueux; ~ di tartufi	~ Périgueux; ~ de trufas
turtle sauce (Madeira sauce with essence of herbs)	Schildkrötensauce (Madeirasauce mit Auszug von Kräutern); Tortue	~ tortue (sauce madère avec infusion d'herbes)	~ tartaruga (salsa madera con infusione di erbe)	~ tortuga (salsa madera con infusión de hierbas)
Tyrolean sauce	Tiroler Sauce	~ tyrolienne	~ tirolese	~ tirolesa
velouté sauce	Samtsauce	~ velouté	~ vellutata	~ velouté
Venetian sauce (white wine sauce with purée of herbs)	venezianische Sauce (Weißweinsauce mit Kräuterpüree)	~ vénitienne (sauce vin blanc avec purée d'herbes)	~ veneziana (salsa di vino bianco con passato di erbe)	~ veneciana (salsa de vino blanco con puré de hierbas)
venison sauce; sauce grand-veneur (poivrade sauce with game extract and redcurrant jelly)	Grand veneur-Sauce (Pfeffersauce mit Wildextrakt und Johannisbeergelee); Wildsauce	~ grand-veneur (sauce poivrade avec extrait de gibier et gelée de groseilles); ~ venaison	~ grand-veneur (salsa poivrade con estratto di selvaggina e gelatina di ribes); ~ di cacciagione	~ grand-veneur (salsa poivrade con extracto de caza y alea de grosellas); ~ de venado
Villeroi sauce (white sauce with essence of mushrooms)	Villeroi-Sauce (weiße Sauce mit Champignonfond)	~ Villeroi (sauce allemande à l'essence de champignons)	~ Villeroi (salsa bianca con essenza di funghi)	~ Villeroi (salsa blanca aromatizada con champiñones)
vinaigrette[1]	Vinaigrette	~ vinaigrette	~ vinaigrette	~ vinagreta
walnut sauce; nut sauce	Walnusssauce	~ aux noix	~ di noci	~ de nueces

1) also vinaigrette dressing and vinaigrette sauce

Sauces

Sauces English	**Saucen** German	**Sauces** French	**Salse** Italian	**Salsas** Spanish
watercress sauce	Kressesauce	sauce au cresson	salsa al crescione	salsa de berros
white sauce	weiße Sauce	~ blanche	~ bianca	~ blanca
~ wine sauce	Weißweinsauce	~ au vin blanc	~ di vino bianco	~ de vino blanco
wild garlic sauce	Bärlauchsauce	~ à l'ail sauvage	~ all'aglio orsino	~ de ajo de oso
yoghurt sauce	Joghurtsauce	~ yaourt	~ allo yogurt	~ de yogur
zingara sauce (tomatoed sauce with strips of ham, ox-tongue, mushrooms)	Zigeunersauce (Tomatensauce mit Paprika, Champignons, Zunge und Schinken)	~ zingara (sauce tomatée au paprika avec julienne de jambon, langue, champignons)	~ alla zingara (salsa al pomodoro con paprica, con filetti di prosciutto, lingua e funghi)	~ gitana (salsa española con tiritas de jamón, lengua, champiñones)

Butters

Butters English	**Buttermischungen** German	**Beurres composés** French	**Burri composti** Italian	**Mantequillas compuestas** Spanish
anchovy butter	Sardellenbutter	beurre d'anchois	burro d'acciughe	mantequilla de anchoas
black butter	schwarze Butter	~ noir	~ nero	~ negra; ~ tostada
brown butter	Nussbutter; braune Butter	~ noisette	~ nocciola	~ dorada
caviar butter	Kaviarbutter	~ de caviar	~ di caviale	~ de caviar
chervil butter	Kerbelbutter	~ de cerfeuil	~ di cerfoglio	~ de perifollo
chive butter	Schnittlauchbutter	~ de ciboulette	~ di erba cipollina	~ de cebollino
crayfish butter	Krebsbutter	~ d'écrevisses	~ di gamberi	~ de cangrejos
cress butter	Kressebutter	~ de cresson	~ al crescione	~ de berro
dill butter	Dillbutter	~ à l'aneth	~ all'aneto	~ de eneldo
garlic butter	Knoblauchbutter	~ d'ail	~ all'aglio	~ de ajo
green butter	grüne Butter	~ vert	~ verde	~ verde
juniper berry butter	Wacholderbutter	~ de genièvre	~ al ginepro	~ de enebro
lime butter	Limettenbutter	~ de citron vert	~ di lime; ~ limetta	~ de lima
lobster butter	Hummerbutter	~ de homard	~ d'astice	~ de bogavante
maître d'hôtel butter (with chopped parsley and lemon juice); parsley butter	Maître d'hôtel-Butter (Butter mit gehackter Petersilie und Zitronensaft); Petersilienbutter	~ maître d'hôtel (beurre avec persil haché et jus de citron); ~ persillé	~ maître d'hôtel (con prezzemolo trito e succo di limone); ~ al prezzemolo	~ maître d'hôtel (con perejil picado y zumo de limón); ~ de perejil
melted butter	zerlassene Butter	~ fondu	~ fuso	~ derretida; ~ fundida
mustard butter	Senfbutter	~ de moutarde	~ di senape	~ de mostaza
orange butter	Orangenbutter	~ à l'orange	~ all'arancia	~ de naranja
parsley butter; maître d'hôtel butter (with chopped parsley and lemon juice)	Maître d'hôtel-Butter (Butter mit gehackter Petersilie und Zitronensaft); Petersilienbutter	~ maître d'hôtel (beurre avec persil haché et jus de citron); ~ persillé	~ maître d'hôtel (con prezzemolo trito e succo di limone); ~ al prezzemolo	~ maître d'hôtel (con perejil picado y zumo de limón); ~ de perejil
sage butter	Salbeibutter	~ de sauge	~ alla salvia	~ de salvia
salmon butter	Lachsbutter	~ de saumon fumé	~ di salmone	~ de salmón
shallot butter	Schalottenbutter	~ Bercy; ~ d'échalote	~ di scalogno	~ de chalote

Butters

Butters English	Buttermischungen German	Beurres composés French	Burri composti Italian	Mantequillas compuestas Spanish
shrimp butter	Garnelenbutter; Krevettenbutter	beurre de crevettes	burro di gamberetti	mantequilla de gambas
thyme butter	Thymianbutter	~ de thym	~ al timo	~ de tomillo
truffle butter	Trüffelbutter	~ de truffes	~ al tartufo	~ de trufas
wild garlic butter	Bärlauchbutter	~ d'ail sauvage	~ all'aglio orsino	~ de ajo de oso

Hors d'œuvres

Hors d'œuvres[1)] English	Vorspeisen German	Hors-d'œuvre French	Antipasti Italian	Entremeses[2)] Spanish
air-dried venison meat	luftgetrocknetes Hirschfleisch	viande séchée de cerf	bresaola di cervo	cecina de venado
anchovy butter	Sardellenbutter	beurre d'anchois	burro d'acciughe	mantequilla de anchoas
~ canapés	Sardellen-Canapés	canapés aux anchois	canapè di acciughe	canapés de anchoas
~ fillets	Sardellenfilets	filets d'anchois	filetti d'acciuga	filetes de anchoa
~ straws	Sardellenstäbchen	allumettes aux anchois	bastoncini all'acciuga	barritas de anchoa
artichokes, marinated	griechische Artischocken (marinierte Artischocken)	artichauts à la grecque (artichauts marinés)	carciofi alla greca (carciofi marinati)	alcachofas a la griega (alcachofas marinadas)
asparagus in jelly	Spargelsülze	asperges en gelée	asparagi in gelatina	espárragos en gelatina
assorted hors d'œuvres	gemischte Vorspeisen	hors-d'œuvre variés	antipasti assortiti	entremeses variados
~ sausages	Wurstplatte	assiette de charcuterie	salumi assortiti	surtido de embutidos
bacon	Bacon; Frühstücksspeck	bacon; lard fumé	bacon; pancetta affumicata	bacón; beicon; tocino ahumado
bear's ham	Bärenschinken	jambon d'ours	prosciutto d'orso	jamón de oso
Bismarck herring[3)]	Bismarckhering	hareng mariné	aringa marinata	arenque marinado
blinis (small buckwheat pancakes)	Blini (Buchweizenpfannkuchen)	blinis (petites crêpes au sarrasin)	blini (frittatine di grano saraceno)	blinis (crepes de trigo sarraceno)
botargo (pressed caviar of mullet roe)	Botarga (Presskaviar aus Meeräscherogen)	poutargue[4)] (caviar d'œufs de mulet)	bottarga (caviale di uova di muggine)	botarga (embuchado de huevas de mújol)
bouchées; patties	Bouchées; Pastetchen	bouchées	bouchées	volovánes; pastelitos (de hojaldre)
bouchée à la reine	Königinpastete	bouchée à la reine	bouchée à la reine	bouchée a la reina
bruschetta (toasted garlic bread)	Bruschetta (geröstetes Knoblauchbrot)	aillade; chapon	bruschetta (pane abbrustolito e agliato)	bruschetta (pan tostado al ajo)
buckling; bloater	Bückling	buckling; hareng saur; craquelot	aringha affumicata	arenque ahumado
canapés	Canapés (belegte Brötchen)	canapés	canapè; tartine	canapés
~, variety of	verschiedene Canapés	~ divers	tartine assortite	~ surtidos

---

1) also starters - 2) también entrantex y entradas - 3) marinated herring fillet - 4) ou boutargue

Hors d'œuvres

Hors d'œuvres English	**Vorspeisen** German	**Hors-d'œuvre** French	**Antipasti** Italian	**Entremeses** Spanish
caviar; caviare	Kaviar	caviar	caviale	caviar
~, pressed	Presskaviar	~ pressé	~ pressato	~ aplastado
celery rémoulade	Sellerie in Remoulade	céleri rémoulade	sedano con maionese	apio nabo en mayonesa
cervelat; saveloy	Zervelatwurst; Cervelatwurst	cervelas	salsiccia affumicata	salchicha ahumada
cheese soufflé	Käsesoufflé; Käseauflauf	soufflé au fromage	soufflé di formaggio	soufflé de queso
~ straws	Käsestangen	allumettes au fromage	bastoncini al formaggio	barritas de queso
~ tartlets; ramekins	Käsetörtchen; Ramequins	ramequins	tartellette al formaggio	tartaletas de queso
chester straws	Chesterstangen	paillettes au chester	bastoncini al chester	barritas de chester
chicken galantine	Geflügelgalantine	galantine de volaille	galantina di pollo	galantina de pollo
~ salad	Geflügelsalat	salade de volaille	insalata di pollo	ensalada de pollo
~ vol-au-vent	Blätterteigpastete mit Geflügel	vol-au-vent de volaille	vol-au-vent di pollo	volován de pollo
cold cuts; ~ meats	Kalte Platte	assiette anglaise; viandes froides	piatto freddo	surtido de fiambres
confit of goose (goose preserved in fat)	Gänseconfit (eingemachtes Gänsefleisch)	confit d'oie	confit d'oca (oca conservata sotto grasso)	confit de oca (oca confitada)
crabmeat cocktail	Krabbencocktail	cocktail de crabe	cocktail di granchi	cóctel de cangrejos
crayfish cocktail	Krebsschwanz-Cocktail	~ d'écrevisses	~ di gamberi	~ de cangrejos
croquettes	Kroketten	croquettes	crocchette	croquetas
croûtes; toast	Crostini (belegtes Röstbrot)	croûtes	crostini	tostada
crudités (raw vegetables)	Rohkostplatte	assiette de crudités	crudità (verdure crude)	crudités (verduras crudas)
duck breast, smoked	geräucherte Entenbrust	poitrine de canard fumée	petto d'anatra affumicato	pechuga de pato ahumada
eel in jelly	Aal in Gelee	anguille en gelée	anguilla in gelatina	anguila en gelatina
~, marinated	marinierter Aal	~ marinée	~ marinata	~ en escabeche
~, smoked	Räucheraal; Spickaal	~ fumée	~ affumicata	~ ahumada
eggs à la russe	russische Eier	œufs à la russe	uova alla russa	huevos a la rusa
~, stuffed	gefüllte Eier	~ durs farcis	~ ripiene	~ rellenos

Hors d'œuvres

Hors d'œuvres English	**Vorspeisen** German	**Hors-d'œuvre** French	**Antipasti** Italian	**Entremeses** Spanish
eggs with mayonnaise	Eier mit Mayonnaise	œufs durs à la mayonnaise	uova con maionese	huevos con mayonesa
~ with sauce tartare	~ mit Tatarensauce	~ à la tartare	~ alla tartara	~ a la tártara
finger food; snacks	Appetithäppchen	amuse-gueule	stuzzichini	tapas; bocados
fish salad	Fischsalat	salade de poisson	insalata di pesce	ensalada de pescado
foie gras; goose liver	Gänseleber	foie gras	fegato d'oca	hígado de ganso
~ gras terrine	~ -Terrine	terrine de foie gras	terrina di fegato d'oca	terrina de foie-gras
fondue	Fondue (Käsefondue)	fondue savoyarde (fondue au fromage)	fondue; fonduta	fondue a la suiza (fondue de queso)
Frankfurters; Wieners	Frankfurter Würstchen	saucisses de Francfort	würstel	salchichas de Francfort
fruit cocktail; ~ cup	Fruchtsalat; Früchtecocktail	cocktail de fruits	cocktail di frutta	cóctel de frutas
game pie; venison pie	Wildpastete	pâté de gibier	pâté di cacciagione	pastel de caza
garlic sausage	Knoblauchwurst	saucisson à l'ail	salame all'aglio	salchichón al ajo
gherkins; pickles	Gewürzgurken; Cornichons	cornichons	cetriolini sott'aceto	pepinillos en vinagre
goose breast, smoked	geräucherte Gänsebrust; Spickgans	poitrine d'oie fumée	petto d'oca affumicato	pechuga de ganso ahumada
~ ham	Gänseschinken	jambon d'oie	prosciutto d'oca	jamón de ganso
~ liver; foie gras	Gänseleber	foie gras	fegato d'oca	hígado de ganso
~ liver mousse	~ -Mousse	mousse de foie gras	mousse di fegato d'oca	espuma de foie-gras
~ paste	Gänsefleischpaste	rillettes d'oie	pâté d'oca	pasta de ganso
~ salami	Gänsesalami	saucisson d'oie	salame d'oca	salami de ganso
grapefruit, iced	eisgekühlte Grapefruit	grapefruit frappé	pompelmo ghiacciato	pomelo helado
Grisons air-dried beef	Bündner Fleisch	viande séchée des Grisons	bresaola dei Grigioni	cecina de los Grisones
ham	Schinken	jambon	prosciutto	jamón
~, bear's	Bärenschinken	~ d'ours	~ d'orso	~ de oso
~, boiled; cooked ham	gekochter Schinken	~ cuit; ~ de Paris	~ cotto	~ de York; ~ dulce; ~ cocido
~ cornets; ~ rolls	Schinken-Röllchen	cornets de jambon	cornetti di prosciutto	rollitos de jamón
~, goose	Gänseschinken	jambon d'oie	prosciutto d'oca	jamón de ganso

Hors d'œuvres

Hors d'œuvres English	**Vorspeisen** German	**Hors-d'œuvre** French	**Antipasti** Italian	**Entremeses** Spanish
ham mousse	Schinken-Mousse	mousse de jambon	mousse di prosciutto	mousse de jamón
~, Parma	Parmaschinken	jambon cru de Parme	prosciutto di Parma	jamón de Parma
~, raw	roher Schinken	~ cru	~ crudo	~ serrano; ~ crudo
~, reindeer	Rentierschinken	~ de renne	~ di renna	~ de reno
~ sandwich	Schinken-Sandwich	sandwich au jambon	sandwich al prosciutto	bocadillo de jamón
~, smoked	geräucherter Schinken	jambon fumé	prosciutto affumicato	jamón ahumado
~, venison (roe)	Rehschinken	~ de chevreuil	~ di capriolo	~ de corzo
~, venison (deer)	Hirschschinken	~ de cerf	~ di cervo	~ de ciervo
~, Westphalian	westfälischer Schinken	~ de Westphalie	~ di Vestfalia	~ de Westfalia
~, wild boar	Wildschweinschinken	~ de sanglier	~ di cinghiale	~ de jabalí
~, York	Yorker Schinken	~ d'York	~ di York	~ de York
herring fillets	Heringsfilets	filets de hareng	filetti d'aringa	filetes de arenque
~, kippered; kipper	Räucherhering	hareng saur; ~ fumé	aringa affumicata	arenque ahumado
~ salad	Heringssalat	salade de hareng	insalata di aringhe	ensalada de arenques
hors d'œuvre trolley	Vorspeisen vom Wagen	chariot de hors-d'œuvre	carrello di antipasti	carrito de entremeses
~ d'œuvres, meatless	fleischlose Vorspeisen	hors-d'œuvre maigres	antipasti di magro	entremeses de vigilia
~ d'œuvres of fish	Fischvorspeisen	~ de poissons	~ di pesce	~ de pescado
Hungarian salami	ungarische Salami	salami hongrois	salame ungherese	salami húngaro
iced grapefruit	eisgekühlte Grapefruit	grapefruit frappé	pompelmo ghiacciato	pomelo helado
~ melon	~ Melone	melon glacé	melone ghiacciato	melón helado
kipper; kippered herring	Räucherhering	hareng saur; ~ fumé	aringa affumicata	arenque ahumado
lapwing eggs	Kiebitzeier	œufs de vanneau	uova di pavoncella	huevos de avefría
liver sausage; liverwurst	Leberwurst	pâté de foie; boudin de foie	pâté di fegato di maiale; salsiccia di fegato	embuchado de hígado; embutido de hígado
lobster boats	Hummer-Schiffchen	barquettes de homard	barchette d'astice	barquitas de bogavante
~ cocktail	~ -Cocktail	cocktail de homard	cocktail d'astice	cóctel de bogavante
~ mayonnaise	~ -Mayonnaise	mayonnaise de homard	maionese d'astice	mayonesa de bogavante
~ salad	~ -Salat	salade de homard	insalata d'astice	ensalada de bogavante

Hors d'œuvres

Hors d'œuvres English	Vorspeisen German	Hors-d'œuvre French	Antipasti Italian	Entremeses Spanish
lumpfish roe	Deutscher Kaviar (vom Seehasen); Lumpfischrogen	œufs de lump	uova di lompo	huevas de lompa
matie herring[1]	Matjeshering	hareng franc; ~ vierge	aringa giovane	arenque joven
meatless hors d'œuvres	fleischlose Vorspeisen	hors-d'œuvre maigres	antipasti di magro	entremeses de vigilia
melon, iced	eisgekühlte Melone	melon glacé	melone ghiacciato	melón helado
mini pizzas	Minipizzas	mini-pizzas	pizzette	pizzetas; mini pizzas
mixed pickles	Mixed Pickles	mixed pickles[2]	sottaceti	encurtidos (en vinagre)
mortadella	Mortadella	mortadelle	mortadella	mortadela
mushroom vol-au-vent	Blätterteigpastete mit Pilzen	vol-au-vent aux champignons	vol-au-vent ai funghi	volován de setas
mushrooms on toast	Champignons auf Toast	croûte aux champignons	funghi sul crostone	champiñones sobre tostada
mussels salad	Miesmuschelsalat	salade de moules	insalata di cozze	ensalada de mejillones
olive paste	Olivenpaste	tapenade	pâté di olive	pasta de aceitunas
olives, black; ripe olives	schwarze Oliven	olives noires	olive nere	aceitunas negras
~, green	grüne Oliven	~ vertes	~ verdi	~ verdes
~, stuffed	gefüllte Oliven	olives farcies	~ farcite	~ rellenas
ox-muzzle salad	Ochsenmaulsalat	museau de bœuf en salade	insalata di muso di bue	ensalada de morro de buey
oysters	Austern	huîtres	ostriche	ostras
oyster boats	~ -Schiffchen	barquettes d'huîtres	barchette d'ostriche	barquitas de ostras
~ bouchées; ~ patties	~ -Pastetchen	bouchées aux huîtres	vol-au-vent d'ostriche	pastelitos de ostras
~ cocktail	~ -Cocktail	cocktail d'huîtres	cocktail d'ostriche	cóctel de ostras
~ patties; ~ bouchées	~ -Pastetchen	bouchées aux huîtres	vol-au-vent d'ostriche	pastelitos de ostras
parfait de foie gras	Gänseleber-Parfait	parfait de foie gras	parfait di fegato d'oca	parfait de foie-gras
Parma ham	Parmaschinken	jambon cru de Parme	prosciutto di Parma	jamón de Parma
~ ham and melon	Schinken mit Melone	melon au jambon de Parme	~ e melone	melón con jamón serrano
parmesan en brochette	Parmesanspießchen	brochettes de Parme	spiedini di parmigiano	brochetas de parmesano
pâté de foie gras	Gänseleber-Pastete	pâté de foie gras	pâté di fegato d'oca	foie-gras (pasta de higado de ganso)

---

1) herring not fully developed - 2) ou pickles

Hors d'œuvres

Hors d'œuvres English	Vorspeisen German	Hors-d'œuvre French	Antipasti Italian	Entremeses Spanish
patties; bouchées	Bouchées; Pastetchen	bouchées	bouchées	volovánes; pastelitos (de hojaldre)
pickled onions	Perlzwiebeln[1] (sauer eingelegt)	petits oignons (au vinaigre)	cipolline sott'aceto	cebollitas en vinagre
~ tongue; salt ox-tongue	Pökelzunge	langue écarlate	lingua salmistrata	lengua salada
pickles; gherkins	Gewürzgurken; Cornichons	cornichons	cetriolini sott'aceto	pepinillos en vinagre
pork paste	Schweinefleischpaste	rillettes de porc (de Tours)	pâté di maiale	pasta de cerdo
portuguese oysters	Portugiesische Austern	huîtres portugaises	ostriche portoghesi	ostras portuguesas
prawn cocktail; shrimp cocktail	Garnelencocktail	cocktail de crevettes	cocktail di gamberetti	cóctel de gambas
quail eggs	Wachteleier	œufs de caille	uova di quaglia	huevos de codorniz
~ eggs with caviar	~ mit Kaviar	~ de caille au caviar	~ di quaglia con caviale	~ de codorniz con caviar
quiche lorraine (flan with bacon & cream)	Quiche lorraine (Lothringer Specktorte)	quiche lorraine (tarte à la crème et au lard)	quiche lorraine (torta con lardo e crema)	quiche lorenesa (tarta de tocino y crema)
rabbit galantine	Kaninchen-Galantine	galantine de lapin	galantina di coniglio	galantina de conejo
radish	Rettich	radis (noir)	rafano; ravanello	rábano
radishes	Radieschen	~ (roses)	ravanelli	rabanitos
ramekins; cheese tartlets	Käsetörtchen; Ramequins	ramequins	tartellette al formaggio	tartaletas de queso
reindeer ham	Rentierschinken	jambon de renne	prosciutto di renna	jamón de reno
rice croquettes	Reiskroketten	croquettes de riz	crocchette di riso	croquetas de arroz
rissoles (fried cakes with meat or fish stuffing)	Rissolen (frittierte Blätterteigtaschen)	rissoles (chaussons farcis)	rissoles (fagottini fritti)	rissoles (empanadillas fritas)
~ with truffles	~ mit Trüffeln	~ aux truffes	~ ai tartufi	~ con trufas
rollmops (rolled herring)	Rollmops	rollmops	rollmops[2]	rollmops[3]
Russian eggs (set on Russian salad)	russische Eier (mit russischem Salat)	œufs à la russe (dressés sur salade russe)	uova alla russa (con insalata russa)	huevos a la rusa (con ensalada rusa)
salami	Salami	salami	salame	salchichón
~, Hungarian	ungarische Salami	~ hongrois	~ ungherese	salami húngaro

[1] auch Silberzwiebeln - [2] aringa arrotolata e marinata - [3] arenque enrollado en escabeche

Hors d'œuvres

Hors d'œuvres English	**Vorspeisen** German	**Hors-d'œuvre** French	**Antipasti** Italian	**Entremeses** Spanish
salmon canapés	Lachs-Canapés	canapés au saumon	canapè al salmone	canapés de salmón
~ caviar	Lachskaviar (Keta-Kaviar)	caviar de saumon	caviale di salmone	caviar de salmón
~ cornets	Lachsröllchen	cornets de saumon	cornetti di salmone	rollitos de salmón
~ mayonnaise	Lachsmayonnaise	mayonnaise de saumon	maionese di salmone	mayonesa de salmón
~ millefeuille	Lachs in Blätterteig	feuilleté de saumon	salmone in crosta	salmón en hojaldre
~ mousse	Lachsmousse	mousse de saumon	mousse di salmone	mousse de salmón
~, smoked	Räucherlachs	saumon fumé	salmone affumicato	salmón ahumado
salt ox-tongue; pickled tongue	Pökelzunge	langue écarlate	lingua salmistrata	lengua salada
sandwich	Sandwich	sandwich	sandwich; panino	bocadillo; emparedado
~, cheese	Käse-Sandwich	~ au fromage	~ al formaggio	~ de queso
sardines in oil	Ölsardinen	sardines à l'huile	sardine sott'olio	sardinas en aceite
sausage	Wurst; Würstchen	saucisse	salsiccia	salchicha
~ rolls	Würstchen in Blätterteig	~ en feuilletage	~ in crosta	~ en hojaldre
~ salad	Wurstsalat	saucisson en salade	insalata di salsicce	ensalada de salchichón
saveloy; cervelat	Zervelatwurst; Cervelatwurst	cervelas	salsiccia affumicata	salchicha ahumada
scalloped chicken	Geflügel in Muschelschalen	coquilles de volaille	conchiglie di pollo	conchas de ave
~ fish	Fisch in Muschelschalen	~ de poisson	~ di pesce	~ de pescado
scampi cocktail	Scampi-Cocktail	cocktail de langoustines	cocktail di scampi	cóctel de cigalas
Scotch woodcock (scrambled egg on anchovy toast)	Scotch woodcock (Rührei auf Sardellentoast)	scotch woodcock (œuf brouillé sur toast à l'anchois)	scotch woodcock (uovo strapazzato su crostino all'acciuga)	scotch woodcock (huevo revuelto sobre tostada de anchoa)
seafood	Meeresfrüchte	fruits de mer	frutti di mare	mariscos
~ salad	Meeresfrüchtesalat	~ de mer en salade	insalata di mare	~ en ensalada
~ vol-au-vent	Blätterteigpastete mit Meeresfrüchten	vol-au-vent aux fruits de mer	vol-au-vent ai frutti di mare	volován de mariscos
shellfish cocktail	Cocktail von Meeresfrüchten	cocktail de fruits de mer	cocktail di frutti di mare	cóctel de mariscos

Hors d'œuvres

Hors d'œuvres English	**Vorspeisen** German	**Hors-d'œuvre** French	**Antipasti** Italian	**Entremeses** Spanish
shells à la financière	Ragoût fin in Muscheln	coquilles à la financière	conchiglie alla finanziera	conchas a la financiera
shrimps	Garnelen	crevettes	gamberetti	gambas; camarones
shrimp boats	Krabbenschiffchen	barquettes de crevettes	barchette di gamberetti	barquitas de gambas
~ cocktail; prawn cocktail	Garnelencocktail	cocktail de crevettes	cocktail di gamberetti	cóctel de gambas
~ salad	Krabbensalat	salade de crevettes	insalata di gamberetti	ensalada de gambas
smoked meet	Rauchfleisch	viande fumée	carne affumicato	carne ahumada
snacks; finger food	Appetithäppchen	amuse-gueule	stuzzichini	tapas; bocados
snails	Schnecken; Weinbergschnecken	escargots	lumache	caracoles
speck (smoked raw ham)	Tiroler Bauernspeck	speck (jambon cru fumé)	speck (prosciutto crudo affumicato)	speck (jamón serrano ahumado)
sturgeon terrine	Störterrine	terrine d'esturgeon	terrina di storione	terrina de esturión
Swedish platter (marinated and smoked fish specialities)	Schwedenplatte (marinierte und geräucherte Fischspezialitäten)	plat suédois (spécialités de poissons marinés et fumés)	piatto svedese (specialità di pesce marinato e affumicato)	plato sueco (surtido de pescados en escabeche y ahumados)
sweetbread vol-au-vent	Kalbsmilch-Pastete	vol-au-vent de ris de veau	vol-au-vent con animelle	volován de mollejas
swordfish, marinated	marinierter Schwertfisch	espadon mariné	pesce spada marinato	pez espada en escabeche
tench au bleu	Schleie blau	tanche au bleu	tinca al blu	tenca au bleu
tenches, marinated	marinierte Schleien	tanches marinées	tinche marinate	tencas en escabeche
terrapin	Dosenschildkröte; Süßwasserschildkröte	terrapin	tartaruga d'acqua dolce	tortuga de agua dulce
toast; croûtes	Crostini (belegtes Röstbrot)	croûtes	crostini	tostada
tomato juice, chilled	eisgekühlter Tomatensaft	jus de tomates glacé	succo di pomodoro ghiacciato	jugo de tomate helado
~ salad	Tomatensalat	tomates à la vinaigrette	pomodori in insalata	tomates en ensalada
trout caviar	Forellenkaviar	caviar de truite	caviale di trota	caviar de trucha
~, smoked	Räucherforelle	truite fumée	trota affumicata	trucha ahumada
tuna in olive oil	Thunfisch in Öl	thon à l'huile	tonno sott'olio	atún en aceite

Hors d'œuvres

Hors d'œuvres English	**Vorspeisen** German	**Hors-d'œuvre** French	**Antipasti** Italian	**Entremeses** Spanish
veal and ham pie	Schinken-Kalbfleischpastete	pâté de veau et de jambon	pâté di vitello e prosciutto	paté de ternera y jamón
venison ham (deer)	Hirschschinken	jambon de cerf	prosciutto di cervo	jamón de ciervo
~ ham (roe)	Rehschinken	~ de chevreuil	~ di capriolo	~ de corzo
~ pie; game pie	Wildpastete	pâté de gibier	pâté di cacciagione	pastel de caza
~ salami	Hirschsalami	salami de cerf	salame di cervo	salami de ciervo
vol-au-vent	Blätterteigpastete; Vol-au-vent	vol-au-vent; bouchée	vol-au-vent	volován; vol-au-vent
~ à la financière (with chicken giblets)	vol-au-vent à la financière (mit Hühnerklein)	~ à la financière (avec abatis de poulet)	~ alla finanziera (con rigaglie di pollo)	~ a la financiera (con menudillos de pollo)
welsh rabbit[1] (dish of melted cheese on toast)	Welsh Rabbit (Röstbrot mit heißem Käse belegt)	welsh rabbit (fromage fondu sur toast)	welsh rabbit (formaggio fuso su pane tostato)	welsh rabbit (queso derretido sobre tostada)
Westphalian ham	westfälischer Schinken	jambon de Westphalie	prosciutto di Vestfalia	jamón de Westfalia
Wieners; Frankfurters	Frankfurter Würstchen	saucisses de Francfort	würstel	salchichas de Francfort
wild boar ham	Wildschweinschinken	jambon de sanglier	prosciutto di cinghiale	jamón de jabalí
~ boar sausage	Wildschweinwürstchen	saucisse de sanglier	salsiccia di cinghiale	salchicha de jabalí
York ham	Yorker Schinken	jambon d'York	prosciutto di York	jamón de York

---

[1] or Welsh rarebit

Soups

Soups English	**Suppen** German	**Potages** French	**Minestre** Italian	**Sopas** Spanish
Bagration soup (cream of veal soup with macaroni)	Bagration-Suppe (Kalbfleischsuppe mit Makkaroni-Einlage)	potage Bagration (velouté de veau garni de tronçons de macaroni)	minestra Bagration (crema di vitello con maccheroncini)	sopa Bagration (crema de ternera con trocitos de macarrones)
barley soup	Gerstensuppe	~ à l'orge	~ d'orzo	~ de cebada
bean purée soup	Bohnenpüreesuppe	~ purée soissonnaise	passato di fagioli	~ puré de judías
~ soup	Bohnensuppe	~ aux haricots	minestra di fagioli	~ de judías
beer soup	Biersuppe	soupe à la bière	~ di birra	~ de cerveza
beetroot soup	Rote-Bete-Suppe	potage aux betteraves	~ di barbabietole	~ de remolachas
bird's nest soup	Schwalbennestersuppe	~ aux nids d'hirondelle	brodo con nidi di rondine	~ con nidos de salangana
black salsify soup	Schwarzwurzelsuppe	~ de salsifis	zuppa di scorzonera	~ de salsifí
bouillabaisse (French fish-soup with saffron)	Bouillabaisse (Fischsuppe mit Safran)	bouillabaisse (soupe de poisson safranée)	~ di pesce provenzale (con zafferano)	bullabesa (potaje de pescado con azafrán)
~ with half lobster	~ mit halber Languste	~ royale (avec demi-langouste)	~ con mezza aragosta	~ con media langosta
bouillon with egg	Bouillon mit Ei; Fleischbrühe mit Ei	bouillon à l'œuf	brodo all'uovo	caldo con huevo; consomé con yema
brain soup	Hirnsuppe	potage de cervelle	minestra di cervella	sopa de sesos
bread soup	Brotsuppe	soupe au pain	zuppa di pane	~ de pan
broccoli soup	Brokkolisuppe	potage aux brocolis	~ di broccoli	~ de bróculi
broth; bouillon; beeftea	Bouillon; Fleischbrühe; Rindsuppe	bouillon	brodo	caldo (de carne); consomé
busecca (tripe and bean soup)	Busecca (Kuttelsuppe mit weißen Bohnen)	busecca (soupe aux tripes de veau et haricots)	busecca (zuppa di trippa e fagioli)	busecca (sopa de callos con judías blancas)
cabbage soup; kale	Kohlsuppe; Weißkohlsuppe	soupe aux choux	zuppa di cavolo	sopa de coles
calf's light soup	Beuschelsuppe	potage au mou de veau	~ di polmone	~ de bofes de ternera
~ tail soup	Kalbsschwanzsuppe	~ queue de veau	brodo di coda di vitello	~ de rabo de ternera
capon broth	Kapaunbrühe	consommé de chapon	~ di cappone	consomé de capón

Soups

Soups English	Suppen German	Potages French	Minestre Italian	Sopas Spanish
Carmen soup (cream of rice coloured with tomato purée)	Carmen-Suppe (passierte Reissuppe mit Tomatenmark gefärbt)	velouté Carmen (velouté à la crème de riz tomatée)	minestra Carmen (vellutata di riso al pomodoro)	sopa Carmen (crema de arroz con tomate)
carrot soup	Karottensuppe	potage de carottes	~ di carote	~ de zanahorias
cauliflower soup	Blumenkohlsuppe	~ au chou-fleur	~ di cavolfiore	~ de coliflor
cepe mushroom soup	Steinpilzsuppe	~ aux cèpes	~ di funghi porcini	~ de setas (boletos)
chervil soup	Kerbelsuppe	~ au cerfeuil	zuppa di cerfoglio	~ de perifollo
chestnut soup	Kastaniensuppe	~ aux marrons	minestra di castagne	~ de castañas
chicken broth	Hühnerbrühe	consommé de volaille	brodo di pollo	caldo de pollo
~ gumbo	Gombosuppe mit Huhn	potage de poulet aux gombos	minestra di gombo e pollo	sopa de gombo y ave
clam chowder	Muschelsuppe (mit Venusmuscheln)	soupe aux clams	zuppa di vongole	~ de almejas
clear rice soup	Reissuppe (klar); Kraftbrühe mit Reiseinlage	potage au riz	riso in brodo	~ con arroz; consomé con arroz
~ soup	klare Suppe	~ clair	minestra chiara	~ clara
cock-a-leekie (soup of chicken and leeks)	schottische Hühnersuppe mit Lauch	soupe au poulet et aux poireaux	zuppa di pollo e porri	~ de pollo y puerros
cold consommé	kalte Kraftbrühe	consommé froid	consommé freddo	consomé frío
consommé	Kraftbrühe	consommé	consommé[1]	consomé; consumado
~ Célestine (with shredded pancake)	~ Célestine (mit Pfannkuchenstreifen); Frittatensuppe	~ Célestine (garni crêpe taillée en julienne)	~ Celestina (frittatine in brodo)	~ Celestina (con una crepe en tiritas)
~, double	doppelte Kraftbrühe	~ double	~ doppio	~ doble
~ in cup	Kraftbrühe in der Tasse	~ en tasse	~ in tazza	~ en taza
~ madrilène (chickenbroth with tomato)	Geflügelbrühe mit Tomaten; Madrider Brühe	~ madrilène (consommé de volaille avec tomate)	~ alla madrilena (brodo di pollame con pomodori)	~ madrileño (consomé de ave con tomate)
~ with beef marrow	Kraftbrühe mit Mark	~ à la moelle	~ con midollo	~ con tuétano

[1] o brodo ristretto

Soups

Soups English	Suppen German	Potages French	Minestre Italian	Sopas Spanish
consommé with liver quenelles	Kraftbrühe mit Lebernockerln	consommé aux noques de foie	gnocchetti di fegato in brodo	consomé con albondiguillas de hígado
~ with marrow quenelles	~ mit Markklößchen	~ aux quenelles à la moelle	~ di midollo in brodo	~ con albondiguillas de tuétano
~ with milt croûtons	Milzschnittensuppe	potage aux croûtons de rate	crostini di milza in brodo	sopa con costrones de bazo
~ with pasta (or rice)	Kraftbrühe mit Einlage	consommé garni	pastina (o riso) in brodo	consomé de pasta (o de arroz)
~ with pasta	~ mit Teigwaren	potage aux pâtes	~ in brodo	sopa con pasta
~ with profiteroles[1]	~ mit Backerbsen; Backerbsensuppe	consommé aux profiteroles	consommé con pasta reale	~ con profiteroles
~ with quenelles; quenelle soup	Nockerlsuppe	potage aux noques; ~ aux quenelles	gnocchetti in brodo	~ de albóndigas
crayfish cream-soup; ~ bisque	Krebscremesuppe	bisque d'écrevisses	crema di gamberi	bisque de cangrejos
cream of asparagus soup	Spargelcremesuppe	Crème Argenteuil; ~ d'asperges	~ d'asparagi	crema de espárragos
~ of barley soup	Gerstenschleimsuppe	~ d'orge	~ d'orzo	~ de cebada
~ of brain soup	Hirncremesuppe	~ de cervelle	~ di cervella	~ de sesos
~ of carrot soup	Karottencremesuppe	potage Crécy	~ di carote	~ de zanahorias
~ of cauliflower soup; Du Barry soup	Blumenkohlcremesuppe	crème Du Barry; ~ de chou-fleur	minestra Du Barry; crema di cavolfiori	sopa Du Barry; crema de coliflor
~ of celery soup	Selleriecremesuppe	~ de céleri	crema di sedani	crema de apio
~ of champignon soup	Champignoncremesuppe	~ de champignons de couche	~ di champignon	~ de champiñones
~ of chicken soup	Königinsuppe; Geflügelcremesuppe	potage à la reine; crème de volaille	~ di pollo	sopa reina; crema de ave
~ of courgette soup	Zucchinicremesuppe	crème de courgettes	~ di zucchine	~ de calabacines
~ of green pea soup	Erbsenpüreesuppe	~ de petits pois	~ di piselli	crema de guisantes

---

[1] pea-sized balls of choux pastry

Soups

Soups English	Suppen German	Potages French	Minestre Italian	Sopas Spanish
cream of leek soup	Lauchcremesuppe	crème de poireaux	crema di porri	crema de puerros
~ of rice soup	Reisschleimsuppe	~ de riz	~ di riso	~ de arroz
~ of spinach soup	Spinatcremesuppe	~ d'épinards	~ di spinaci	~ de espinacas
~ of vegetable soup	Gemüsecremesuppe	~ de légumes	~ di verdure	~ de legumbres
~ soup	Cremesuppe	crème; velouté	crema; vellutata	crema
cress soup; watercress soup	Kressesuppe; Brunnenkressesuppe	potage au cresson; ~ cressonnière	minestra di crescione	sopa de berros
cucumber soup	Gurkensuppe	~ aux concombres	~ di cetrioli	~ de pepinos
Darblay soup (potato soup with shredded vegetables)	Darblay-Suppe (Kartoffelsuppe mit Gemüsestreifen)	~ julienne Darblay (potage Parmentier garni julienne de légumes)	~ Darblay (minestra di patate con julienne di verdure)	~ Darblay (sopa de patatas con tiritas de verdura)
double consommé	doppelte Kraftbrühe	consommé double	consommé doppio	consomé doble
Du Barry soup; cream of cauliflower soup	Blumenkohlcremesuppe	crème Du Barry; ~ de chou-fleur	minestra Du Barry; crema di cavolfiori	sopa Du Barry; crema de coliflor
eel soup	Aalsuppe	potage à l'anguille	zuppa d'anguilla	~ de anguila
egg-drop soup	Einlaufsuppe	soupe stracciatella	stracciatella	~ de huevos batidos
elder soup	Holundersuppe	potage au sureau	zuppa di sambuco	~ de saúco
fennel soup	Fenchelsuppe	~ aux fenouils	~ di finocchi	~ de hinojos
fish soup	Fischsuppe	soupe de poisson	~ di pesce	~ de pescado
frog soup	Froschsuppe	~ aux grenouilles	~ di rane	~ de ranas
game consommé in pastry crust	Wildbrühe mit Teighaube	consommé de gibier en croûte	consommé di selvaggina in crosta	consomé de caza en costra
~ soup	Jägersuppe; Wildsuppe	potage chasseur; ~ de gibier	minestra del cacciatore; ~ di selvaggina	sopa del cazador; ~ de caza
garbanzo soup	Kichererbsensuppe	~ aux pois chiches	zuppa di ceci	~ de garbanzos
garlic soup	Knoblauchsuppe	soupe à l'ail	~ d'aglio	~ de ajo
garnished bouillon	Bouillon mit Einlage	bouillon garni	brodo con pastina (o riso o altro)	consomé guarnecido

Soups

Soups English	Suppen German	Potages French	Minestre Italian	Sopas Spanish
gazpacho (soup of uncooked vegetables with vinegar & oil)	Gazpacho (kalte Suppe aus rohem Gemüse mit Öl und Essig)	gaspacho (potage non cuit de légumes crus avec huile et vinaigre)	gazpacho (minestra fredda di verdure crude con olio e aceto)	gazpacho (sopa fría de legumbres crudos con aceite y vinagre)
germiny soup (sorrel soup bound with egg-yolks & cream)	Germiny-Suppe (Sauerampfersuppe, stark mit Eigelb und Sahne legiert)	potage Germiny (potage à l'oseille avec double liaison de crème et œufs)	minestra Germiny (zuppa di acetosa, legata con molta panna e rossi d'uovo)	sopa Germiny (sopa de acedera, ligada con mucha crema y yemas de huevo)
giblet soup	Suppe aus Geflügelklein	~ aux abattis de volaille	~ di rigaglie	~ de menudillos
goulash soup (highly seasoned soup of beef & potatoes)	Gulaschsuppe	~ goulache (potage très relevé avec dés de bœuf)	~ di gulasch (minestra piccante con pezzetti di carne)	~ de gulasch (sopa picante con trozos de carne y patatas)
green spelt soup	Grünkernsuppe	soupe d'épeautre vert	zuppa di farro verde	~ de farro verde
Gumbo (with okra pods)	Gombosuppe	potage aux gombos	minestra di gombo	~ de gombo
haricot soup	Bohnensuppe (aus weißen Bohnen)	~ aux haricots blancs	~ di fagioli bianchi	~ de judías blancas
herb soup	Kräutersuppe	~ aux herbes	~ alle erbe	~ de hierbas
julienne	Juliennesuppe	~ julienne	zuppa julienne; minestra di verdura	~ juliana; ~ de hierbas
kale; cabbage soup	Kohlsuppe; Weißkohlsuppe	soupe aux choux	~ di cavolo	~ de coles
kangaroo-tail soup	Känguruschwanzsuppe	potage queue de kangourou	brodo di coda di canguro	~ de rabo de canguro
kidney soup	Nierensuppe	~ aux rognons	minestra di rognone	~ de riñones
kohlrabi soup	Kohlrabisuppe	soupe au chou-rave	zuppa di cavolo rapa	~ de colinabo
leek soup	Lauchsuppe	potage aux poireaux	~ di porri	~ de puerros
lenten soup; soup maigre	Fastensuppe	~ maigre	minestra di magro	~ de vigilia[1]
lentil soup	Linsensuppe	~ Conti (aux lentilles)[2]	~ di lenticchie	~ de lentejas
liver dumpling soup	Leberknödelsuppe	~ aux boulettes de foie	canederli di fegato in brodo	~ con albóndigas de hígado
~ soup	Lebersuppe	~ au foie de veau	zuppa di fegato	~ de hígado
lobster bisque	Hummersuppe	bisque de homard	~ d'astice	~ de bogavante

[1] o sopa de viernes - [2] ou Esaü

Soups

Soups English	**Suppen** German	**Potages** French	**Minestre** Italian	**Sopas** Spanish
Londonderry soup (consommé with Madeira and diced calf's head)	Londonderry-Suppe (mit Madeira und Kalbskopfwürfeln)	potage Londonderry (consommé au madère, garni tête de veau en dés)	consommé Londonderry (brodo al madera con dadi di testina di vitello)	sopa Londonderry (caldo al madera con dados de cabeza de ternera)
minestrone (thick vegetable soup with pasta or rice)	Minestrone (Gemüsesuppe mit Reis- oder Teigwaren-Einlage)	minestrone (potage aux légumes divers garni riz ou pâtes)	minestrone (minestra di verdura con riso o pasta)	minestrone (sopa de verduras con pasta o arroz)
mock-turtle soup	falsche Schildkrötensuppe	potage fausse tortue	brodo di finta tartaruga	sopa de tortuga falsa
morel soup	Morchelsuppe	~ aux morilles	minestra di spugnole	~ de colmenillas
mulligatawny (soup) (curry soup with chicken)	Mulligatawny-Suppe (Currysuppe mit Huhn)	~ mulligatawny (soupe de poulet au curry)	~ mulligatawny (minestra di pollo al curry)	~ mulligatawny (sopa de ave al curry)
mushroom soup	Pilzsuppe	~ aux champignons	~ di funghi	~ de setas
mussel soup	Muschelsuppe (mit Miesmuscheln)	soupe aux moules	zuppa di cozze	~ de mejillones
nettle soup	Brennnesselsuppe	~ d'orties	~ di ortiche	~ de ortiga
noodle soup	Nudelsuppe	potage aux pâtes	pastina in brodo	~ de fideos
~ soup with chicken	~ mit Huhn	poule au pot aux nouilles	pollo e taglierini in brodo	~ de tallarines con ave
oatmeal soup	Haferschleimsuppe	crème d'avoine	crema d'avena	crema de avena
onion soup	Zwiebelsuppe	soupe à l'oignon	zuppa di cipolle	sopa de cebolla
~ soup, baked	~ überbacken	~ gratinée	~ di cipolle gratinata	~ de cebolla gratinada
oxtail soup	Ochsenschwanzsuppe[1]	oxtail; potage queue de bœuf	brodo di coda di bue	~ de rabo de buey
oyster soup	Austernsuppe	soupe aux huîtres	zuppa d'ostriche	~ de ostras
pea soup	Erbsensuppe	potage Saint-Germain	minestra di piselli	~ de guisantes
peasant-style soup (vegetable soup)	Bauernsuppe (Gemüsesuppe)	~ à la paysanne (potage aux légumes)	zuppa alla contadina (zuppa di verdura)	~ campesina (sopa de verduras)
pheasant consommé	Fasanen-Kraftbrühe	consommé de faisan	consommé di fagiano	consomé de faisán

---

1) auch Oxtailsuppe

Soups

Soups English	**Suppen** German	**Potages** French	**Minestre** Italian	**Sopas** Spanish
Philadelphia pepper pot (soup of tripe highly seasoned)	Philadelphier Kuttelsuppe (stark gepfeffert)	potage aux tripes de Philadelphie (très épicé)	zuppa Filadelfia (zuppa di trippa molto pepata)	sopa de callos con pimienta
Portuguese soup (tomato soup)	Portugiesische Suppe (Tomatensuppe)	~ à la portugaise (purée de tomates)	minestra alla portoghese (minestra di pomodoro)	~ portuguesa (sopa de tomate)
pot-au-feu (broth with meat and vegetables)	Potaufeu (Eintopf aus Fleisch und Gemüse); Suppentopf	pot-au-feu; petite marmite	pot-au-feu (brodo con verdure e pezzi di lesso)	pot-au-feu (cocido de carne de vaca)
potato soup	Kartoffelsuppe	potage Parmentier	minestra di patate	sopa de patatas
princess soup (cream of chicken soup with asparagus tips)	Prinzessin-Suppe (Geflügelcremesuppe mit Spargelspitzen)	crème princesse (crème de volaille garnie de pointes d'asperges)	crema principessa (crema di pollo con punte d'asparagi)	~ princesa (crema de ave con puntas de espárragos)
pumpkin soup	Kürbissuppe	soupe au potiron	zuppa di zucca	~ de calabaza
quenelle soup; consommé with quenelles	Nockerlsuppe	potage aux noques; ~ aux quenelles	gnocchetti in brodo	~ de albóndigas
ramson soup	Bährlauchsuppe	~ à l'ail sauvage	zuppa di aglio orsino	~ de ajo de oso
ravioli soup	Ravioli-Suppe	~ aux ravioli	ravioli in brodo	~ de ravioles
real turtle soup	Schildkrötensuppe	~ tortue	brodo di tartaruga	~ de tortuga
rice and pea soup	Risi-Pisi[1]	~ de riz aux petits pois	risi e bisi	~ de arroz y guisantes
royale soup (with egg custard)	Kraftbrühe mit Eierstich	consommé royale (garni de royale)	consommé reale (con dadini di crema reale)	consomé real (con dados de flan)
santé soup (potato purée with sorrel)	Gesundheitssuppe (Kartoffelsuppe mit Sauerampfer)	potage santé (purée Parmentier à l'oseille)	minestra santé (passato di patate con acetosa)	sopa de la salud (puré de patatas con acedera)
sauerkraut soup	Sauerkrautsuppe	soupe de choucroute	zuppa di crauti	~ de chucrut
Scotch broth (soup of mutton[2] and pearl-barley)	Schottische Brühe (Hammelbouillon mit Graupen)	pot-au-feu écossais (soupe de mouton à l'orge)	brodo scozzese (brodo di montone con orzo)	caldo escocés (caldo de carnero con cebada)

---
1) auch Risibisi - 2) or beef

Soups

Soups English	Suppen German	Potages French	Minestre Italian	Sopas Spanish
seafood soup	Meeresfrüchtesuppe	soupe aux fruits de mer	zuppa di frutti di mare	sopa de mariscos
semolina dumpling soup	Grießnockerlsuppe	potage aux quenelles de semoule	gnocchetti di semolino in brodo	~ con albondiguillas de sémola
~ soup	Grießsuppe	~ à la semoule	minestra di semolino	~ de sémola
shark's fin soup	Haifischflossensuppe	consommé aux nageoires de requin	zuppa di pinne di pesce	~ de aletas de tiburón
shellfish bisque	Bisque von Krustentieren	bisque de crustacés	bisque di crostacei	bisque de crustacéos
shrimp soup	Krabbensuppe	soupe aux crevettes	zuppa di gamberetti	sopa de gambas
snail soup	Schneckensuppe	potage aux escargots	~ di lumache	~ de caracoles
sorrel soup	Sauerampfersuppe	~ à l'oseille	~ di acetosa	~ de acedera
soup maigre; lenten soup	Fastensuppe	~ maigre	minestra di magro	~ de vigilia[1]
~ of the day	Tagessuppe	~ du jour	~ del giorno	~ del día
spelt soup	Dinkelsuppe	soupe d'épeautre	~ di farro	~ de espelta
spring soup	Frühlingssuppe	potage printanier	zuppa primaverile	~ de primavera
squid soup	Tintenfischsuppe	soupe aux calmars	~ di calamari	~ de calamares
tapioca soup	Tapiokasuppe	potage au tapioca	minestra di tapioca	~ de tapioca
tomato consommé	Tomatenbrühe	consommé à la tomate	consommé al pomodoro	consomé de tomate
~ soup	Tomatensuppe	potage à la tomate	minestra di pomodori	sopa de tomate
tripe soup	Kuttelsuppe	soupe aux tripes	zuppa di trippa	~ de callos
turbot soup	Steinbuttsuppe	~ de turbot	~ di rombo	~ de rodaballo
turtle soup Lady Curzon (flavoured with curry & covered with whipped cream)	Schildkrötensuppe Lady Curzon (mit Curry gewürzt und mit Schlagsahne bedeckt)	potage tortue Lady Curzon (relevé au curry et couvert de crème fouettée)	brodo di tartaruga Lady Curzon (condito con curry e coperto di panna montata)	~ de tortuga Lady Curzon (aromatizada con curry y cubierta de nata batida)
~ soup, real	Schildkrötensuppe	~ tortue	~ di tartaruga	~ de tortuga
Tyrolean dumpling soup	Knödelsuppe	~ aux boulettes tyroliennes	canederli in brodo	~ con albóndigas del Tirol
vegetable broth	Gemüsebrühe	bouillon de légumes	brodo vegetale	caldo de verduras
~ purée soup	Gemüsepüreesuppe	potage purée de légumes	passato di verdura	sopa puré de verduras

---

[1] o sopa de viernes

Soups

Soups English	**Suppen** German	**Potages** French	**Minestre** Italian	**Sopas** Spanish
vegetable soup	Gemüsesuppe	potage aux légumes	minestra di verdura	sopa de verduras
velvet soup (carrot purée with tapioca)	Samtsuppe (Karottenpüree mit Tapioka)	~ velours (purée Crécy avec tapioca)	vellutata di carote e tapioca	crema de zanahorias y tapioca
vermicelli soup	Vermicelli-Suppe; Kraftbrühe mit Fadennudeln	consommé au vermicelle; potage au vermicelle	vermicelli in brodo	consomé con fideos; sopa de fideos
vichyssoise (iced cream of potato soup)	Vichyssoise (Kartoffel-Lauch-Suppe, kalt serviert)	vichyssoise (potage aux poireaux et aux pommes, servi froid)	vichyssoise (minestra di porri e patate, servita fredda)	vichyssoise (sopa de puerros y patatas servida fría)
watercress soup; cress soup	Kressesuppe; Brunnenkressesuppe	potage au cresson; ~ cressonnière	minestra di crescione	sopa de berros
wild mushroom soup	Waldpilzsuppe	~ aux champignons sauvages	zuppa di funghi di bosco	~ de setas silvestres
wine soup	Weinsuppe	soupe au vin	minestra di vino	~ de vino
zuppa pavese (beefbroth with slices of fried bread and an egg poached in it)	Zuppa pavese (Bouillon mit gerösteten Brotscheiben, darauf ein pochiertes Ei)	zuppa pavese (consommé avec tranches de pain grillé et un œuf cassé dessus)	zuppa alla pavese (brodo con fette di pane abbrustolito e sopra un uovo affogazo)	zuppa pavese (caldo con huevo y rebanadas de pan frito)

Eggs

Eggs English	Eierspeisen German	Œufs French	Uova Italian	Huevos Spanish
artichoke omelette	Omelett mit Artischocken	omelette aux artichauts	omelette coi carciofi	tortilla de alcachofas
asparagus omelette	~ mit Spargelspitzen	~ aux pointes d'asperges	~ con punte d'asparagi	~ de espárragos
bacon and eggs	Eier mit Bacon	œufs au bacon	uova al bacon	huevos con bacón
~ omelet	Omelett mit Speck	omelette au lard	omelette con pancetta	tortilla con tocino
cheese and potato omelette	~ auf savoyische Art (mit Kartoffeln und Käse)	~ à la savoyarde (avec gruyère et pommes)	~ alla savoiarda (con patate e groviera)	~ a la saboyarda (con queso y patatas)
~ omelette	~ mit Käse	~ au fromage	~ al formaggio	~ de queso
chicken liver omelette	~ mit Geflügelleber	~ aux foies de volaille	~ con fegatini di pollo	~ de higadillos
cold eggs tartare sauce	Eier mit Tatarensauce	œufs froids à la tartare	uova alla tartara	huevos fríos a la tártara
~ eggs with mayonnaise	~ mit Mayonnaise	~ durs à la mayonnaise	~ sode con maionese	~ duros con mayonesa
crayfish omelette	Omelett mit Krebsfleisch	omelette Nantua (aux écrevisses)	omelette con gamberi	tortilla de cangrejos
egg salad	Eiersalat	œufs durs en salade	uova sode in insalata	huevos duros en ensalada
eggs à la russe	Russische Eier	~ à la russe	~ alla russa	~ a la rusa
~ Benedict (poached eggs with ham and hollandaise sauce)	Eier auf Benediktinerart (verlorene: mit Schinken und Sauce Hollandaise)	pochés bénédictine (avec jambon et sauce hollandaise)	~ affogate alla benedettina (con prosciutto e salsa olandese)	~ escalfados a la benedictina (con jamón y salsa holandesa)
~ cooked to order	~ nach Wunsch	~ au choix	~ a piacere	~ a elección; ~ a gusto
~, curried	Curryeier	~ au curry	~ al curry	~ al curry
~ en cocotte	Eier in Cocotte (pochierte Eier)	~ en cocotte	~ in cocotte	~ en cocotte
~ en cocotte, creamed	~ in Sahne (in Förmchen)	~ en cocotte à la crème	~ in cocotte alla panna	~ en cocotte a la crema
~ in jelly	~ in Aspik	~ en gelée	~ in gelatina	~ en gelatina
~ mimosa (stuffed eggs)	~ Mimosa (gefüllte Eier)	~ mimosa (œufs durs farcis)	~ mimosa (uova sode ripiene)	~ mimosa (huevos duros rellenos)
Florentine omelette; spinach omelette	Omelett mit Spinat	omelette à la florentine	omelette con spinaci	tortilla de espinacas
fried eggs (in deep fat)	frittierte Eier	œufs frits	uova fritte	huevos fritos

Eggs

Eggs English	**Eierspeisen** German	**Œufs** French	**Uova** Italian	**Huevos** Spanish
fried eggs[1]	Spiegeleier; Setzeier	œufs sur le plat; ~ poêlés; ~ au plat; ~ au miroir	uova al tegamino; ~ al piatto; ~ al burro	huevos al plato; ~ estrellados
~ eggs Bercy (with grilled sausage and tomato sauce)	Eier Bercy (Spiegeleier mit Bratwürstchen und Tomatensauce)	~ sur le plat Bercy (garnis d'une saucisse grillée, sauce tomate)	~ al piatto Bercy (con una piccola salsiccia e salsa di pomodoro)	~ estrellados Bercy (con salchicha y salsa de tomate)
~ eggs Meyerbeer (with grilled kidney)	~ Meyerbeer (Setzeier mit gegrillter Lammniere und Trüffelsauce)	~ sur le plat Meyerbeer (au rognon grillé et sauce Périgueux)	~ al tegame Meyerbeer (con rognone d'agnello e salsa di tartufi)	~ al plato Meyerbeer (con riñones y salsa de trufas)
~ eggs Turbigo (with sausage)	~ Turbigo (Spiegeleier mit Bratwürstchen)	~ sur le plat Turbigo (avec saucisse)	~ al tegame Turbigo (con una salsiccia)	~ al plato Turbigo (con salchicha)
~ eggs with bacón	~ auf amerikanische Art (Spiegeleier mit Speck)	~ sur le plat à l'américaine (au bacon)	all'americana (al tegame con bacon)	~ a la americana (al plato con bacón)
~ eggs with chicken livers	türkische Eier (Spiegeleier mit Geflügelleber)	~ sur le plat à la turque (aux foies de volaille)	~ al tegame alla turca (con fegatini)	~ al plato a la turca (con higadillos)
ham and eggs (fried or scrambled)	Eier mit Schinken (Spiegeleier oder Rühreier)	~ au jambon (sur le plat ou brouillés)	~ al prosciutto (al tegame o strapazzate)	~ con jamón (al plato o revueltos)
~ omelette	Omelett mit Schinken	omelette au jambon	omelette al prosciutto	tortilla de jamón
hard-boiled eggs	hart gekochte Eier	œufs durs	uova sode	huevos duros
herb omelette; savoury omelette	Omelett mit Kräutern	omelette aux fines herbes	omelette alle erbe; ~ verde (con erbe)	tortilla finas hierbas
kidney omelette	~ mit Nieren	~ aux rognons	~ col rognone	~ de riñones
lapwing eggs	Kiebitzeier	œufs de vanneau	uova di pavoncella	huevos de avefría
medium-boiled eggs	Fünfminuten-Eier; wachsweiche Eier	~ mollets	~ bazzotte	~ mollets; ~ encerados; ~ blandos
mushroom omelette	Omelett mit Pilzen	omelette aux champignons	omelette con funghi	tortilla con setas
nettle omelet	~ mit Brennnessel	~ à l'ortie	~ all' ortica	~ de ortiga
omelette (unfolded)	Eierkuchen	~ plate	frittata	tortilla
omelette; omelet	Omelett[2]	omelette	omelette; frittata	tortilla; ~ española

[1] Am. sunny-side up eggs - [2] auch Omelette

Eggs

Eggs English	Eierspeisen German	Œufs French	Uova Italian	Huevos Spanish
omelette with ceps	Omelett mit Steinpilzen	omelette aux cèpes	omelette con funghi porcini	tortilla de setas
~ with champignons	~ mit Champignons	~ aux champignons	~ con champignon	~ de champiñones
onion omelette	~ mit Zwiebeln	~ à la lyonnaise	~ con cipolle	~ de cebolla
pancake	Pfannkuchen	pannequet; crêpe	crêpe; crespella	crepe
peasant's omelette (omelette with sorrel, potato & bacon, not folded)	Omelett nach Bauernart (Eierkuchen mit Speckwürfeln, Kartoffeln und Sauerampfer)	omelette à la paysanne (omelette plate avec lardons, pommes de terre et oseille)	omelette alla campagnola (non ripiegata, con lardo, patate e acetosa)	tortilla paisana (tortilla española de patatas, acedera y tocino)
plain omelette	~ natur	~ nature	~ al naturale; ~ semplice	~ francesa; ~ sencilla; ~ al natural
poached eggs	pochierte Eier; verlorene Eier	œufs pochés	uova affogate; ~ in camicia	huevos escalfados
~ eggs Florentine (eggs on bed of leaf-spinach)	florentinische Eier (verlorene Eier auf Blattspinat)	~ pochés a la florentine (œufs gratinés sur lit d'épinards)	~ affogate alla fiorentina (uova gratinate su spinaci)	~ a la florentina (huevos escalfados sobre espinacas)
~ eggs Mornay (au gratin)	Eier Mornay (verlorene Eier gratiniert)	~ Mornay (œufs pochés au gratin)	~ Mornay (affogate al gratin)	~ Mornay (huevos escalfados al gratén)
~ eggs on toast	~ auf Toast (pochierte)	~ pochés sur toast	~ affogate su toast	~ escalfados sobre tostada
potato omelette	Omelett mit Kartoffeln	omelette Parmentier	omelette con patate	tortilla de patatas
quail eggs	Wachteleier	œufs de caille	uova di quaglia	huevos de codorniz
~ eggs in jelly	~ in Aspik	~ de caille en gelée	~ di quaglia in gelatina	~ de codorniz en gelatina
~ eggs with caviar	~ mit Kaviar	~ de caille au caviar	~ di quaglia al caviale	~ de codorniz al caviar
sausage omelette	Omelett mit Würstchen	omelette à la saucisse	omelette con salsiccia	tortilla de salchicha
savoury omelette; herb omelette	~ mit Kräutern	~ aux fines herbes	~ alle erbe; ~ verde (con erbe)	~ finas hierbas
Savoy omelette (cheese and potato omelette, not folded)	~ auf savoyische Art (Eierkuchen mit Kartoffeln und Käse)	~ à la savoyarde (omelette plate avec gruyére et pommes)	~ alla savoiarda (non ripiegata, con patate e groviera)	~ a la saboyarda (tortilla española con queso y patatas)

Eggs

Eggs English	Eierspeisen German	Œufs French	Uova Italian	Huevos Spanish
scrambled eggs	Rühreier	œufs brouillés	uova strapazzate	huevos revueltos
~ eggs with asparagus	Eier mit Spargel (Rühreier)	~ brouillés Argenteuil (aux asperges)	~ strapazzate con asparagi	~ revueltos con espárragos
~ eggs with mushrooms	~ mit Champignons (Rühreier)	~ brouillés aux champignons	~ strapazzate ai funghi	~ revueltos con champiñones
~ eggs with prawns	Krabbenrührei	~ brouillés aux crevettes	~ strapazzate ai gamberetti	~ revueltos con gambas
~ eggs with tomatoes	Eier mit Tomaten (Rühreier)	~ brouillés portugaise (aux tomates)	~ strapazzate al pomodoro	~ revueltos con tomate
soft-boiled eggs	Dreiminuten-Eier; weich gekochte Eier	~ à la coque	~ alla coque; ~ al guscio	~ pasados por agua[1]
sorrel omelette	Omelett mit Sauerampfer	omelette à l'oseille	omelette all'acetosella	tortilla de acedera
Spanish omelette (flat omelette with onion, pimiento & tomato)	~ auf spanische Art (Eierkuchen mit Tomaten, Zwiebeln und Paprika)	~ espagnole (omelette plate avec tomates, oignons et pimients)	~ alla spagnola (non ripiegata, con pomodori, cipolle e peperoni)	~ española ((con tomate, cebolla y pimiento morrón)
spinach omelette; Florentine omelette	~ mit Spinat	~ à la florentine	~ con spinaci	~ de espinacas
stuffed eggs	gefüllte Eier	œufs farcis	uova ripiene	huevos rellenos
~ eggs Chimay (eggs au gratin with mushroom stuffing)	Eier Chimay (überbackene Eier mit Champignonfüllung)	~ farcis Chimay (œfs durs gratinés, farcis de champignons)	~ ripiene alla Chimay (uova gratinate ripiene di funghi)	~ Chimay (huevos al gratén rellenos de champiñones)
tomato omelette	Omelett mit Tomaten	omelette portugaise	omelette con pomodori	tortilla de tomate
truffle omelette	~ mit Trüffeln	~ aux truffes	~ al tartufo	~ de trufas
wild mushroom omelet	~ nach Försterinart (mit Waldpilzen)	~ à la forestière (aux champignons des bois)	~ alla forestale (con funghi di bosco)	~ a la forestal (con setas silvestres)

---

[1] o huevos en cáscara

Fish and shellfish

Fish and shellfish English	Fische und Schaltiere German	Poissons et crustacés French	Pesci e crostacei Italian	Pescados y crustáceos Spanish
abalones; ormers; sea ears	Meerohren	ormeaux; oreilles de mer	orecchie di mare	orejas de mar
allice shad; shad	Alse; Maifisch	alose	cheppia; alosa	sábalo; alosa
anchovies	Sardellen	anchois	alici; acciughe	boquerones; anchoas
angler-fish; frogfish	Seeteufel; Anglerfisch; Lotte	lotte (de mer); baudroie	pescatrice; coda di rospo[1]	rape[2]
~, broiled	~ vom Grill	~ grillée	~ alla griglia	~ a la parrilla
~ flan	Flan von Seeteufel	flan de baudroie	flan di pescatrice	flan de rape
~ fricassee	Seeteufelfrikassee	fricassée de lotte	fricassea di pescatrice	fricasé de rape
~ medallion	Seeteufelmedaillon	médaillon de lotte	medaglione di pescatrice	medallón de rape
barbel	Barbe	barbeau	barbo; barbio	barbo
bass; sea bass	Wolfsbarsch; Loup; Seebarsch	bar; loup (de mer)	branzino; spigola	lubina; róbalo
~, grilled	~ vom Rost	~ grillée	spigola in gratella	~ a la parrilla
~ with mayonnaise, cold	~ mit Mayonnaise	~ froid mayonnaise	~ lessa con maionese	~ fría con mayonesa
bergylt; redfish; rosefish; red perch	Rotbarsch; Goldbarsch	sébaste; rascasse du nord	scorfano atlantico; ~ di fondale; sebaste	gallineta; perae de mar
black bass	Forellenbarsch	perche truitée	persico trota	perca atruchada
bleaks	Ukeleie; Silberfische	ablettes	alborelle	albures
~, fried	gebackene Ukeleie	friture d'ablettes	~ fritte	~ fritos
boiled trout; trout au bleu	Forelle blau	truite au bleu	trota bollita; ~ al blu	trucha azulada; ~ hervida
bonito	Bonito	bonite; pélamide	bonito; palamita	bonito
brandade of salt cod (purée of salt cod)	Stockfisch-Brandade (Stockfischpüree)	brandade de morue (purée de morue)	baccalà mantecato (crema di baccalà)	brandada de bacalao (puré de bacalao); arenques a la provenzal
bream	Brasse[3]	brème	abramide	brema
brill	Glattbutt	barbue	rombo liscio	rémol; barbuda; rodaballo menor
brook trout	Bachsaibling	saumon de fontaine; omble	salmerino di fonte	salvelino; umbla
brown trout[4]	Bachforelle	truite de rivière	trota di fiume; ~ di torrente	trucha de río

---

[1] o rana pescatrice - [2] o pejesapo - [3] auch Brachse - [4] Am. speckled trout

Fish and shellfish

Fish and shellfish English	Fische und Schaltiere German	Poissons et crustacés French	Pesci e crostacei Italian	Pescados y crustáceos Spanish
buckling; bloater	Bückling	buckling; hareng saur; craquelot	aringha affumicata	arenque ahumado
bullheads; miller's thumbs	Kaulköpfe[1]	chabots	scazzoni; magnaroni	cotos
burbot; eelpout	Trüsche; Quappe; Aalquappe[2]	lotte de rivière	bottatrice; lota	lota
calamaries; squids	Kalmare	calmars; encornets	calamari	calamares
~, stewed	geschmorte Kalmare	~ à l'étuvée	~ in umido	~ estofados
carp	Karpfen	carpe	carpa	carpa
~ au bleu	~ blau	~ au bleu	~ al blu	~ al azul; ~ au bleu
~, fried	gebackener Karpfen	~ frite	~ fritta	~ frita
~ in beer sauce	Karpfen in Bier	~ à la bière	~ alla birra	~ a la cerveza
~, soft roe of	Karpfenmilch	laitances de carpe	latte di carpa	lechas de carpa
~, sweet and sour	Karpfen süß-sauer	carpe aigre-doux	carpa in agrodolce	carpa en agridulce
carpaccio of fresh salmon	Carpaccio von frischem Lachs	carpaccio de saumon frais	carpaccio di salmone fresco	carpaccio de salmón fresco
catch of the day	fangfrischer Fisch	marée du jour	pesce di giornata	pescado del día
catfish	Zwergwels	poisson-chat[3]	~ gatto	siluro
char[4]	Saibling; Seesaibling	omble chevalier	salmerino	salvelino; umbla
~, oven-cooked	~ aus dem Ofen	~ chevalier au four	~ al forno	~ al horno
~, potted	eingemachter Saibling	conserve d'omble chevalier en pot	pâté di salmerino	conserva de umbla
~ sauté	sautierter Saibling	omble chevalier sauté	salmerino sauté	salvelino salteado
chub	Döbel	chevaine; chevesne	cavedano	cacho
cioppino (stew of fish and shellfish in tomato sauce)	Cioppino (Fischragout in Tomatensauce)	cioppino (ragoût de poisson et de fruits de mer à la tomate)	cioppino (stufato di pesce e frutti di mare al pomodoro)	cioppino (guiso de pescado y mariscos al tomate)
clams	Venusmuscheln	clams; palourdes	vongole	almejas
~ fritters	Muschelbeignets	beignets de clams	frittelle di vongole	buñuelos de almejas

1) auch Groppen - 2) auch Aalraupe - 3) dit aussi silure nain - 4) also charr

Fish and shellfish

Fish and shellfish English	Fische und Schaltiere German	Poissons et crustacés French	Pesci e crostacei Italian	Pescados y crustáceos Spanish
coalfish; coley; saithe	Seelachs; Köhler	lieu noir; colin; charbonnier	merlano nero; merluzzo	carbonero; faneca
~ brochettes	Seelachsspieß	~ noir en brochette	spiedino di merlano nero	brocheta de carbonero
cockles	Herzmuscheln	coques; bucardes	cuori di mare	berberechos
cod; codfish	Kabeljau; Dorsch	cabillaud	merluzzo	bacalao (fresco)
~, fried	gebackener Kabeljau	~ frit	~ fritto	~ frito
~ parsley sauce, boiled	Kabeljau mit Petersiliensauce	~ sauce persil	~ con salsa al prezzemolo	~ con salsa de perejil
~ with mayonnaise, cold	~ mit Mayonnaise	~ froid mayonnaise	~ lesso con maionese	~ frío con mayonesa
cold bass with mayonnaise	Wolfsbarsch mit Mayonnaise	bar froid mayonnaise	spigola lessa con maionese	lubina fría con mayonesa
~ cod with mayonnaise	Kabeljau mit Mayonnaise	cabillaud froid mayonnaise	merluzzo lesso con maionese	bacalao frío con mayonesa
conger eel[1]	Meeraal	congre	grongo	congrio
crabs; green crabs; shore crabs	Krabben; Strandkrabben	crabes; ~ verts	granchi	cangrejos de mar; cámbaros
crab	Taschenkrebs	tourteau	granciporro; granchio paguro	buey de mar[2]; pato
crayfish	Krebse; Flusskrebse	écrevisses	gamberi (di fiume)	cangrejos de río
~ in their broth[3]	~ im Sud	~ à la nage	~ nel loro brodo	~ en su caldo
~ pyramid	Krebspyramide	~ en buisson	~ in piramide	pirámide de cangrejos
~ stew	Ragout von Flusskrebsen	ragoût d'écrevisses	stufato di gamberi di fiume	ragú de cangrejos de río
croaker; drumfish	Umberfisch	ombrine	ombrina	verrugato
crucian	Karausche	carassin	carassio	carpín; carasio
cuttlefish	Tintenfische	seiches	seppie	jibias
~ brochettes	Tintenfischspieße	~ en brochettes	spiedini di seppie	brochetas de jibias
~, small	Tintenfische (klein)	chipirons; sépioles	seppioline	chipirones
~, stuffed	gefüllte Tintenfische	seiches farcies	seppie ripiene	jibias rellenas
dab	Limande; Kliesche	limande	limanda	lengua; limanda
danube salmon; huchen	Donaulachs; Huchen	saumon de Danube; huchon	salmone del Danubio	salmón del Danubio

1) or conger - 2) o masera - 3) also swimming crayfish

Fish and shellfish

Fish and shellfish English	Fische und Schaltiere German	Poissons et crustacés French	Pesci e crostacei Italian	Pescados y crustáceos Spanish
date-shells	Steindatteln; Meerdatteln	dattes de mer	datteri di mare	dátiles de mar
dentex	Zahnbrasse	denté	dentice	dentón
dogfish; smooth hound	Glatthai	émissole; moutelle	palombo	musola
dolphin fish; dorado	Goldmakrele	coriphène	lampuga; corifena	lampuga; dorado
dorado; dolphin fish	Goldmakrele	coriphène	lampuga; corifena	lampuga; dorado
Dory; John Dory	Petersfisch; Heringskönig	saint-pierre; dorée	sampietro; pesce San Pietro	pez de San Pedro; gallo
drumfish; croaker	Umberfisch	ombrine	ombrina	verrugato
eel	Aal	anguille	anguilla	anguila
~, fried	gebackener Aal	~ frite	~ fritta	~ frita
~ in dill sauce	Aal in Dillsauce	~ à l'aneth	~ in salsa all'aneto	~ en salsa de enelgo
~ in green sauce	~ grün	~ au vert	~ al verde	~ al verde
~, matelote of (eel stew)	Aalragout	~ en matelote	~ alla marinara	~ en estofado
~ on the spit	Aal vom Spieß	~ à la broche	~ allo spiedo	~ al asador
~, roast	gebratener Aal	~ rôtie	~ arrosto	~ asada
eelpout; burbot	Trüsche; Quappe; Aalquappe[1]	lotte de rivière	bottatrice; lota	lota
electric ray; torpedo fish	Zitterrochen	torpille; raie électrique	torpedine	torpedo
elvers; silver eels	Glasaale	civelles; pibales; alevins d'anguille	anguillette; cieche	angulas
fillets of hake	Seehechtfilets	filets de colin	filetti di nasello	filetes de merluza
~ of sole	Seezungenfilets	~ de sole	~ di sogliola	~ de lenguado
~ of sole Orly (deep-fried, served with tomato sauce)	~ Orly (frittiert und mit Tomatensauce angerichtet)	~ de sole Orly (filets frits servis avec sauce tomate)	~ di sogliola Orly (filetti fritti e serviti con salsa di pomodoro)	~ de lenguado Orly (filetes fritos con salsa de tomate)
finnan haddock; smoked haddock	Haddock; geräucherter Schellfisch	haddock (églefin fumé)	eglefino affumicato	eglefino ahumado
fish balls; ~ cakes	Fischbuletten; Fischfrikadellen	boulettes de poisson	polpette di pesce	albóndigas de pescado; croquetas de pescado

---

[1] auch Aalraupe

Fish and shellfish

Fish and shellfish English	Fische und Schaltiere German	Poissons et crustacés French	Pesci e crostacei Italian	Pescados y crustáceos Spanish
fish brochettes	Fischspieße	brochettes de poisson	spiedini di pesce	brochetas de pescado
~ cakes; ~ balls	Fischbuletten; Fischfrikadellen	boulettes de poisson	polpette di pesce	albóndigas de pescado; croquetas de pescado
~ fricassee	Fischfrikassee	fricassée de poisson	fricassea di pesce	fricasé de pescado
~ grill	Fischgrillade	grillade de poissons	grigliata di pesce	parrillada de pescado
~ mayonnaise	Fischmayonnaise	mayonnaise de poisson	maionese di pesce	mayonesa de pescado
~ mousse	Fischmousse	mousse de poisson	mousse di pesce	mousse de pescado
~ rolls	Fischröllchen	paupiettes de poisson	involtini di pesce	rollitos de pescado
~ stew	Fischragout	ragoût de poisson	stufato di pesce	ragú de pescado
flounder	Flunder	flet	passera di mare; pianuzza	platija
fresh-water fish	Süßwasserfisch	poisson d'eau douce	pesce d'acqua dolce	pez de agua dulce
fried fish fillet	gebackenes Fischfilet	filet de poisson frit	filetto di pesce fritto	filete de pescado frito
frog legs	Froschschenkel	cuisses de grenouilles	rane; cosce di rana	ranas; ancas de rana
~ legs, fried	gebackene Froschschenkel	~ de grenouilles frites	~ fritte	~ fritas
~ legs sauté	gebratene Froschschenkel	grenouilles sautées	~ al burro	~ salteadas
frogfish; angler-fish	Seeteufel; Anglerfisch; Lotte	lotte (de mer); baudroie	pescatrice; coda di rospo[1]	rape[2]
garfish; needlefish	Hornhecht	orphie; aiguille de mer	aguglia	aguja
gilthead	Goldbrasse; Dorade	daurade; dorade	orata	dorada
~, baked	~ aus dem Ofen	~ au four	~ al forno	~ al horno
~ in salt crust	~ in Salzkruste	~ au sel	~ al sale	~ a la sal
~, roast	gebratene Goldbrasse	~ rôtie	~ arrosto	~ asada
goby	Meergrundel	gobie	ghiozzo	gobio; pez del diablo
grayling	Äsche	ombre	temolo	tímalo
greater weever; weever	Drachenfisch; Petermännchen	vive	tracina; trachino; ragno	araña
green cod; pollack	Pollack	lieu jaune; merlan jaune	merlano giallo	abadejo
~ crabs; crabs; shore crabs	Krabben; Strandkrabben	crabes; ~ verts	granchi	cangrejos de mar; cámbaros

---

[1] o rana pescatrice - [2] o pejesapo

Fish and shellfish

Fish and shellfish English	**Fische und Schaltiere** German	**Poissons et crustacés** French	**Pesci e crostacei** Italian	**Pescados y crustáceos** Spanish
grey mullet	Meeräsche	mulet; muge	cefalo; muggine	mujol; cabezudo
~ mullet, broiled	gegrillte Meeräsche	~ grillé	~ ai ferri	~ a la parrilla
grouper	Zackenbarsch	mérou	cernia	mero
gudgeons	Gründlinge	goujons	gobioni; ghiozzi di fiume	gobios
gurnard; gurnet	Knurrhahn	grondin	gallinella; pesce cappone	rubio; gallina de mar
haddock	Schellfisch	églefin; aiglefin	eglefino	eglefino
~, smoked; finnan haddock	Haddock; geräucherter Schellfisch	haddock (églefin fumé)	~ affumicato	~ ahumado
hake	Seehecht	colin; merlu	nasello; merluzzo	merluza[1]
~, fillets of	Seehechtfilets	filets de colin	filetti di nasello	filetes de merluza
~ meunière	Seehecht in Butter gebraten	colin meunière	nasello al burro	merluza a la molinera
~, poached	pochierter Seehecht	~ poché	~ lesso	~ cocida
halibut	Heilbutt	flétan	halibut; ippoglosso	halibut; hipogloso
~, grilled	~ vom Rost	~ grillé	~ ai ferri	~ a la parrilla
hard roe; roe	Rogen	œufs de poisson	uova di pesce	huevas
herring	Hering	hareng	aringa	arenque
~, kippered; kipper	Räucherhering	~ saur; ~ fumé	~ affumicata	~ ahumado
~, marinated; soused herring	marinierter Hering	~ mariné	~ marinata	~ marinado; ~ en escabeche
horse mackerel; scad	Bastardmakrele; Stöcker	saurel; chinchard	suro; sugherello	chicharro; jurel
huchen; danube salmon	Donaulachs; Huchen	saumon de Danube; huchon	salmone del Danubio	salmón del Danubio
John Dory; Dory	Petersfisch; Heringskönig	saint-pierre; dorée	sampietro; pesce San Pietro	pez de San Pedro; gallo
Kedgeree (dish of rice, fish and hard-boiled eggs)	Kedgeree (Reisgericht mit Fisch und harten Eiern)	Kedgeree (riz garni de poisson et d'œufs durs)	Kedgeree (riso con pesce e fettine di nuova sode)	Kedgeree (carroz con pescado y huevos duros)
king prawns	Riesengarnelen	crevettes rouges; gambas	gamberoni; spannocchi	langostinos
kipper; kippered herring	Räucherhering	hareng saur; ~ fumé	aringa affumicata	arenque ahumado
lake trout	Seeforelle	truite de lac	trota di lago	trucha de lago
~ trout, grilled	~ vom Grill	~ de lac grillée	~ di lago alla griglia	~ de lago a la parrilla

[1] o pescada

Fish and shellfish

Fish and shellfish English	Fische und Schaltiere German	Poissons et crustacés French	Pesci e crostacei Italian	Pescados y crustáceos Spanish
lamprey	Neunauge	lamproie	lampreda	lamprea
lemon sole	Rotzunge	limande-sole	limanda	mendo
limpets	Napfschnecken	patelles	patelle	lapas
ling	Leng; Lengfisch	lingue; julienne	molva	maruca; arbitán; molva
loach	Schmerle; Bartgrundel; Steinbeißer	loche[1]	cobite	locha
lobster	Hummer	homard	astice	bogavante
~, American style (in rich tomato sauce)	~ auf amerikanische Art (in Tomatensauce)	~ à l'américaine (saute aux tomates)	~ all'americana (in salsa di pomodoro e cognac)	~ a la americana (en salsa de tomate)
~ Catalan style	katalanische Languste	langouste à la catalane	aragosta alla catalana	langosta a la catalana
~ flambé	flambierter Hummer	homard flambé	astice alla fiamma	bogavante flameado
~ in aspic	Hummer in Aspik	aspic de homard	~ in gelatina	~ en gelatina
~ mayonnaise	~ -Mayonnaise	mayonnaise de homard	maionese d'astice	mayonesa de bogavante
~ medallion	Hummermedaillon	médaillon de homard	medaglione d'astice	medallón de bogavante
~ thermidor (lobster meat baked in the lobster shell)	Hummer Thermidor (Hummerfleisch in der Schale überbacken)	homard thermidor (escalopes gratinées dans la carapace)	astice alla termidoro (fette d'astice gratinate nella corazza)	bogavante Termidor (carne de bogavante gratinada en el caparazón)
mackerel	Makrele	maquereau	sgombro[2]	caballa
~ en papillote	~ in Folie	~ en papillote	~ al cartoccio	~ en papillote
~ with black butter sauce	~ mit brauner Buttersauce	~ au beurre noir	~ al burro nero	~ con mantequilla negra
mantis shrimps; squills	Heuschreckenkrebse	squilles	canocchie; pannocchie	galeras
miller's thumbs; bullheads	Kaulköpfe[3]	chabots	scazzoni; magnaroni	cotos
mirror carp	Spiegelkarpfen	carpe miroir	carpa a specchio	carpa de espejo
mixed fried fish	Fischfrittüre	friture de poisson	frittura di pesce	fritura de pescado
moray eel	Muräne	murène	murena	morena; murena
murices	Stachelschnecken	rochers épineux	murici; garusoli	cañadillas
mussels	Miesmuscheln	moules	cozze; mitili	mejillones
~ au gratin; ~ mornay	gratinierte Miesmuscheln	~ au gratin	~ gratinate	~ al gratén

1) ou loche de rivière - 2) o scombro - 3) auch Groppen

Fish and shellfish

Fish and shellfish English	**Fische und Schaltiere** German	**Poissons et crustacés** French	**Pesci e crostacei** Italian	**Pescados y crustáceos** Spanish
mussels, farmed	Zuchtmuscheln	moules de bouchot	cozze d'allevamento	mejillones de vivero
~ in white wine	Miesmuscheln in Weißwein	~ marinières (au vin blanc)	~ al vino bianco	~ al vino blanco
~ mornay; ~ au gratin	gratinierte Miesmuscheln	~ au gratin	~ gratinate	~ al gratén
~ with cream sauce	Miesmuscheln in Sahnesauce	~ à la crème	~ alla panna	~ a la crema
needlefish; garfish	Hornhecht	orphie; aiguille de mer	aguglia	aguja
octopus; poulp[1]	Krake; Seepolyp	poulpe; pieuvre	polpo *n*	pulpo
~ vinaigrette	~ in Vinaigrette	~ en vinaigrette	~ insalata	~ en vinagreta
ormers; abalones; sea ears	Meerohren	ormeaux; oreilles de mer	orecchie di mare	orejas de mar
oysters	Austern	huîtres	ostriche	ostras
~, fried	gebackene Austern	~ frites	~ fritte	~ fritas
~ Mornay	gratinierte Austern	~ gratinées; ~ Mornay	~ gratinate	~ al gratén
~, portuguese	portugiesische Austern	~ portugaises	~ portoghesi	~ portuguesas
perch	Barsch; Flussbarsch	perche	pesce persico	perca
~, boiled; ~ au bleu	~ blau	~ au bleu	~ persico al blu	~ azulada
periwinkles; winkles	Strandschnecken	bigorneaux; vignots	lumache di mare; littorine	bígaros
piddocks	Dattelmuscheln; Bohrmuscheln	pholades	foladi	barrenas
pike	Hecht	brochet	luccio	lucio
~ balls; ~ quenelles	Hechtklößchen	quenelles de brochet	polpettine di luccio	albóndigas de lucio
~ in white butter	Hecht in weißer Buttersauce	brochet au beurre blanc	luccio al burro bianco	lucio con mantequilla blanca
pike-perch	Zander; Schill	sandre; perche-brochet	lucioperca[2]	lucioperca
~ au bleu	~ blau	~ au bleu	~ al blu	~ au bleu
~ au gratin	überbackener Zander	~ au gratin	~ al gratin	~ al gratén
~ fillets	Zanderfilets	filets de sandre	filetti di lucioperca	filetes de lucioperca
~ fricassee	Zanderfrikassee	fricassée de sandre	fricassea di lucioperca	fricasé de lucioperca
~, grilled	Zander vom Grill	sandre grillé	lucioperca alla griglia	lucioperca a la parrilla
~ roll	Roulade vom Zander	roulade de sandre	rotolo di lucioperca	rollo de lucioperca

---

[1] also poulpe - [2] o lucioperca, sandra

Fish and shellfish

Fish and shellfish English	**Fische und Schaltiere** German	**Poissons et crustacés** French	**Pesci e crostacei** Italian	**Pescados y crustáceos** Spanish
pike-perch, stuffed	gefüllter Zander	sandre farci	lucioperca farcita	lucioperca rellena
pike quenelles; ~ balls	Hechtklößchen	quenelles de brochet	polpettine di luccio	albóndigas de lucio
pilchards; sardines	Sardinen	sardines	sardine; sarde	sardinas
pilchard fritters	frittierte Sardinen	~ en beignets	frittelle di sarde	buñuelos de sardinas
plaice	Scholle	plie; carrelet	platessa; passera	platija; solla
poached turbot	pochierter Steinbutt	turbot poché	rombo lesso	rodaballo cocido
pollack; green cod	Pollack	lieu jaune; merlan jaune	merlano giallo	abadejo
pompano	Gabelmakrele	liche	leccia stella	palometa blanca
porbeagle[1]	Heringshai[2]	touille; taupe; lamie	smeriglio	cailón; marrajo
poulp[3]; octopus	Krake; Seepolyp	poulpe; pieuvre	polpo	pulpo
prawns[4]	Garnelen; Steingarnelen	crevettes (roses)	gamberetti (rosa)	gambas
~, curried	~ in Currysauce	~ au curry	~ al curry	~ al curry
queen scallops	Kammmuscheln	pétoncles; vanneaux	canestrelli; pettini	volandeiras; zamburiñas
ragout of salt cod	Stockfischragout	morue en ragoût	baccalà in umido	bacalao en ragú
rainbow trout	Regenbogenforelle	truite arc-en-ciel	trota arcobaleno	trucha arco iris
ray; skate	Rochen	raie	razza	raya
razor shells; ~ clams	Messermuscheln; Scheidenmuscheln	couteaux	cannolicchi; cannelli	navajas
red mullet[5]	Meerbarbe; Rotbarbe	rouget; rouget-barbet	triglia (di fango)	salmonete; barbo de mar
~ mullet; surmullet[6]	Meerbarbe; Streifenbarbe	~ de roche; surmulet	~ di scoglio	~ de roca
~ mullet en papillote	~ in Folie	~ en papillote	~ al cartoccio	~ en papillote
~ mullet, grilled	gegrillte Meerbarbe	~ grillé	~ in gratella	~ emparrillado
~ mullet with parsley butter, grilled	Meerbarbe mit Kräuterbutter	~ à la maître d'hôtel	~ con burro al prezzemolo	~ con mantequilla de perejil
~ prawns	Hummerkrabben	gambas; crevettes rouges	gamberi imperiali	gambas; langostinos
~ sea-bream	Rotbrasse	pageau; pageot; pagel	pagello	besugo; breca
redfish; rosefish; bergylt; red perch	Rotbarsch; Goldbarsch	sébaste; rascasse du nord	scorfano atlantico; ~ di fondale; sebaste	gallineta; perae de mar

---

1) also mackerel shark - 2) auch Kalbfisch - 3) also poulpe - 4) Am. shrimps - 5) Am. goatfish - 6) also striped surmullet

Fish and shellfish

Fish and shellfish English	Fische und Schaltiere German	Poissons et crustacés French	Pesci e crostacei Italian	Pescados y crustáceos Spanish
redfish fillet, fried	gebackenes Rotbarschfilet	filet de rascasse frit	filetto di scorfano fritto	filete de gallineta frito
rhine salmon	Rheinsalm	saumon du Rhin	salmone del Reno	salmón del Rin
roach	Plötze; Rotauge	gardon	leucisco	bermejuela
roast pike	gebratener Hecht	brochet rôti	luccio arrosto	lucio asado
rockling; sea loach	Seequappe	loche de mer; motelle	motella	bertorella; barbada; motela
roe; hard roe	Rogen	œufs de poisson	uova di pesce	huevas
rolled sole fillets; sole roulades	Seezungenröllchen	paupiettes de sole	involtini di sogliola	rollos de lenguado; popietas de lenguado
rosefish; redfish; bergylt; red perch	Rotbarsch; Goldbarsch	sébaste; rascasse du nord	scorfano atlantico; ~ di fondale; sebaste	gallineta; perae de mar
~ fillet, fried	gebackenes Goldbarschfilet	filet de sébaste frit	filetto di sebaste fritto	filete de perca de mar frito
saithe; coalfish; coley	Seelachs; Köhler	lieu noir; colin; charbonnier	merlano nero; merluzzo	carbonero; faneca
salmon	Lachs	saumon	salmone	salmón
~, boiled	gekochter Lachs	~ au court-bouillon	~ lesso	~ cocido
~ cutlet	Lachskotelett	côtelette de saumon	costoletta di salmone	chuleta de salmón
~, danube; huchen	Donaulachs; Huchen	saumon de Danube; huchon	salmone del Danubio	salmón del Danubio
~, dill marinated	Lachs in Dillmarinade	~ mariné à l'aneth	~ marinato all'aneto	~ marinado a l'eneldo
~ goulash	Lachsgulasch	goulache de saumon	gulasch di salmone	gulasch de salmón
~, grilled	Lachs vom Rost	saumon grillé	salmone ai ferri	salmón emparrillado
~ in champagne	~ in Champagner	~ au champagne	~ allo champagne	~ al champañ
~ in pastry	~ in Blätterteig	feuilleté de saumon	~ in crosta	~ en hojaldre
~ in salt crust	~ in Salzkruste	saumon en croûte de sel	~ al sale	~ a la sal
~ medallion	Lachsmedaillon	médaillon de saumon	medaglione di salmone	medallón de salmón
~ of the Baltic Sea	Ostseelachs	saumon de la Baltique	salmone del Baltico	salmón del Báltico
~ pie	Lachspastete (warm)	pâté de saumon en croûte	pâté di salmone in crosta	pastel de salmón
~, poached	pochierter Lachs	saumon poché	salmone lesso	salmón cocido
~ rolls	Lachsröllchen	paupiettes de saumon	involtini di salmone	rollitos de salmón
~ steak	Lachssteak	darne de saumon	trancio di salmone	tajada de salmón

Fish and shellfish

Fish and shellfish English	Fische und Schaltiere German	Poissons et crustacés French	Pesci e crostacei Italian	Pescados y crustáceos Spanish
salmon tartare	Lachstatar	tartare de saumon	tartara di salmone	salmón a la tártara
~ trout	Lachsforelle	truite saumonée	trota salmonata	trucha asalmonada
~, wild	Wildlachs	saumon sauvage	salmone selvaggio	salmón salvaje
salt cod; stockfish	Stockfisch	morue	baccalà; stoccafisso	bacalao (seco)
~ cod in cream	~ in Rahmsauce	~ à la crème	~ alla crema	~ a la crema
~ cod in tomato sauce	~ in Tomatensauce	~ sautée aux tomates	~ in umido	~ en salsa de tomate
~ cod, ragout of	Stockfischragout	~ en ragoût	~ in umido	~ en ragú
sand smelts; silversides	Ährenfische	prêtres; nonnats	latterini	pejerrey; abichones
sardines; pilchards	Sardinen	sardines	sardine; sarde	sardinas
scad; horse mackerel	Bastardmakrele; Stöcker	saurel; chinchard	suro; sugherello	chicharro; jurel
scallops	Jakobsmuscheln	coquilles Saint-Jacques	capesante	vieiras
scallop brochettes	Jakobsmuschelspieß	brochettes de Saint-Jacques	spiedini di capesante	brochetas de vieiras
scallops au gratin	gratinierte Jakobsmuscheln	coquilles Saint-Jacques gratinées	capesante gratinate	vieiras gratinadas
~, queen	Kammmuscheln	pétoncles; vanneaux	canestrelli; pettini	volandeiras; zamburiñas
scampi[1]	Scampi; Kaisergranat	langoustines; scampi	scampi	cigalas
~, curried	~ mit Curry	~ au curry	~ al curry	~ al curry
~, fried	frittierte Scampi	~ frites	~ fritti	~ fritas
~, steamed	Scampi im Dampf gegart	~ à la vapeur	~ al vapore	~ al vapor
scorpion-fish	Drachenkopf	rascasse	scorfano	rascacio; escorpena
sea bass; bass	Wolfsbarsch; Loup; Seebarsch	bar; loup (de mer)	branzino; spigola	lubina; róbalo
~ bass in salt crust	~ in Salzkruste	~ au sel	~ al sale	~ a la sal
~ bass meunière	~ nach Müllerinart	~ meunière; ~ au beurre	~ alla mugnaia	~ a la molinera
~ bass, poached	pochierter Wolfsbarsch	~ poché	~ lesso	~ cocida
~ bass with herbs	Wolfsbarsch mit Kräutern	~ aux herbes	~ alle erbe	~ con hierbas
sea-bream	Meerbrasse	pagre	pagro	pagro; pargo
sea ears; ormers; abalones	Meerohren	ormeaux; oreilles de mer	orecchie di mare	orejas de mar

[1] also Dublin Bay prawns

Fish and shellfish

Fish and shellfish English	Fische und Schaltiere German	Poissons et crustacés French	Pesci e crostacei Italian	Pescados y crustáceos Spanish
sea-fish	Seefisch	poisson de mer	pesce di mare	pez marino
~ loach; rockling	Seequappe	loche de mer; motelle	motella	bertorella; barbada; motela
~ trout	Meerforelle	truite de mer	trota di mare	trucha de mar; reo
~ urchins	Seeigel	oursins; châtaignes de mer	ricci di mare	erizos de mar
seafood; shellfish	Meeresfrüchte	fruits de mer	frutti di mare	mariscos
shad; allice shad	Alse; Maifisch	alose	cheppia; alosa	sábalo; alosa
~ roe	Maifischrogen	œufs d'alose	uova di cheppia	huevas de sábalo
sheatfish; wels; catfish	Wels; Waller	silure glane; glane	siluro	siluro
shellfish; seafood	Meeresfrüchte	fruits de mer	frutti di mare	mariscos
shore crabs; crabs; green crabs	Krabben; Strandkrabben	crabes; ~ verts	granchi	cangrejos de mar; cámbaros
shrimps	Garnelen	crevettes	gamberetti	gambas; camarones
~ creole	~ auf kreolische Art	~ à la créole	~ alla creola	camarones a la criolla
~, curried	~ in Currysauce	~ au curry	~ al curry	~ al curry
silver eels; elvers	Glasaale	civelles; pibales; alevins d'anguille	anguillette; cieche	angulas
silversides; sand smelts	Ährenfische	prêtres; nonnats	latterini	pejerrey; abichones
skate; ray	Rochen	raie	razza	raya
~ with black butter	~ mit schwarzer Butter	~ au beurre noir	~ al burro nero	~ con mantequilla negra
~ with caper sauce	~ mit Kapernsauce	~ sauce aux câpres	~ con salsa di capperi	~ con salsa de alcaparras
slipper lobster	Bärenkrebs	cigale de mer; scyllare	cicala di mare; magnosa	cigarra
smelt	Stint	éperlan	sperlano; eperlano	eperlano
~ brochettes	Stintspießchen	éperlans en brochettes	spiedini di sperlani	brochetas de eperlanos
smooth hound; dogfish	Glatthai	émissole; moutelle	palombo	musola
snails	Schnecken; Weinbergschnecken	escargots	lumache	caracoles
~ in garlic butter	Weinbergschnecken mit Kräuterbutter	~ à la bourguignonne	~ con burro all'aglio	~ en mantequilla de ajo

Fish and shellfish

Fish and shellfish English	Fische und Schaltiere German	Poissons et crustacés French	Pesci e crostacei Italian	Pescados y crustáceos Spanish
soft roe of carp	Karpfenmilch	laitances de carpe	latte di carpa	lechas de carpa
soft-shell crabs	weichschalige Strandkrabben	crabes mous (en mue)	mollecche	cámbaros mollares
sole	Seezunge	sole	sogliola	lenguado
~ Colbert (breaded, fried, filled with parsley butter)	~ Colbert (paniert, gebacken und mit Kräuterbutter gefüllt)	~ Colbert (panée, frite fourrée de beurre maître d'hôtel)	~ Colbert (panata, fritta e farcita di burro maître d'hôtel)	~ Colbert (lenguado frito relleno de mantequilla maître d'hôtel)
~ fillets in white wine	Seezungenfilets in Weißwein	filets de sole au vin blanc	filetti di sogliola al vino bianco	filetes de lenguado al vino blanco
~, fillets of	Seezungenfilets	~ de sole	~ di sogliola	~ de lenguado
~ Florentine	Seezunge auf Spinat	sole à la florentine	sogliola agli spinaci	lenguado con espinacas
~, fried	frittierte Seezunge	~ frite	~ fritta	~ frito
~, grilled	gegrillte Seezunge	~ grillée	~ alla griglia	~ a la parrilla
~ in salt crust	Seezunge in Salzkruste	~ en croûte de sel	~ al sale	~ a la sal
~ meunière	~ nach Müllerinart	~ à la meunière	~ alla mugnaia	~ a la molinera
~ Mornay	gratinierte Seezunge	~ au gratin; ~ mornay	~ gratinata	~ al gratén
~ Orly, fillets of (deep-fried, served with tomato sauce)	Seezungenfilets Orly (frittiert und mit Tomatensauce angerichtet)	filets de sole Orly (filets frits servis avec sauce tomate)	filetti di sogliola Orly (filetti fritti e serviti con salsa di pomodoro)	filetes de lenguado Orly (filetes fritos con salsa de tomate)
~ roulades; rolled sole fillets	Seezungenröllchen	paupiettes de sole	involtini di sogliola	rollos de lenguado; popietas de lenguado
~, steamed	gedämpfte Seezunge	sole à la vapeur	sogliola al vapore	lenguado al vapor
soused herring; marinated herring	marinierter Hering	hareng mariné	aringa marinata	arenque marinado; ~ en escabeche
spider crabs	Meerspinnen	araignées de mer	grancevole; granceole	centollas[1]
spiny dogfish; spur-dog	Dornhai	aiguillat	spinarolo	mielga; galludo
~ lobster[2]	Languste	langouste	aragosta	langosta

---

[1] o centollos - [2] also rock lobster and crawfish

Fish and shellfish

Fish and shellfish English	**Fische und Schaltiere** German	**Poissons et crustacés** French	**Pesci e crostacei** Italian	**Pescados y crustáceos** Spanish
spiny lobster en bellevue (lobster meat in jelly)	Languste Bellevue (Schwanzscheiben in Gelee)	langouste à la parisienne[1] (escalopes à la gelée)	aragosta in bella vista (fette di aragosta in gelatina)	langosta a la parisiense (rodajas en gelatina)
~ lobster in jelly	~ Bellevue in Aspik	~ en bellevue	~ in bella vista	~ a la parisiense
~ lobster mayonnaise	~ mit Mayonnaise	~ à la mayonnaise	~ con maionese	~ con mayonesa
~ lobster medallions	Langustenmedaillons	médaillons de langouste	medaglioni di aragosta	medallones de langosta
spotted dogfish	Katzenhai	roussette	gattuccio	pintarroja
sprats	Sprotten	sprats	spratti; papaline; sarde	espadines
~, smoked	~ (Kieler Sprotten)	~ fumés	~ affumicati	~ ahumados
spur-dog; spiny dogfish	Dornhai	aiguillat	spinarolo	mielga; galludo
squids; calamaries	Kalmare	calmars; encornets	calamari	calamares
~, fried	frittierte Kalmare	friture de calmars	~ fritti	~ fritos
~, small	Kalmare (kleine)	supions	calamaretti	chipirones
squills; mantis shrimps	Heuschreckenkrebse	squilles	canocchie; pannocchie	galeras
sterlet	Sterlet	sterlet	sterletto[2]	esturión esterlete
stockfish; salt cod	Stockfisch	morue	baccalà; stoccafisso	bacalao (seco)
stonebass; wreckfish	Wrackbarsch	cernier[3]	cernia di scoglio	cherna
sturgeon	Stör	esturgeon	storione	esturión
~, smoked	geräucherter Stör	~ fumé	~ affumicato	~ ahumado
~ steak, grilled	Störschnitte vom Grill	darne d'esturgeon grillée	trancio di storione ai ferri	~ a la parrilla
surmullet[4]; red mullet	Meerbarbe; Streifenbarbe	rouget de roche; surmullet	triglia di scoglio	salmonete de roca
sweet and sour carp	Karpfen süß-sauer	carpe aigre-doux	carpa in agrodolce	carpa en agridulce
swordfish	Schwertfisch	espadon	pesce spada	pez espada; emperador
~ carpaccio	Schwertfischcarpaccio	carpaccio d'espadon	carpaccio di pesce spada	carpaccio de pez espada
tench	Schleie	tanche	tinca	tenca
~ au bleu	~ blau	~ au bleu	~ al blu	~ au bleu
~ au gratin	überbackene Schleie	~ gratinée	~ gratinata	~ al gratén

---

1) ou langouste en bellevue - 2) o sterlatto - 3) ou mérou des Basques - 4) also striped surmullet

Fish and shellfish

Fish and shellfish English	Fische und Schaltiere German	Poissons et crustacés French	Pesci e crostacei Italian	Pescados y crustáceos Spanish
terrapin	Dosenschildkröte; Süßwasserschildkröte	terrapin; tortue diamant	tartaruga d'acqua dolce	tortuga de agua dulce
terrine of fish	Fischterrine	terrine de poisson	terrina di pesce	terrina de pescado
torpedo fish; electric ray	Zitterrochen	torpille; raie électrique	torpedine	torpedo
trout	Forelle	truite	trota	trucha
~ amandine	~ mit Mandeln	~ aux amandes	~ con le mandorle	~ con almendras
~ au bleu; boiled trout	~ blau	~ au bleu	~ bollita; ~ al blu	~ azulada; ~ hervida
~ en papillote	~ in Folie	~ en papillote	~ al cartoccio	~ en papillote
~, fried	gebackene Forelle	~ frite	~ fritta	~ frita
~ in cream sauce	Forelle in Sahnesauce	~ à la crème	~ alla panna	~ a la crema
~ in jelly	~ in Aspik	~ en gelée	~ in gelatina	~ en gelatina
~ in red wine	~ in Rotwein	~ au vin rouge	~ al vino rosso	~ al vino tinto
meunière	~ nach Müllerinart	~ meunière	~ alla mugnaia	~ a la molinera
~, smoked	geräucherte Forelle	~ fumée	~ affumicata	~ ahumada
~, smoked fillets of	~ Forellenfilets	filets de truite fumés	filetti di trota affumicati	filetes de trucha ahumados
~, stuffed	gefüllte Forelle	truite farcie	trota ripiena	trucha rellena
trouts, farmed; ~ from the fish-tank	Zuchtforellen	truites d'élevage	trote d'allevamento; ~ di vivaio	truchas de vivero
tuna; tunny	Thunfisch[1]	thon	tonno	atún
~ fish, grilled	~ vom Grill	~ grillé	~ ai ferri	~ a la parrilla
~ with mushrooms, braised	geschmorter Thunfisch mit Pilzen	~ braisé aux champignons	~ in umido coi funghi	~ estofado con champiñones
turbot	Steinbutt	turbot	rombo	rodaballo
~ au gratin	überbackener Steinbutt	~ gratiné	~ gratinato	~ gratinado
~, braised	geschmorter Steinbutt	~ braisé	~ brasato	~ estofado
~, grilled	Steinbutt vom Grill	~ grillé	~ grigliato; ~ in gratella	~ a la parrilla
~ in white wine	~ in Weißwein	~ au vin blanc	~ al vino bianco	~ al vino blanco
~ roulade	Steinbuttroulade	roulade de turbot	rotolo di rombo	rollo de rodaballo

[1] auch Tunfisch

Fish and shellfish

Fish and shellfish English	Fische und Schaltiere German	Poissons et crustacés French	Pesci e crostacei Italian	Pescados y crustáceos Spanish
turbot sauce hollandaise, poached	gekochter Steinbutt mit holländischer Sauce	turbot poché sauce hollandaise	rombo lesso con salsa olandese	rodaballo cocido con salsa holandesa
~ soufflé	Steinbuttsoufflé	soufflé de turbot	soufflé di rombo	soufflé de rodaballo
turtle	Schildkröte	tortue	tartaruga	tortuga
velvet swim crabs	Schwimmkrabben	étrilles	granchi di arena	nécoras
venus clams	warzige Venusmuscheln	praires	tartufi di mare	escupiñas; verigüetos
~ clams, stuffed	gefüllte Venusmuscheln	~ farcies	~ di mare ripieni	~ rellenas
weever; greater weever	Drachenfisch; Petermännchen	vive	tracina; trachino; ragno	araña
wels; sheatfish; catfish	Wels; Waller	silure glane; glane	siluro	siluro
whitebaits, fried	frittierte Weißfischchen	friture de blanchailles	frittura di bianchetti	fritura de chanquetes
whitefish	Felchen; Renke; Maräne	corégone; lavaret; marène	coregono; lavarello; marena	lavareto; corégono
whiting	Merlan; Wittling	merlan	merlano; merlango	merlán[1]
~, fried	gebackener Merlan	~ frit	~ fritto	~ frito
~ in white wine	Merlan in Weißwein	~ au vin blanc	~ al vino bianco	~ al vino blanco
~ meunière	~ Müllerinart	~ à la meunière	~ alla mugnaia	~ a la molinera
~ ravigote sauce	~ mit Vinaigrette	~ ravigote	~ alla vinaigrette	~ a la vinagreta
wild salmon	Wildlachs	saumon sauvage	salmone selvaggio	salmón salvaje
winkles; periwinkles	Strandschnecken	bigorneaux; vignots	lumache di mare; littorine	bígaros
wrasse	Lippfisch	vieille; labre	tordo; labro	tordo; merlo; labro
wreckfish; stonebass	Wrackbarsch	cernier[2]	cernia di scoglio	cherna

---

1) o plegonero, pescadilla - 2) ou mérou des Basques

Meat

Meat English	Fleisch German	Viandes French	Carni Italian	Carnes Spanish
baby lamb; spring lamb	Milchlamm	agneau de lait	agnello di latte	cordero lechal; lechazo; ternasco
beef	Rindfleisch	bœuf	manzo; bue	vaca; buey
colt	Fohlen	poulain	puledro	potro
horse	Pferdefleisch	cheval	cavallo	caballo
kid	Zicklein; Kitz	chevreau; cabri	capretto	cabrito; choto
lamb	Lammfleisch	agneau	agnello	cordero
moufflon; mouflon	Mufflon	mouflon	muflone	muflón
mutton	Hammelfleisch; Schöpsenfleisch	mouton	montone; castrato	carnero
ostrich	Strauß	autruche	struzzo	avestruz
pork	Schweinefleisch	porc	maiale	cerdo
spring lamb; baby lamb	Milchlamm	agneau de lait	agnello di latte	cordero lechal; lechazo; ternasco
sucking pig; suckling pig	Spanferkel	chochon de lait; porcelet	maialino di latte	cochinillo; lechón; tostón (gebratenes)
veal	Kalbfleisch	veau	vitello	ternera

Meat dishes

Meat dishes English	**Fleischgerichte** German	**Plats de viande** French	**Piatti di carne** Italian	**Platos de carne** Spanish
beef à la mode (braised with carrots, onions and calf's foot)	Bœuf à la mode (Rinderschmorbraten, Rindfleisch mit Karotten und Kalbsfuß geschmort)	bœuf à la mode (braisé avec carottes et pied de veau)	Manzo alla moda (brasato con carote, cipolline e piede di vitello)	vaca a la moda (braseada con zanahorias y pies de ternera)
~, boiled; prime boiled beef	gekochtes Rindfleisch; Tafelspitz; Suppenfleisch	~ bouilli	bollito di manzo; manzo bollito; ~ lesso	carne del cocido
~, braised; pot-roast	Rinderschmorbraten; Schmorbraten	~ braisé[1]	manzo brasato	estofado de vaca; ~ de buey
~ carpaccio (thin slices of raw beef filled seasoned with oil and Parmesan)	Rindercarpaccio; Carpaccio (rohe Filetscheiben mit Öl und Parmesan)	carpaccio (tranches très minces de bœuf ou servies avec huile et parmesan)	carpaccio (felte fottili di filetto crudo condite con olio e parmigiano)	carpaccio de carne (lonjas de solomillo crudo con aceite y parmesano)
~ cheeks	Ochsenwangen	bajoues de bœuf	guance di manzo	carrillos de buey
~ jardinière[2] (with cooked vegetables)	Rinderfilet nach Gärtnerinart (mit Gemüse)	filet de bœuf à la jardinière (aux légumes)	filetto di manzo alla giardiniera (con verdure)	solomillo a la jardinera (con legumbres)
~ olives; ~ roulades	Rinderrouladen	paupiettes de bœuf	involtini di manzo	rollitos de buey; popietas de vaca
~ stew; ragout of beef	Rinderragout	ragoût de bœuf[3]	stufato di manzo	estofado de vaca
~ Stroganoff (beef stew in sour cream sauce)	Filetgulasch Stroganow (in saurer Sahne)	bœuf Stroganov (sauté de bœf à la crème aigre)	manzo alla Stroganov (con panna acida)	buey Stroganov (estofado en crema agria)
~ vinaigrette	Rindfleischsalat	~ vinaigrette	~ in insalata	ensalada de buey
~ Wellington[4] (baked in pastry)	Rinderfilet Wellington (in Blätterteighülle)	filet de bœuf Wellington (en croûte de feuilletage)	filetto di manzo in crosta; ~ di manzo Wellington (in involucro di pasta sfoglia)	solomillo Wellington (envuelto en pasta de hojaldre)
beefsteak; steak	Beefsteak	bifteck; steak	bistecca (di manzo)	bistec; steak
~ with a fried egg	~ mit Spiegelei	steak à cheval (avec un œuf poêlé dessus)	~ alla Bismarck (con un uovo sopra)	~ a caballo (con un huevo al plato)

---

1) ou bœuf en daube - 2) also fillet of beef jardinière - 3) ou estouffade (de bœuf) - 4) also fillet of beef Wellington

Meat dishes

Meat dishes English	**Fleischgerichte** German	**Plats de viande** French	**Piatti di carne** Italian	**Platos de carne** Spanish
Bitoke (kind of Hamburg steak)	Bitok (russisches Hacksteak)	bitoke (beefsteak haché, sauté au beurre)	bitoke (polpetta di manzo)	bitoque (bistec de picadillo)
black pudding[1]	Blutwurst	boudin noir	sanguinaccio	morcilla
blanquette of veal	Kalbsragout in weißer Sauce	blanquette de veau	fricassea di vitello	ternera en salsa blanca
bœuf bourguignon (beef stew in red wine)	Bœuf bourguignon (Rinderragout in Rotwein)	bœuf bourguignon	bue alla borgognona (stufato nel vino rosso)	vaca a la borgoñona (estofado al vino tinto)
brain fritters	Hirnbeignets	fritots de cervelle	frittelle di cervella	buñuelos de sesos
brains meunière	gebratenes Kalbshirn	cervelle à la meunière	cervello alla mugnaia	sesos a la molinera
~ with black butter	Kalbshirn in schwarzer Buttersauce	~ au beurre noir	~ al burro nero	~ con mantequilla negra
brisket of beef; breast of beef	Rinderbrust	poitrine de bœuf	petto di manzo	pecho de vaca
bubble and squeak (cabbage, potato and sometimes meat fried together)	Bubble and squeak (Kohl, Kartoffeln und manchmal Fleisch zusammen aufgebraten)	bubble and squeak (choux et pommes de terre sautés, parfois avec de la viande)	bubble and squeak (cavoli, patate e talvolta carne rosolati assieme)	bubble and squeak (coles, patatas y a veces carne, salteados juntos)
Burgundy beef stew (stewed in red wine with mushrooms and small onions)	Rindfleisch auf Burgunder Art (in Rotwein mit Zwiebelchen und Champignons geschmort)	bœuf bourguignon (sauté au vin rouge avec champignons et petits oignons)	bue alla borgognona (brasato nel vino rosso con funghi e cipolline)	vaca a la borgoñona (estofado al vino tinto con cebollitas y champiñones)
calf's brains	Kalbshirn	cervelle de veau	cervello di vitello	sesos de ternera
~ brains, fried	frittiertes Kalbshirn	~ frite	~ fritto	~ fritos
~ brains with egg	Hirn mit Ei	~ de veau à l'œuf	~ di vitello all'uovo	~ con huevo
~ ears	Kalbsohren	oreilles de veau	orecchie di vitello	orejas de ternera
~ feet	Kalbsfüße	pieds de veau	piedini di vitello	pies de ternera
~ feet, fried	gebackene Kalbsfüße	~ de veau frits	piedi di vitello fritti	~ de ternera fritos
~ feet, grilled	Kalbsfüße vom Rost	~ de veau grillés	piedini di vitello grigliati	~ de ternera a la parrilla
~ gristle	Kalbsbrustknorpel	tendrons de veau	tenerume di vitello	ternillas de ternera

---

[1] also blood sausage

Meat dishes

Meat dishes English	**Fleischgerichte** German	**Plats de viande** French	**Piatti di carne** Italian	**Platos de carne** Spanish
calf's gristle, braised	geschmorter Kalbsbrustknorpel	tendrons de veau braisés	tenerume di vitello brasato	ternillas braseadas
~ head	Kalbskopf	tête de veau	testina di vitello	cabeza de ternera
~ head, boiled	gekochter Kalbskopf	~ de veau au court-bouillon	~ bollita	~ cocida
~ head en tortue (garnished with olives, mushrooms, gherkins)	Kalbskopf auf Schildkrötenart (mit Oliven, Champignons, Essiggurken)	~ de veau en tortue (garnie olives, champignons, cornichons)	~ di vitello en tortue (guarnita di olive, funghi, cetriolini)	~ de ternera en tortue (con aceitunas, champiñones, pepinillos)
~ head, fried	frittierter Kalbskopf	~ de veau frite	~ di vitello fritta	~ de ternera frita
~ head vinaigrette	Kalbskopf mit Vinaigrette	~ de veau vinaigrette	~ di vitello in salsa vinaigrette	~ de ternera a la vinagreta
~ heart	Kalbsherz	cœur de veau	cuore di vitello ai	corazón de ternera
~ heart, grilled	~ vom Rost	~ de veau grillé	~ di vitello ai ferri	~ de ternera a la parrilla
~ kidney	Kalbsniere	rognon de veau	rognone di vitello	riñones de ternera
~ kidney flambé	flambierte Kalbsniere	~ de veau flambé	~ alla fiamma	~ de ternera flameados
~ kidney, grilled	gegrillte Kalbsniere	~ de veau grillé	~ di vitello alla griglia	~ asados a la parrilla
~ kidney in white wine	Kalbsniere in Weißweinsauce	~ de veau au vin blanc	~ al vino bianco	~ en vino blanco
~ kidney sauté	sautierte Kalbsniere	~ de veau sauté	~ di vitello saltato	~ de ternera salteados
~ kidney Turbigo (garnished with mushrooms and sausage)	Kalbsniere Turbigo (mit Champignons und Bratwürtchen)	~ de veau Turbigo (garni de champignons et d'une saucisse)	~ alla Turbigo (guarnito di funghi e di una salsiccia)	riñone de ternera Turbigo (con champiñones y salchicha)
~ lights	Kalbslunge	mou de veau	polmone di vitello	bofes de ternera
~ liver	Kalbsleber	foie de veau	fegato di vitello	hígado de ternera
~ liver and apples	~ nach Berliner Art (mit Äpfeln)	~ à la berlinoise (aux pommes fruits)	~ di vitello alla berlinese (con mele)	~ de ternera a la berlinesa (con manzanas)
~ liver and bacon	~ auf englische Art (mit Speckscheiben)	~ à l'anglaise (sauté au bacon)	~ all'inglese (con fettine di pancetta)	~ de ternera a la inglesa (con tocino)

Meat dishes

Meat dishes English	Fleischgerichte German	Plats de viande French	Piatti di carne Italian	Platos de carne Spanish
calf's liver en brochette	Kalbsleber am Spießchen	brochettes de foie de veau	spiedini di fegato	hígado de ternera en brocheta
~ liver, fried	gebackene Kalbsleber	foie de veau frit	fegato di vitello fritto	~ de ternera frito
~ liver, grilled	gegrillte Kalbsleber	~ de veau grillé	~ di vitello grigliato	~ de ternera a la parrilla
~ liver kebabs	Kalbsleberspieße	brochettes de foie de veau	spiedini di fegato	brochetas de hígado
~ liver sauté	gebratene Kalbsleber	foie de veau sauté	fegato di vitello al burro	hígado de ternera salteado
~ liver Tyrolean style (fried liver in sour cream sauce)	Tiroler Leber (Kalbsleberscheiben in Sauerrahmsauce)	~ de veau à la tyrolienne (sauté, nappé sauce crème aigre)	~ di vitello alla tirolese (in salsa di panna acida)	~ de ternera a la tirolesa (en salsa de crema agria)
~ sweetbreads	Kalbsbries; Kalbsmilch	ris de veau	animelle di vitello	mollejas de ternera
~ sweetbreads with mushrooms	~ mit Champignons	~ de veau aux champignons	~ coi funghi	~ de ternera con champiñones
~ tongue	Kalbszunge	langue de veau	lingua di vitello	lengua de ternera
~ tongue ragout	Kalbszungen-Ragout	~ de veau en ragoût	~ di vitello in umido	~ de ternera estofada
~ tripe	Kalbskutteln	tripes de veau	trippa di vitello	callos de ternera
cassoulet (casserole of beans and various meats)	Cassoulet (Bohnenragout mit Schweine- oder Gänsefleisch)	cassoulet (ragoût de haricots blancs avec viande de porc ou d'oie)	cassoulet (stufato di fagioli bianchi con carne di maiale o d'oca)	cassoulet (estofado de judías blancas con carne de cerdo o de oca)
charbroiled meats	Fleisch vom Holzkohlengrill	grillades au feu de bois	carni alla brace	carnes a la brasa
chateaubriand (double thick fillet steak)	Chateaubriand (doppelt dickes Filetsteak)	chateaubriand[1]	chateaubriand (bistecca doppia di filetto)	chateaubriand (filete doble de solomillo)
chili con carne (chili-falvowed stew of minced beef and beans)	Chili con carne (mit Chillies gewürztes Fleischragout mit Bohnen)	chili con carne (ragoût de bœuf haché au piment et aux haricots)	chili con carne (stufato di manzo tritato e fagioli al peperoncino)	chile con carne (estofado de vaca con guindilla y judías)
chipped veal in cream; creamed sliced veal	Geschnetzeltes in Sahnesauce	émincé de veau (zurichoise)	striscioline di vitello alla panna; vitello alla zurighese	tiras de ternera a la crema; lonjas de ternera a la crema

---

[1] ou châteaubriant

Meat dishes

Meat dishes English	Fleischgerichte German	Plats de viande French	Piatti di carne Italian	Platos de carne Spanish
cold cuts; ~ meats	Kalte Platte	assiette anglaise; viandes froides	piatto freddo	surtido de fiambres
~ roast veal	Kalbsbraten kalt	rôti de veau froid	arrosto freddo	asado de ternera frío
~ veal in tuna sauce	Kalbfleisch in Thunfischsauce	veau froid au thon	vitello tonnato	ternera con salsa de atún
colt steak	Fohlensteak	steak de poulain	bistecca di puledro	steak de potro
cornish pasty	Fleischpastete	petit pâté en croûte	pâté di carne in crosta	pastel de carne
cottage pie; shepherd's pie (minced meat topped with mashed potato)	Hirtenpastete (Kartoffelpüree auf Hackfleisch)	hachis parmentier (gratin de viande hachée et de purée de pommes)	pasticcio del pastore (gratin di carne tritata e di purè di patate)	~ del pastor (picadillo cubierto de puré de patatas y gratinado)
cracklings	Grieben	grattons; frittons	ciccioli	chicharrones
creamed sliced veal; chipped veal in cream	Geschnetzeltes in Sahnesauce	émincé de veau (zurichoise)	striscioline di vitello alla panna; vitello alla zurighese	tiras de ternera a la crema; lonjas de ternera a la crema
crown of lamb; ~ roast of lamb	Kronenbraten vom Lamm; gebratener Lammkranz	couronne d'agneau rôtie	corona d'agnello arrosto	corona de cordero asada
double sirloin steak	doppeltes Entrecote	entrecôte double	costata doppia	entrecot doble
easter lamb	Osterlamm	agneau pascal	agnello pasquale	cordero pascual
egg roll; spring roll	Frühlingsrolle	rouleau de printemps	involtino primavera	rollo de primavera
entrecôte[1]	Entrecote	entrecôte	costata di manzo	entrecot
~ lyonnaise (with fried onions); sirloin steak lyonnaise (with fried onions)	~ nach Lyoner Art (mit Zwiebeln)	~ à la lyonnaise (aux oignons)	~ alla lionese (con cipolle)	~ a la lionesa (con cebollas)
escalope of veal	Kalbsschnitzel	escalope de veau	scaloppina di vitello	escalope de ternera
~ of veal, breaded	paniertes Kalbsschnitzel	~ de veau panée	~ di vitello impanata	~ de ternera empanado
~ of veal chasseur (with mushrooms)	Jägerschnitzel (mit Champignons)	~ de veau chasseur (aux champignons)	~ alla cacciatora (con funghi)	~ a la cazadora (con champiñones)

---

[1] also sirloin steak

Meat dishes

Meat dishes English	Fleischgerichte German	Plats de viande French	Piatti di carne Italian	Platos de carne Spanish
escalope of veal Cordon bleu (filled with ham & cheese)	Cordon bleu (Kalbsschnitzel mit Schinken-Käsefüllung)	escalope de veau Cordon bleu (farcie de jambon et de fromage)	scaloppina Cordon bleu (farcita di prosciutto e formaggio)	escalope Cordon bleu (relleno de jamón y queso)
~ of veal, gipsy-style (with strips of ham, tungue and mushrooms)	Zigeuner-Schnitzel (mit feinen Schinkenstreifen, Zunge und Champignons)	~ de veau zingara (garnie julienne de jambon, langue et champignons)	~ di vitello alla zingara (con filetti di prosciutto, lingua e funghi)	~ de ternera a la gitana (con tiritas de jamón, lengua y champiñones)
~ of veal Holstein (with a fried egg and anchovy fillets)	Holstein-Schnitzel (mit Setzei und Sardellenfilets)	~ de veau Holstein (garnie œuf poêlé et filets d'anchois)	~ alla Holstein (con filetti d'acciuga e un uovo al piatto)	~ Holstein (con un huevo al plato y filetes de anchoas)
~ of veal, Parisienne (dipped in beaten egg & fried)	Pariser Schnitzel (in verquirltes Ei getaucht und gebacken)	~ de veau à la parisienne (panée à l'œuf et frite)	~ alla parigina (passata nell'uovo sbattuto e fritta)	~ de ternera a la parisiense (pasada en huevo batido y frita)
~ of veal sauté	Naturschnitzel; Kalbsschnitzel natur	~ de veau sautée	~ di vitello al burro	~ de ternera salteada
filett of pork	Schweinefilet	filet de porc	filetto di maiale	lomo de cerdo
fillet of beef; sirloin; tenderloin	Rinderfilet	~ de bœuf	~ di manzo	solomillo (de buey)
~ of beef in jelly	~ in Aspik	~ de bœuf en gelée	~ di manzo in gelatina	~ en gelatina
~ of beef in Madeira	~ in Madeirasauce	~ de bœuf au madère	~ di manzo al madera	~ al madera
~ of beef Portuguese (with stuffed tomatoes)	~ auf portugiesische Art (mit Tomaten)	~ de bœuf portugaise (aux tomates farcies)	~ di manzo alla portoghese (con pomodori)	~ a la portuguesa (con tomates)
~ of lamb in pastry	Lammfilet in Teigkruste	~ d'agneau en croûte	~ d'agnello in crosta	~ de cordero en costra
~ of veal	Kalbsfilet	~ de veau	~ di vitello	~ de ternera
~ of veal, larded	gespicktes Kalbsfilet	~ de veau piqué	~ di vitello lardellato	~ de ternera mechado
~ steak	Filetsteak	filet-steak; filet grillé	bistecca di filetto	bistec de solomillo
Flemish stew (slices of beef stewed in beer)	flämische Karbonaden (Rinderschnitzel in Bier geschmort)	carbonnades à la flamande (tranches de bœuf à la bière)	brasato alla fiamminga (fette di manzo brasate nella birra)	carbonada flamenca (bistecs braseados en cerveza)

Meat dishes

Meat dishes English	**Fleischgerichte** German	**Plats de viande** French	**Piatti di carne** Italian	**Platos de carne** Spanish
fondue bourguignonne	Fleischfondue	fondue bourguignonne	fondue bourguignonne	fondue borgoñón
Frankfurters; Wieners	Frankfurter Würstchen	saucisses de Francfort	würstel	salchichas de Frankfurt
fricandeau of veal[1]	Kalbsfrikandeau[2]	fricandeau (de veau)	fricandò di vitello	fricandó de ternera
fried brains	gebackenes Hirn	cervelle de veau frite	cervello fritto	sesos fritos
garnished sauerkraut ; sauerkraut with pork meats	garniertes Sauerkraut	choucroute alsacienne	crauti all'alsaziana	chucrut a la alsaciana
gigot; leg of mutton	Hammelkeule	gigot de mouton	cosciotto di montone	pierna de carnero
goulash	Gulasch	goulache	gulasch	gulasch
~, Hungarian	ungarisches Gulasch	~ à la hongroise	~ all' ungherese	~ húngaro
~ of pork	Schweinegulasch	~ de porc	~ di maiale	~ de cerdo
~, veal	Kalbsgulasch	~ de veau	~ di vitello	~ de ternera
grenadines (braised larded slices of veal)	Grenadins (gespickte Kalbsschnitzel)	grenadins de veau (escalopes piquées)	grenadine (scaloppine lardellate)	escalopes mechados
grills; grilled meats	Grillgerichte; Grilladen	grillades	grigliata di carne	parrillada de carne
grilled entrecôte with parsley butter; ~ sirloin steak with parsley butter	Entrecote vom Grill mit Kräuterbutter	entrecôte grillée maître d'hôtel	costata alla griglia con burro al prezzemolo; ~ alla griglia con burro maître d'hôtel	entrecot con mantequilla al perejil; ~ a la mayordoma (con mantequilla maître d'hôtel)
~ lamb chop	Lammkotelett vom Rost	côtelette d'agneau grillée	costoletta d'agnello alla griglia	chuleta de cordero a la parrilla
~ meats; grills	Grillgerichte; Grilladen	grillades	grigliata di carne	parrillada de carne
~ sausages	Bratwürste vom Grill	saucisses grillées	salsicce ai ferri	salchichas a la parrilla
~ sirloin steak with parsley butter; ~ entrecôte with parsley butter	Entrecote vom Grill mit Kräuterbutter	entrecôte grillée maître d'hôtel	costata alla griglia con burro al prezzemolo; ~ alla griglia con burro maître d'hôtel	entrecot con mantequilla al perejil; ~ a la mayordoma (con mantequilla maître d'hôtel)

1) slice of braised larded veal - 2) Schnitte von gespickter Kalbsnuss

Meat dishes

Meat dishes English	Fleischgerichte German	Plats de viande French	Piatti di carne Italian	Platos de carne Spanish
grilled steak	Beefsteak vom Grill; Grillsteak; Rostbraten	bifteck grillé; steak grillé	bistecca ai ferri	bistec a la parrilla
~ tournedos	Filetschnitte vom Grill	tournedos grillé	tournedos alla griglia	tournedó a la parrilla
haggis (sheep's offal boiled in the animal's stomach)	Haggis (Innereien vom Schaf in Schafsmagen gekocht)	haggis (fressure de bebris bouillie dans la parse de l'animal)	haggis (frattaglie di pecora bollite nello stomaco dell'animale)	haggis (asaduras de oveja cocidas en lo stómago del animal)
ham	Schinken	jambon	prosciutto	jamón
~ in jelly	~ in Aspik	~ en gelée	~ in gelatina	~ en gelatina
~ in Madeira sauce	~ in Madeirasauce	~ braisé au madère	~ al madera	~ al madera
~ in pastry	~ in Teigkruste	~ en croûte	~ in crosta	~ en pasta
~ medallions	Schinkenmedaillons	médaillons de jambon	medaglioni di prosciutto	medallones de jamón
~ steak	Schinkensteak	steak de jambon	bistecca di prosciutto	bistec de jamón
~ with sauerkraut	Schinken mit Sauerkraut	jambon à la choucroute	prosciutto con crauti	jamón con chucruta
~ with spinach	~ mit Spinat	~ aux épinards	~ con spinaci	~ con espinacas
Hamburger	Hamburger (Frikadelle, Hacksteak); deutsches Beefsteak	Hamburger	Hamburger (polpetta in forma di medaglione)	Hamburguesa (bistec de picadillo)
hash calf's lights	Lungen-Haschee	hachis de mou de veau	polmone di vitello tritato	bofes de ternera picados
horse steak	Pferdesteak	steak de cheval	bistecca di cavallo	steak de caballo
hot pot; single-dish meal; hotchpotch	Eintopf; Eintopfgericht	plat unique; potée	piatto unico	plato único; puchero
hotpot (stew of mutton and potato)	Hammelragout mit Kartoffeln	ragoût de monton aux pommes	stufato di montone e patate	estofado de carnero y patatas
Irish stew (mutton stew with onion & potato)	Irishstew (Eintopf aus Hammelfleisch)	irish stew (ragoût de mouton)	irish stew (stufato di montone)	irish stew (estofado de carnero)
kebabs; shashliks (meat on skewers)	Schaschliks (Hammelspießchen)	kebabs (brochettes de mouton)	spiedini di montone	brochetas de cordero

Meat dishes

Meat dishes English	Fleischgerichte German	Plats de viande French	Piatti di carne Italian	Platos de carne Spanish
kidney in Madeira sauce	Kalbsniere in Madeirasauce	rognon de veau au madère	rognone di vitello al madera	riñones de ternera al madera
~ kebabs; kidneys en brochette	Nierenspießchen	rognons en brochettes	spiedini di rognone	~ en brochetas
lamb chop; ~ cutlet	Lammkotelett	côtelette d'agneau	costoletta d'agnello	chuleta de cordero
~ chop, breaded	paniertes Lammkotelett	~ d'agneau panée	~ d'agnello impanata	~ de cordero empanada
~ chops	Lammrippchen	côtelettes d'agneau	costine d'agnello	costillas de cordero
~ curry	Lammcurry	curry d'agneau	curry d'agnello	curry de cordero
~ fricassee	Lammfrikassee	fricassée d'agneau	fricassea d'agnello	fricasé de cordero
~ kebabs	Lammspieße	brochettes d'agneau	spiedini d'agnello	brochetas de cordero
~ noisettes	Lammnüsschen	noisettes d'agneau	nocette d'agnello	medallones de cordero
~ pluck	Beuschel von Lamm; Lamminnereien	fressure d'agneau	interiora d'agnello; coratella d'agnello	asaduras de cordero
~ stew	Lammragout	sauté d'agneau	spezzatino d'agnello	estofado de cordero
~ stew with spring vegetables	~ auf Frühlingsart (mit jungem Gemüse)	~ d'agneau printanier (aux primeurs)	~ d'agnello primaverile (con verdure novelle)	~ de cordero primaveral (con verduras)
lamb's brains	Lammhirn	cervelles d'agneau	cervella d'agnello	sesos de cordero
~ brains meunière	gebratenes Lammhirn	~ d'agneau à la meunière	~ d'agnello alla mugnaia	~ de cordero salteados
~ head	Lammkopf	tête d'agneau	testina d'agnello	cabeza de cordero
~ kidneys	Lammnieren	rognons d'agneau	rognoni d'agnello	riñones de cordero
~ sweetbreads	Lammbries	ris d'agneau	animelle d'agnello	mollejas de cordero
larded fillet of veal	gespicktes Kalbsfilet	filet de veau piqué	filetto di vitello lardellato	solomillo de ternera mechado
leg of lamb	Lammkeule	gigot d'agneau	cosciotto d'agnello	pierna de cordero
~ of mutton; gigot	Hammelkeule	~ de mouton	~ di montone	~ de carnero
~ of mutton, braised	geschmorte Hammelkeule	~ de mouton braisé	~ di montone brasato	~ de carnero braseada
~ of pork (pickled)	Eisbein; Surhaxe; Schweinskeule	jambonneau	~ di maiale	codillo de cerdo

Meat dishes

Meat dishes English	Fleischgerichte German	Plats de viande French	Piatti di carne Italian	Platos de carne Spanish
leg of pork and pea purée	Eisbein mit Erbsenpüree	jambonneau à la purée de pois	cosciotto di maiale con purè di piselli	codillo de cerdo con puré de guisantes
~ of pork with dried fruit	~ mit Backobst	~ aux fruits secs	~ di maiale con frutta secca	~ de cerdo con frutos secos
~ of pork with sauerkraut	~ mit Sauerkraut	~ à la choucroute	~ di maiale con crauti	~ de cerdo con chucrut
~ of veal	Kalbskeule; Kalbsschlegel	cuisseau de veau	coscia di vitello	pierna de ternera
liver sausage; liverwurst	Leberwurst	pâté de foie; boudin de foie	pâté di fegato di maiale; salsiccia di fegato	embuchado de hígado; embutido de hígado
loin of lamb	Lammkarree	carré d'agneau	carré d'agnello	lomo de cordero
~ of pork; ribs of pork	Schweinskarree	~ de porc	~ di maiale	~ de cerdo
~ of pork, smoked	Räucherkarree	~ de porc fumé	~ di maiale affumicato	carré de cerdo ahumado
~ of pork with sauerkraut	Schweinskarree mit Sauerkraut	~ de porc à l'alsacienne	~ di maiale con crauti	lomo de cerdo con chucrut
~ of veal	Kalbskarree; Kalbslende	~ de veau; longe de veau	~ di vitello; lombata di vitello	~ de ternera
~ of veal, braised	geschmorte Kalbsnuss	noix de veau braisée	noce di vitello brasata	nuez de ternera braseada
~ of veal in jelly	gesülzte Kalbsnuss	~ de veau en gelée	~ di vitello in gelatina	~ de ternera en gelatina
~ of veal, roast	gebratene Kalbsnuss	~ de veau rôtie	~ di vitello arrosto	~ de ternera asada
~ of veal, roasted	Kalbsnierenbraten	longe de veau rôtie	lombata di vitello arrosto	lomo de ternera asado
meat-filled cabbage rolls	Kohl-Rouladen	paupiettes de choux	involtini di cavolo	popietas de coles
meatballs; meat cakes	Buletten; Fleischklöße; Frikadellen; Hackbällchen	boulettes; fricadelles	polpette (di carne)	albóndigas (de carne)
~ in savoury sauce	Königsberger Klopse	~ de bœuf en sauce piquante	~ di carne in salsa piccante	~ de carne en salsa picante
meatloaf	Hackbraten	rôti haché; pain de bœuf	polpettone arrosto	rollo de carne picada; pastel casero
medallion of veal[1]	Kalbsmedaillon	médaillon de veau	medaglione di vitello	medallón de ternera
~ of veal with mushrooms	~ mit Champignons	~ de veau aux champignons	~ di vitello con funghi	~ de ternera con champiñones

---

[1] also veal noisettes

Meat dishes

Meat dishes English	Fleischgerichte German	Plats de viande French	Piatti di carne Italian	Platos de carne Spanish
minced steak	Hacksteak	steak haché	svizzera	bistec de carne picada
minute sirloin steak	Entrecote minute	entrecôte minute	costata al minuto	entrecot al minuto
~ steak	Minutensteak	~ minute	bistecca al minuto	bistec al minuto
mixed grill	Mixed Grill	mixed-grill	grigliata mista	parrillada mixta
mutton chop	Hammelkotelett	côtelette de mouton	costoletta di montone	chuleta de carnero
~ stew	Hammelragout	ragoût de mouton; navarin	stufato di montone; spezzatino di montone	estofado de carnero
~ trotters	Hammelfüße	pieds de mouton	piedini di montone	pies de carnero
old-fashioned veal fricassee	Kalbsfrikassee altmodisch	fricassée de veau à l'ancienne	fricassea di vitello all'antica	fricasé de ternera a la antigua
olives	Rouladen	paupiettes	involtini	popietas
ossobuco (braised slice of veal shank)	Ossobuco (Kalbshaxe in Scheiben gedünstet)	osso-buco (rouelle de jarret de veau braisée)	Ossobuco (garretto di vitello col midollo cotto in umido)	ossobuco (rodaja braseada de jarrete de ternera)
our special terrine	Terrine nach Art des Hauses	terrine maison	terrina della casa	terrina de la casa
ox kidney	Rindernieren	rognons de bœuf	rognoni di manzo	riñones de buey
~ liver	Rinderleber	foie de bœuf	fegato di manzo	hígado de buey
~ tongue	Ochsenzunge	langue de bœuf	lingua di bue	lengua de vaca
~ tongue, braised	geschmorte Ochsenzunge	~ de bœuf braisée	~ di bue brasata	~ de vaca braseada
~ tongue in Madeira	Ochsenzunge in Madeirasauce	~ de bœuf au madère	~ di bue al madera	~ de vaca al madera
oxtail	Ochsenschwanz	queue de bœuf	coda di bue	rabo de buey
pepper steak	Pfeffersteak	steak au poivre	bistecca al pepe	steak a la pimienta
piccata (slice of veal fried in butter with parsley and lemon)	Piccata (kleines Naturschnitzel mit Petersilie und Zitrone)	piccata de veau (petite escalope de veau sautée au persil et au citron)	piccata (fettina di vitello al burro con prezzemolo e limone)	piccata (escalope pequeño con perejil y zumo de imón)
pickled pork; salt pork	Pökelfleisch; Surfleisch	salé; petit salé	carne salata (di maiale)	carne salada (de cerdo)
~ tongue	Pökelzunge	langue écarlate	lingua salmistrata	lengua salada

Meat dishes

Meat dishes English	**Fleischgerichte** German	**Plats de viande** French	**Piatti di carne** Italian	**Platos de carne** Spanish
pig's ears	Schweinsohren	oreilles de porc	orecchie di maiale	orejas de cerdo
~ ears with peas	~ mit Erbsenbrei	~ de porc à la purée de pois	~ di maiale con piselli	~ de cerdo con guisantes
~ trotter, boiled	gekochter Schweinefuß	pied de porc bouilli	piedino di maiale lesso	pata de cerdo hervida
pluck	Innereien	fressure	interiora	asaduras
pork cheeks	Schweinebacken	bajoues de porc	guance di maiale	carrillos de cerdo
~ chop, breaded	paniertes Schweinekotelett	côte de porc panée	costoletta di maiale impanata	chuleta de cerdo empanada
~ chop, grilled; broiled pork cutlet	gegrilltes Schweinekotelett	~ de porc grillée	~ di maiale ai ferri	~ de cerdo a la parrilla
~ chop paprika sauce	Schweinekotelett in Paprikasauce	~ de porc au paprika	~ di maiale alla paprica	~ de cerdo al pimentón
~ chop, smoked; smoked spare-rib	Kasseler Rippenspeer	~ de porc fumée	braciola di maiale affumicata	costillas de cerdo ahumadas
~ chop with mustard	Schweinekotelett mit Senfsauce	~ de porc à la moutarde	costoletta di maiale alla senape	chuleta de cerdo con mostaza
~ chop with savoy	Schweinsrippchen mit Wirsingkohl	côtelette de porc au chou frisé	braciola di maiale alle verze	costilla de cerdo con coles
~ cutlet; ~ chop	Schweinekotelett; Schweinerippchen	côte de porc; côtelette de porc	costoletta di maiale[1]	chuleta de cerdo
~ cutlet in jelly	Sülzkotelett	~ de porc en gelée	braciola di maiale in gelatina	~ de cerdo en gelatina
~ escalope	Schweineschnitzel	escalope de porc	scaloppina di maiale	escalope de cerdo
~ goulash with sauerkraut	Szegediner Gulasch	goulache de porc à la choucroute	gulasch di maiale con crauti	gulasch de cerdo con chucrut
~ liver	Schweinsleber	foie de porc	fegato di maiale	hígado de cerdo
~ with horse-radish, boiled	Krenfleisch	porc bouilli au raifort	maiale lesso con rafano	cerdo con rábano picante
pot-roast; braised beef	Rinderschmorbraten; Schmorbraten	bœuf braisé[2]	manzo brasato	estofado de vaca; ~ de buey

---

[1] o braciola di maiale - [2] ou bœuf en daube

Meat dishes

Meat dishes English	Fleischgerichte German	Plats de viande French	Piatti di carne Italian	Platos de carne Spanish
prime boiled beef; boiled beef	gekochtes Rindfleisch; Tafelspitz; Suppenfleisch	bœuf bouilli	bollito di manzo; manzo bollito; ~ lesso	carne del cocido
ragout of beef; beef stew	Rinderragout	ragoût de bœuf[1]	stufato di manzo	estofado de vaca
~ of oxtail	Ochsenschwanzragout	queue de bœuf en ragoût	coda di bue in umido	rabo de buey en estofado
~ of tongue	Zungenragout	langue en ragoût	lingua in umido	lengua estofada
ribs of pork; loin of pork	Schweinskarree	carré de porc	carré di maiale	lomo de cerdo
roast beef	Rinderbraten[2]; Ochsenbraten	rôti de bœuf	arrosto di manzo	asado de vaca
~ beef	Roastbeef	rosbif	roastbeef	rosbif
~ beef fillet	gebratenes Rinderfilet	filet de bœuf rôti	filetto di manzo arrosto	solomillo asado
~ kid	Kitzbraten; Zickleinbraten	chevreau rôti	capretto arrosto	cabrito asado
~ lamb	Lammbraten	rôti d'agneau	arrosto d'agnello	asado de cordero
~ leg of lamb	gebratene Lammkeule	gigot d'agneau rôti	cosciotto d'agnello arrosto	pierna de cordero asada
~ leg of mutton (with onions & potatoes)	Hammelkeule nach Bäckerinart (mit Kartoffeln und Zwiebeln im Backofen gebraten)	~ de mouton boulangère (rôti avec pommes de terre et oignons)	~ di montone alla fornaia (cotto in forno con patate e cipolle)	~ de carnero a la panadera (asada con patatas y cebollas)
~ mutton	Hammelbraten	rôti de mouton	arrosto di montone	asado de carnero
~ pork	Schweinebraten[3]	~ de porc	~ di maiale	~ de cerdo
~ pork sausage	Bratwurst	saucisse rôtie	salsiccia arrostita	salchicha asada
~ saddle of lamb	gebratener Lammrücken	selle d'agneau rôtie	sella d'agnello arrosto	silla de cordero asada
~ shank	gebratene Schweinshaxe	jarret de porc rôti	stinco di maiale arrosto	pierna de cerdo asada
~ sirloin	Lendenbraten	aloyau rôti	lombata arrosto	solomillo asado
~ stuffed sucking-pig	gefülltes Spanferkel	porcelet farci rôti	maialino di latte farcito	cochinillo relleno asado
~ sucking pig	gebratenes Spanferkel	~ rôti	~ di latte arrosto	~ asado[4]
~ veal	Kalbsbraten	rôti de veau	arrosto di vitello	asado de ternera
~ veal, cold	~ kalt	~ de veau froid	~ freddo	~ de ternera frío

---

1) ou estouffade (de bœuf) - 2) auch Rindsbraten, Rindsbrust usw. (bes. südd., österr.) - 3) auch Schweinsbraten usw (bes. südd., österr.) - 4) o tostón

Meat dishes

Meat dishes English	Fleischgerichte German	Plats de viande French	Piatti di carne Italian	Platos de carne Spanish
rolled roast veal	Kalbsrollbraten	roulade de veau	rotolo di vitello; rollè di vitello	rollo de ternera asado; asado arrollado
rump-steak	Rumpsteak[1]	rumsteck; romsteck	bistecca di manzo	bistec de vaca
saddle of mutton	Hammelrücken	selle de mouton	sella di montone	silla de carnero
~ of veal	Kalbsrücken	~ de veau	~ di vitello	~ de ternera
~ of veal chartreuse (with mixed vegetables cooked in moulds)	~ nach Kartäuser Art (mit verschiedenen Gemüsen, in Becherformen gekocht)	~ de veau en chartreuse (aux légumes variés)	~ di vitello alla certosina (con verdure miste cotte in uno stampo)	~ de ternera a la cartuja (con variedad de verduras cocidas en un molde)
~ of veal Orlov (braised sliced saddle browned in hot oven with onion purée)	~ Orlow (braisiert, in Scheiben geschnitten und mit Zwiebelmus glaciert)	~ de veau Orlov (braisée, excalopée, glacée au four avec une purée Soubise)	~ di vitello Orlov (brasata, affettata e glassata al forno con purè di cipolle)	~ de ternera Orlov (braseada, tajada en lonjas y glaseada al horno con puré de cebollas)
salt pork; pickled pork	Pökelfleisch; Surfleisch	salé; petit salé	carne salata (di maiale)	carne salada (de cerdo)
~ pork with cabbage	~ mit Kohl	petit salé aux choux	~ salata e cavolo	~ salada con coles
~ ribs of pork	Pökelkarree	carré de porc salé	carré di maiale salato	costillar de cerdo salado
saltimbocca (escalope with ham and sage)	Saltimbocca (Schnitzel mit Schinken und Salbei)	saltimbocca (escalope de veau au jambon et à la sauge)	saltimbocca (scaloppina con prosciutto e salvia)	saltimbocca (escalope con jamón y salvia)
sauerbraten (braised beef, previously marinated in vinegar)	Sauerbraten (in Essigbeize vorgehandelter Schmorbraten)	bœuf braisé à l'aigre (bœuf mariné au vinaigre et braisé)	manzo brasato all'agro (manzo marinato nell'aceto e brasato)	estofado de vaca al vinagre
sauerkraut with pork meats; garnished sauerkraut	garniertes Sauerkraut	choucroute alsacienne	crauti all'alsaziana	chucrut a la alsaciana
sausages in white wine	Würstchen in Weißwein	saucisses au vin blanc	salsicce al vino bianco	salchichas al vino blanco
~ with cabbage	~ mit Kohl	~ au chou	~ e cavoli	~ con coles
shank; shin	Schweinshaxe	jarret de porc	stinco di maiale	pierna de cerdo

---

[1] in Deutschland bezeichnet das Rumpsteak oft ein Entrecôte (simple)

Meat dishes

Meat dishes English	**Fleischgerichte** German	**Plats de viande** French	**Piatti di carne** Italian	**Platos de carne** Spanish
shashliks (meat on skewers); kebabs	Schaschliks (Hammelspießchen)	kebabs (brochettes de mouton)	spiedini di montone	brochetas de cordero
shepherd's pie (minced meat topped with mashed potato); cottage pie	Hirtenpastete (Kartoffelpüree auf Hackfleisch)	hachis parmentier (gratin de viande hachée et de purée de pommes)	pasticcio del pastore (gratin di carne tritata e di purè di patate)	pastel del pastor (picadillo cubierto de puré de patatas y gratinado)
shin; shank	Schweinshaxe	jarret de porc	stinco di maiale	pierna de cerdo
~ of beef	Rinderhaxe	~ de bœuf	~ di bue	jarrete de buey
~ of veal; veal shank	Kalbshaxe; Kalbsstelze	~ de veau	~ di vitello	~ de ternera
shoulder of lamb	Lammschulter	épaule d'agneau	spalla d'agnello	paletilla de cordero; espaldilla de cordero
~ of pork	Schweineschulter	~ de porc	~ di maiale	espaldilla de cerdo
single-dish meal; hot pot; hotchpotch	Eintopf; Eintopfgericht	plat unique; potée	piatto unico	plato único; puchero
sirloin; fillet of beef; tenderloin	Rinderfilet	filet de bœuf	filetto di manzo	solomillo (de buey)
~ steak in red wine sauce	Entrecote nach Weinhändlerart (in Rotweinsauce)	entrecôte marchand de vin (au vin rouge)	costata al vino rosso	entrecot a la vinatera (con salsa de vino tinto)
~ steak lyonnaise (with fried onions); entrecôte lyonnaise (with fried onions)	~ nach Lyoner Art (mit Zwiebeln)	~ à la lyonnaise (aux oignons)	~ alla lionese (con cipolle)	~ a la lionesa (con cebollas)
~ steak Mirabeau (with anchovy fillets & olives)	~ Mirabeau (mit Sardellenfilets und Oliven)	~ Mirabeau (garnie filets d'ancois et olives)	~ Mirabeau (con filetti d'acciuga e olive)	~ Mirabeau (con filetes de anchoas y aceitunas)
~ steak with cress	~ mit Kresse	~ vert pré (au cresson)	~ con crescione	~ con berros
smoked meat	Rauchfleisch	viande fumée	carne affumicata	carne ahumada
~ pork meat	Kaiserfleisch	~ de porc fumée	~ di maiale affumicata	~ de cerdo ahumada

Meat dishes

Meat dishes English	Fleischgerichte German	Plats de viande French	Piatti di carne Italian	Platos de carne Spanish
smoked tongue	Räucherzunge	langue fumée	lingua affumicata	lengua ahumada
sour calf's head	Kalbskopf sauer	tête de veau à l'aigre	testina di vitello all'agro	cabeza de ternera en salsa agria
~ calf's lights	Wiener Beuschel (Saure Lunge)	mou de veau à l'aigre	polmone di vitello all'agro	bofes de ternera a la vienesa (en salsa agria)
~ calf's liver	saure Leber	foie de veau à l'aigre	fegato di vitello all'agro	hígado en salsa agria
~ tripe	~ Kutteln	tripes à l'aigre	trippa all'agro	callos en salsa agria
spare-rib, smoked; smoked pork chop	Kasseler Rippenspeer	côte de porc fumée	braciola di maiale affumicata	costillas de cerdo ahumadas
spinal marrow of veal	Rückenmark vom Kalb	amourettes de veau	schienali di vitello	tuétanos de ternera
spitted roast; spit-roasted meat	Spießbraten	rôti à la broche	arrosto allo spiedo	carne al asador
spring roll; egg roll	Frühlingsrolle	rouleau de printemps	involtino primavera	rollo de primavera
steak; beefsteak	Beefsteak	bifteck; steak	bistecca (di manzo)	bistec; steak
~ and kidney pie	Steak- und Nierenpastete	pâté de bœuf et de rognon en croûte	pâté di manzo e di rognone in crosta	pastel de bistec y de riñon
~, stewed	Schmorsteak	steak étuvé; stew-steak	bistecca brasata	bistec braseado
~ tartare (raw minced beefsteak topped with egg)	Tatarbeefsteak (rohes Hacksteak mit Eigelb)	~ tartare (steak cru haché avec un jaune d'œuf dessus)	~ alla tartara (bistecca di carne cruda tritata con uova sopra)	steak tártaro (bistec de picadillo crudo con encima un huevo); bistec a la tartara
~ with fried onions[1]	Wiener Rostbraten; Zwiebelrostbraten	~ à la viennoise (aux oignons)[2]	~ di manzo alla viennese (con cipolle)	bistec a la vienesa (con cebollas)
~ with vegetables	garniertes Beefsteak	bifteck garni	~ con contorno	~ con guarnición
stew	Tajine (Schmorragout)	tajine	stufato	estofado
stewed pork	Schweinefleischragout	ragoût de porc	~ di maiale	ragú de cerdo
stuffed breast of lamb	gefüllte Lammbrust	poitrine d'agneau farcie	petto d'agnello farcito	pecho de cordero relleno
~ breast of veal	~ Kalbsbrust	~ de veau farcie	~ di vitello farcito	~ de ternera relleno

[1] also sirloin steak with fried onions - [2] ou entrecôte à la viennoise

Meat dishes

Meat dishes English	**Fleischgerichte** German	**Plats de viande** French	**Piatti di carne** Italian	**Platos de carne** Spanish
stuffed shoulder of veal	gefüllte Kalbsschulter	épaule de veau farcie	spalla di vitello ripiena	paletilla de ternera rellena
~ veal escalope	~ Kalbsschnitzel	escalope de veau farcie	scaloppina di vitello farcita	escalope de ternera relleno
sucking pig chop	Spanferkelkotelett	côtelette de porcelet	braciola di maialino	costilla de cochinillo
sweetbreads	Bries	ris	animelle	mollejas
sweetbread in pastry	Kalbsbries in Blätterteig	feuilleté de ris de veau	~ in crosta	~ en hojaldre
sweetbreads with peas	~ mit Erbsen	ris de veau Clamart	~ coi piselli	~ con guisantes
tenderloin; fillet of beef; sirloin	Rinderfilet	filet de bœuf	filetto di manzo	solomillo (de buey)
terrine of veal	Kalbfleischterrine	terrine de veau	terrina di vitello	terrina de ternera
toad-in-the-hole (sausages baked in batter)	Würstchen in Teig	saucisses en pâte	salsicce nella pastella	salchichas en pasta
tournedos (small fillet of beef)	Rinderfiletschnitte	tournedos (médaillon de filet de bœuf)	tournedos (medaglione di filetto di bue)	tournedó (medallón de solomillo)
~ arlésienne (with aubergines, onions and tomatoes)	Filetschnitte auf arlesische Art (mit Auberginen, Zwiebeln, Tomaten)	~ à l'arlésienne (garni d'aubergines, oignons et tomates)	~ all'arlesiana (guarnito di melanzane, cipolle e pomodori)	~ a la arlesiana (con berenjenas, cebollas y tomates)
~ Clamart (with artichoke bottoms filled with peas)	~ Clamart (dazu Artischockenböden gefüllt mit Erbsen)	~ Clamart (aux fonds d'artichauts remplis de pois)	~ Clamart (con fondi di carciofo, riempiti di piselli)	tournedós Clamart (con guisantes sobre fondos de alcachofas)
~ for gourmets (with foie gras)	~ nach Feinschmeckerart (mit Gänseleber)	~ des gourmets (fourré escalope de foie gras)	~ del buongustaio (con fegato d'oca)	tournedó de los gastrónomos (con foie-gras)
~ Helder (with tomatoes & parisienne potatoes)	~ Helder (mit Tomaten und Pariser Kartoffeln garniert)	~ Helder (aux tomates concassées et pommes parisienne)	~ Helder (guarnito di pomodori e di patate alla parigina)	tournedós Helder (con tomates y patatas a la parisiense)

Meat dishes

Meat dishes English	Fleischgerichte German	Plats de viande French	Piatti di carne Italian	Platos de carne Spanish
tournedos Henry IV (a: chipped potatoes, sauce béarnaise. b: artichoke bottoms, noisette potatoes)	Filetschnitte Heinrich IV. (a: Pommes frites, Béarner Sauce. b: Artischockenböden, Nusskartoffeln)	tournedos Henri IV (a: pommes pont-neuf, sauce béarnaise. b: fonds d'artichauts, pommes noisettes)	tournedos Enrico IV (a: patate fritte, salsa bearnese. b: fondi di carciofo, patate nocciola)	tournedós Enriquo IV (a: con patatas fritas y salsa bearnesa. b: con fondos de alcachofas rellenos de patatas)
~ in Madeira sauce	~ in Madeirasauce	~ sauté au madère	~ al madera	tournedó al madera
~ mascotte (with quartered artichokes & potatoes)	~ Mascotte (mit geviertelten Artischocken, Kartoffeln und Trüffeln)	~ mascotte (aux quartiers d'artichauts, pommes et truffes)	~ mascotte (con spicchi di carciofo, patate e tartufi)	tournedós mascotte (con fondos de alcachofas, patatas y trufas)
~ Masséna (with artichoke bottoms and marrow, truffle sauce)	~ Masséna (mit Artischockenböden und Rindermark)	~ Masséna (aux fonds d'artichauts et à la moelle, sauce Périgueux)	~ Massena (con fondi di carciofo e midollo, salsa di tartufi)	tournedó Masséna (con fondos de alcachofas y tuétano)
~ Portuguese (with tomatoes)	~ auf portugiesische Art (mit Tomaten)	~ à la portugaise (aux tomates farcies)	~ alla portoghese (guarnito di pomodori)	~ a la portuguesa (con tomates)
~ Rossini (with slice of foie gras and truffles, Madeira sauce)	~ Rossini (mit Gänseleberscheibe und Trüffeln, Madeirasauce)	~ Rossini (garni de foie gras et de truffes, sauce madère)	~ Rossini (con foie gras e fettine di tartufo, salsa al madera)	~ Rossini (con lonja de foie-gras y trufas, salsa madera)
~ sauce béarnaise, broiled	~ vom Grill mit Béarner Sauce	~ béarnaise	~ alla bearnese (con salsa bearnese)	tournedós a la bearnesa (con salsa bearnesa)
~ with marrow	~ mit Mark	~ à la moelle	~ al midollo	tournedó con tuétano
tripe	Kutteln; Kaldaunen	tripes[1] *pl*	trippa	callos
~ and onions	~ mit Zwiebeln	~ à la lyonnaise (aux oignons)	~ con le cipolle	~ con cebollas
~ of kid	Zickleinkutteln	~ de chevreau	~ di capretto	~ de cabrito
Tyrolean sirloin steak (with tomatoes & fried onion rings)	Entrecote nach Tiroler Art (mit Tomaten und Zwiebelringen garniert)	entrecôte tyrolienne (garnie tomates et rondelles d'oignons frits)	costata alla tirolese (guarnita di pomodori e di cipolle fritte)	entrecot a la tirolesa (con tomates y cebollas fritas)

---

[1] ou gras-double *sing.*

Meat dishes

Meat dishes English	Fleischgerichte German	Plats de viande French	Piatti di carne Italian	Platos de carne Spanish
veal and ham pie (hot)	Kalbfleisch-Schinken-Pastete im Teig	pâté de veau et jambon en croûte	pâté di vitello e prosciutto in crosta	pastel de ternera y jamón
~ chop; ~ cutlet	Kalbskotelett	côte de veau	costoletta di vitello	chuleta de ternera
~ chop, grilled	gegrilltes Kalbskotelett	~ de veau grillée	~ di vitello ai ferri	~ a la parrilla
~ cutlet en papillote	Kalbskotelett in Folie	~ de veau en papillote	~ di vitello al cartoccio	~ en papillote
~ cutlet in jelly	~ Bellevue (in Aspik)	~ de veau en bellevue (en gelée)	~ di vitello in bella vista (in gelatina)	~ de ternera en bella vista (en gelatina)
~ cutlet Milanese (breaded cutlet)	~ nach Mailänder Art (paniertes Kotelett)	~ de veau milanaise (côte de veau panée)	~ alla milanese (costoletta impanata)	~ a la milanesa (chuleta empanada)
~ cutlet Pojarski (minced veal cutlet)	~ Pojarski (gehacktes Kotelett)	~ de veau Pojarski (côte de veau hachée)	~ di vitello Pojarski (costoletta tritata)	~ de ternera Pojarski (chuleta de picadillo)
~ cutlet sauté	gebratenes Kalbskotelett (natur)	~ de veau sautée	~ di vitello sauté	~ de ternera salteada
~ escalope, creamed; ~ escalope in cream sauce	Kalbsschnitzel in Sahnesauce; Rahmschnitzel; Sahneschnitzel	escalope de veau à la crème	scaloppina di vitello alla panna	escalope de tenera a la crema
~ escalope with paprika	Paprikaschnitzel	~ de veau au paprika	~ di vitello alla paprica	~ de ternera con pimentón
~ fricassee	Kalbsfrikassee	fricassée de veau	fricassea di vitello	fricasé de ternera
~ galantine	Kalbfleischgalantine	galantine de veau	galantina di vitello	galantina de ternera
~ meatballs; ~ balls	Kalbsfrikadellen	fricadelles de veau	polpette di vitello	albóndigas de ternera
~ noisette au gratin	gratinierte Kalbsnüsschen	noisette de veau gratinée	medaglione di vitello gratinato	medallón de ternera gratinado
~ pie	Kalbfleischpastete	pâté de veau	pâté di vitello	pastel de ternera
~ roulades[1]	Kalbsrouladen; Kalbfleischröllchen	paupiettes de veau	involtini di vitello	rollitos de ternera; popietas de ternera
~ roulades in vine leaves	~ in Weinblättern	~ de veau aux feuilles de vigne	~ di vitello in foglia di vite	~ de ternera en hojas de vid

---

1) slices of veal rolled up with stuffing & stewed

Meat dishes

Meat dishes English	Fleischgerichte German	Plats de viande French	Piatti di carne Italian	Platos de carne Spanish
veal sausages; white sausages	Weißwürste	boudins blancs de veau	salsicce di vitello	salchichas de ternera
~ shank; shin of veal	Kalbshaxe; Kalbsstelze	jarret de veau	stinco di vitello	jarrete de ternera
~ shank, braised	geschmorte Kalbshaxe	~ de veau braisé	~ di vitello brasato	~ de ternera estofado
~ steak	Kalbssteak	steak de veau	bistecca di vitello	bistec de ternera
~ stew	Kalbsragout	sauté de veau	spezzatino di vitello	estofado de ternera
~ stew chasseur (with mushrooms and tomatoes); ~ stew, hunter's style	~ nach Jägerart (mit Champignons und Tomaten)	~ de veau chasseur (aux champignons et tomates)	~ di vitello alla cacciatora (con funghi e pomodori)	~ de ternera a la cazadora (con champiñones y tomates)
~ stew Marengo (with tomato and white wine)	~ Marengo (mit Tomaten und Weißwein)	~ de veau Marengo (aux tomates et au vin blanc)	~ di vitello Marengo (con pomodori e vino bianco)	~ de ternera Marengo (con tomates y vino blanco)
~ stew with peas	~ mit Erbsen	veau aux petits pois	~ di vitello con piselli	~ de ternera con guisantes
~ stew with spring vegetables	~ mit Frühlingsgemüse	sauté de veau printanier (aux primeurs)	~ di vitello primaverile (con verdure novelle)	~ de ternera primaveral (con verduras)
white sausages; veal sausages	Weißwürste	boudins blancs de veau	salsicce di vitello	salchichas de ternera
Wieners; Frankfurters	Frankfurter Würstchen	saucisses de Francfort	würstel	~ de Frankfurt
Wiener schnitzel[1] (breaded veal slice)	Wiener Schnitzel (paniertes Kalbsschnitzel)	escalope viennoise (escalope de veau panée)	cotoletta alla milanese (scaloppina di vitello impanata)	escalope vienés[2] (escalope de ternera empanado)
zampone (pork sausage enwrapped in the skin of a pig's trotter)	Zampone (Wurst in der Haut eines ganzen Schweinsfußes)	zampone (saucisson enveloppé dans la peau d'un pied de porc)	zampone (salume insaccato nella zampa del maiale)	zampone (embutido en la piel de la pata entera de cerdo)
~ with lentils	~ mit Linsen	~ aux lentilles	~ con lenticchie	~ con lentejas
~ with sauerkraut	~ mit Sauerkraut	~ à la choucroute	~ con crauti	~ con chucrut

---

1) or Vienna schnitzel - 2) o escalope milanés

Poultry

Poultry English	**Geflügel** German	**Volailles** French	**Pollame** Italian	**Aves** Spanish
aromatic chicken	Hühnchen mit Aromen	poulet aux aromates	pollo agli aromi	pollo con especias
capon	Kapaun	chapon	cappone	capón
~, roast truffled	getrüffelter Kapaun	~ truffé rôti	~ arrosto tartufato	~ asado trufado
casserole of chicken	geschmortes Hühnchen; Hühnchen in der Kasserolle	poulet en cocotte	pollo stufato; ~ en casseruola	pollo estofado; ~ en cacerola
chaud-froid of chicken[1]	Geflügel-Chaudfroid	chaud-froid de poulet	chaud-froid di pollo	~ en gelatina
chicken	Hühnchen	poulet	pollo	pollo
~ à la King (in cream sauce with mushrooms and sherry)	~ nach Königsart (in Rahmsauce mit Champignons und Sherry)	~ à la royale (en sauce crème avec champignons et xérès)	~ alla reale (in salsa di panna con funghi e sherry)	~ a la real (en salsa de crema con champiñones y jerez)
~, boiled	gekochtes Hühnchen	~ bouilli	~ lesso	~ cocido
~, boned stuffed	ausgebeintes und gefülltes Hühnchen	~ désossé et farci	~ disossato e ripieno	~ deshuesado y relleno
~ breast[2]	Hühnerbrust[3]	suprême de volaille[4]	petti di pollo[5]	pechuga de pollo[6]
~ breast in cream	~ in Sahne	~ de volaille à la crème	~ di pollo alla panna	~ de pollo a la crema
~ breast Maryland (with sweetcorn fritters & fried bananas)	Hühnerbrustfilet Maryland (mit kleinen Maisbeignets und gebratenen Bananen)	suprêmes de volaille Maryland (aux beignets de maïs et bananes frites)	~ di pollo Maryland (con frittelle di mais e banane fritte)	supremas de pollo Maryland (con galletas de maíz y plátanos fritos)
~ breast with salt ox-tongue	Hühnerbrust mit Pökelzunge	suprême de volaille à l'écarlate	~ di pollo con lingua salmistrata	~ de pollo con lengua salada
~ creole (with rice, tomatoes and green peppers)	Hühnchen auf kreolische Art (mit Reis, Tomaten, Paprikaschoten)	poulet à la créole (au riz avec tomates et poivron)	pollo alla creola (con riso, pomodori e peperoni)	pollo a la criolla (con arroz, tomates y pimientos)
~ croquettes	Geflügelkroketten	croquettes de volaille	crocchette di pollo	croquetas de pollo
~ curry	Curryhuhn	curry de poulet	pollo al curry	pollo al curry

[1] filleted poultry served in jelly - [2] or chicken fillets - [3] auch Hühnerbrustfilet - [4] ou blanc de poulet, filets de volaille - [5] o suprême di pollo - [6] o supremas de pollo

Poultry

Poultry English	Geflügel German	Volailles French	Pollame Italian	Aves Spanish
chicken cutlet	Geflügelkotelett	côtelette de volaille	cotoletta di pollo	chuleta de pollo
~ fricassee	Hühnerfrikassee	fricassée de poulet	fricassea di pollo	fricasé de pollo
~ galantine	Geflügel-Galantine	galantine de volaille	galantina di pollo	galantina de pollo
~ , hunter's style; hunter's chicken (with mushrooms)	Hühnchen nach Jägerart (mit Pilzen)	poulet chasseur (aux champignons)	pollo alla cacciatora (con funghi)	pollo a la cazadora (con champiñones)
~ in champagne	~ in Champagner	~ au champagne	~ allo champagne	~ al champaña
~ in cream sauce	~ in Rahmsauce	~ sauté à la crème	~ alla panna	~ a la crema
~ in jelly	~ in Aspik	~ en gelée	~ in gelatina	~ en gelatina
~ in pastry	~ im Teigmantel	~ en pâte	~ in crosta	~ en costra
~ in salt crust	~ in Salzkruste	~ en croûte de sel	~ al sale	~ a la sal
~ in wine sauce	~ in Weinsauce	~ au vin	~ con salsa al vino	~ al vino
~ jambolaya	Jambeya von Huhn	jambelage de poulet	jambelaye di pollo	jambalaya de pollo
~ leg	Hühnerkeule	cuisse de poulet	coscia di pollo	muslo de pollo
~ liver kebabs	Geflügelleber am Spießchen	brochettes de foies de volaille	spiedini di fegatini	brochetas de higadillos
~ liver pâté	Hühnerleberpastete	pâté de foies de volaille	pâté di fegatini	paté de higadillos
~ livers	Geflügelleber	foies de volaille	fegatini (di pollo)	higadillos (de ave)
~ Marengo (with mushrooms, wine and tomatoes)	Hühnchen Marengo (mit Champignons, Wein und Tomaten)	poulet Marengo (aux champignons, vin et tomates)	pollo alla Marengo (con funghi, vino e pomodori)	pollo a la Marengo (con champiñones, vino y tomate)
~ Maryland (with sweetcorn fritters & fried bananas)	~ Maryland (mit kleinen Maisbeignets und gebratenen Bananen)	~ Maryland (aux beignets de maïs et bananes frites)	~ Maryland (con frittelle di mais e banane fritte)	~ Maryland (con galletas de maíz y plátanos fritos)
~ mayonnaise	Hühnermayonnaise	mayonnaise de volaille	maionese di pollo	mayonesa de pollo
~ mousse	Geflügelmousse	mousse de volaille	mousse di pollo	mousse de pollo; espuma de ave
~ pie	Hühnerpastete	pâté de poulet	pâté di pollo	pastel de ave

Poultry

Poultry English	Geflügel German	Volailles French	Pollame Italian	Aves Spanish
chicken pilaw	Hühnerpilaf	pilaf de volaille	pilaf di pollo	pilav de pollo
~, roast stuffed	gefülltes Hühnchen (gebraten)	poulet farci rôti	pollo ripieno arrosto	pollo relleno asado
~ roulades	Geflügelröllchen	paupiettes de volaille	involtini di pollo	rollitos de pollo
~ sauté	sautiertes Hühnchen	poulet sauté	pollo sauté	pollo salteado; ~ guisado
~ stew	Schmorragout von Huhn	tajine de poulet	stufato di pollo	estofado de pollo
~ wings	Hühnerflügel	ailes de volaille	ali di pollo	alas de pollo
~ with bacon, broiled	Hühnchen auf amerikanische Art (vom Rost, mit Speck)	poulet grillé à l'américaine (au bacon)	pollo alla griglia all'americana (con bacon)	pollo a la americana (a la parrilla con tocino)
~ with mayonnaise	~ mit Mayonnaise	~ froid mayonnaise	~ con maionese	~ con mayonesa
~ with paprika; paprika chicken	~ mit Paprika; Paprikahuhn	~ au paprika	~ alla paprica	~ con pimentón
cockscombs	Hahnenkämme	crêtes de coq	creste di gallo	crestas de gallo
confit of duck (duck preserved in fat)	Entenconfit (eingemachtes Entenfleisch)	confit de canard	confit d'anatra (anatra conservata sotto grasso)	confit de pato (pato confitado)
~ of goose (goose preserved in fat)	Gänseconfit (eingemachtes Gänsefleisch)	~ d'oie	~ d'oca (oca conservata sotto grasso)	~ de oca (oca confitada); conserva de ganso
deviled spring chicken (broiled chicken)	Hühnchen nach Teufelsart (vom Grill)	poulet grillé à la diable (sauce diable à part)	pollo alla diavola (cotto in gratella)	pollo a la diabla (asado a la parrilla)
duck	Ente	canard[1]	anatra; anitra	pato
~ breast	Entenbrust	suprême de canard	petto d'anatra	pechuga de pato
~ leg	Entenkeule	cuisse de canard	coscia d'anatra	muslo de pato
~ pâté	Entenpastete	pâté de canard	pâté d'anatra	paté de pato
~ with olives, braised	Ente mit Oliven	caneton aux olives	anatra con le olive	pato con aceitunas
~ with orange sauce	~ mit Orangensauce	canard à l'orange	~ all'arancia	~ a la naranja
~ with red cabbage	~ mit Rotkohl	~ au chou rouge	~ con cavoli rossi	~ con col lombarda

---

[1] auf den Speisekarten fast immer „caneton" = junge Ente

Poultry

Poultry English	**Geflügel** German	**Volailles** French	**Pollame** Italian	**Aves** Spanish
duck with turnips	Ente mit weißen Rüben; ~ mit Mairübchen	canard aux navets	anatra con le rape	pato con nabos
duckling	junge Ente	canette; caneton	~ novella	~ joven
escalope of foie gras	Gänseleber-Scheibe	escalope de foie gras	scaloppa di foie gras	escalope de foie-gras
foie gras; goose liver	Gänseleber	foie gras	fegato d'oca	hígado de ganso
fresh foie gras	~ (frische)	~ gras frais	foie gras fresco	foie-gras fresco
fricassee of turkey	Putenfrikassee	blanquette de dinde	fricassea di tacchino	blanqueta de pavo
fried chicken	Backhähnchen	poulet frit	pollo fritto	pollo frito
~ spring chicken	Wiener Backhendl	~ frit à la viennoise	pollastrino fritto	~ frito
giblets	Geflügelklein	abattis	rigaglie di pollo	menudillos
gizzards	Geflügelmagen	gésiers	ventrigli	buche
goose	Gans	oie	oca	ganso; oca
~ cracklings	Gänsegrieben	grattons d'oie	ciccioli d'oca	chicharrones de oca
~ giblets	Gänseklein	abattis d'oie	rigaglie d'oca	menudillos de ganso
~ liver; foie gras	Gänseleber	foie gras	fegato d'oca	hígado de ganso
~ with sauerkraut, braised	Gans auf elsässische Art (mit Sauerkraut)	oie à l'alsacienne (à la choucroute)	oca all'alsaziana (con crauti)	ganso a la alsaciana (con chucrut)
grilled chicken	Grillhähnchen; gegrilltes Hühnchen	poulet grillé	pollo alla griglia	pollo emparrillado; ~ a la parrilla
guinea fowl; ~ hen	Perlhuhn	pintade	faraona	pintada[1]
~ fowl breast	Perlhuhnbrust	suprême de pintade	petto di faraona	pechuga de pintada
~ fowl galantine	Perlhuhngalantine	galantine de pintade	galantina di faraona	galantina de pintada
~ fowl with cabbage	geschmortes Perlhuhn mit Kohl	pintade braisée au chou	faraona brasata con cavoli	pintada estofada con coles
guinea-hen en papillote	Perlhuhn en Papillote	~ en papillote	~ al cartoccio	~ en papillote
guinea hen in cream	~ in Rahmsauce	~ à la crème	~ alla panna	~ a la crema
hen	Henne	poule	gallina	gallina

---

[1] o gallina de Guinea

Poultry

Poultry English	Geflügel German	Volailles French	Pollame Italian	Aves Spanish
hunter's chicken (with mushrooms); chicken, hunter's style	Hühnchen nach Jägerart (mit Pilzen)	poulet chasseur (aux champignons)	pollo alla cacciatora (con funghi)	pollo a la cazadora (con champiñones)
Maryland fried chicken (garnished with fried bacon)	Backhähnchen Maryland (mit gebratenem Speck garniert)	~ frit Maryland (garni de tranches frites de bacon)	~ fritto Maryland (con fettine di pancetta fritte)	~ frito Maryland (con lonjas fritas de tocino)
minute pigeon; pigeon sauté	sautierte Taube	pigeon à la minute	piccione al minuto	pichón al minuto
mousse of duck	Entenmousse	mousse de canard	mousse d'anatra	mousse de pato
musk duck	Barbarie-Ente; Moschusente	canard de Barbarie; ~ musqué	anatra muta	pato de Berbería; ~ mudo
paprika chicken; chicken with paprika	Hühnchen mit Paprika; Paprikahuhn	poulet au paprika	pollo alla paprica	pollo con pimentón
parfait de foie gras	Gänseleber-Parfait	parfait de foie gras	parfait di fegato d'oca	parfait de foie-gras
pâté de foie gras	~ -Pastete	pâté de foie gras	pâté di fegato d'oca	foie-gras (pasta de hígado de ganso)
peking duck	Pekingente	canard laqué	anatra laccata	pato laqueado
pigeon	Taube	pigeon	piccione	pichón
~ breast	Taubenbrust	suprême de pigeon	petto di piccione	pechuga de pichón
~, broiled	Taube vom Grill	pigeon à la crapaudine	piccione in gratella	pichón asado a la parrilla
~ pâté; ~ pie	Taubenpastete	pâté de pigeons	pâté di piccione	paté de pichón; pastel de pichón
~ sauté; minute pigeon	sautierte Taube	pigeon à la minute	piccione al minuto	pichón al minuto
poulard; poularde	Poularde; Masthuhn	poularde	pollastra	pularda
~, boiled	gekochte Poularde	~ pochée	~ lessa	~ cocida
~, braised	geschmorte Poularde	~ en cocotte	~ brasata	~ estofada
~ in bladder	Poularde in der Schweinsblase	~ en vessie; ~ en chemise	~ in camicia	~ en vejiga

Poultry

Poultry English	Geflügel German	Volailles French	Pollame Italian	Aves Spanish
poulard Suvorov (stuffed with foie gras & truffles)	Poularde Suworow (mit Gänseleber und Trüffeln)	poularde Souvarov (farcie de foie gras et truffes)	pollastra Suvarov (ripiena di fegato d'oca e tartufi)	pularda Suvarov (rellena de foie-gras y trufas)
~ with rice	~ mit Reis	~ au riz	~ col riso	~ con arroz
~ with tarragon	~ mit Estragon	~ à l'estragon	~ al dragoncello	~ con estragón
pressed duck	Ente in der Presse	canard à la presse; ~ au sang	anatra al torchio	pato a la sangre
ragout of goose	Gänseragout	ragoût d'oie	stufato d'oca	ragú de oca
roast chicken	Brathähnchen; gebratenes Hühnchen	poulet rôti	pollo arrosto	pollo asado
~ duck	gebratene Ente	caneton rôti	anatra arrosto	pato asado
~ goose	~ Gans	oie rôtie	oca arrosto	ganso asado
~ goose with apple sauce	Gans auf englische Art (mit Apfelmus)	~ à l'anglaise (rôtie, sauce aux pommes)	~ arrosto all'inglese (con salsa di mele)	~ asado a la inglesa (con salsa de manzanas)
~ guinea fowl	gebratenes Perlhuhn	pintade rôtie	faraona arrosto	pintada asada
~ turkey	Putenbraten	dinde rôtie	tacchino arrosto	pavo asado
~ turkey with chestnut stuffing	Truthahn mit Kastanienfüllung	~ farcie aux marrons	~ ripieno di marroni	~ relleno de castañas
rolled roast turkey	Putenrollbraten	roulade de dinde	rotolo di tacchino	rollo de pavo asado
saffron chicken	Safranhuhn	poulet au safran	pollo allo zafferano	pollo al azafrán
salmi of guinea-hen	Perlhuhnragout	pintade en salmis	faraona in salmi	pintada en slamorejo
spit-roasted chicken; spring chicken on the spit	Hühnchen vom Spieß	poulet à la broche	pollo allo spiedo	pollo al asador
~ pigeon	Taube vom Spieß	pigeon rôti à la broche	piccione allo spiedo	pichón al asador
spitted turkey	Truthahn vom Spieß	dindonneau à la broche	tacchinotto allo spiedo	pavipollo al asador
spring chicken	Hähnchen	poulet nouveau	pollastrino ; pollo novello	pollo joven
~ chicken on the spit; spit-roasted chicken	Hühnchen vom Spieß	~ à la broche	pollo allo spiedo	~ al asador
squab; young pigeon	junge Taube	pigeonneau	piccione novello	pichón joven

Poultry

Poultry English	Geflügel German	Volailles French	Pollame Italian	Aves Spanish
stewed chicken	Schmorhuhn	poulet en cocotte	pollo stufato	pollo estofado
stuffed chicken	gefülltes Hühnchen	~ farci	~ ripieno	~ relleno
~ goose neck	gefüllter Gänsehals	cou d'oie farci	collo d'oca farcito	cuello de ganso relleno
~ pigeon	gefüllte Taube	pigeon farci	piccione farcito	pichón relleno
~ turkey	gefüllter Truthahn	dinde farcie	tacchino ripieno	pavo relleno
~ winglets	~ Hühnerflügel	ailerons farcis	alette di pollo ripiene	alones rellenos
terrine de foie gras	Gänseleber-Terrine	terrine de foie gras	terrina di fegato d'oca	terrina de foie-gras
truffled chicken breast	Hühnerbrust mit Trüffeln	suprême de volaille aux truffes	petti di pollo al tartufo	pechuga de pollo con trufas
~ poulard	getrüffelte Poularde	poularde truffée	pollastra tartufata	pularda trufada
~ turkey	getrüffelter Truthahn	dinde truffée	tacchino tartufato	pavo trufado
turkey	Truthahn	dinde	tacchino	pavo
~, boiled	gekochter Truthahn	~ pochée	~ lesso	~ cocido
~, braised	geschmorter Truthahn	~ braisée	~ brasato	~ estofado
~ breast[1]	Putenbrust[2]	suprême de dinde[3]	petto di tacchino[4]	pechuga de pavo
~ escalope	Putenschnitzel	escalope de dinde	scaloppina di tacchino	escalope de pavo
~ galantine	Truthahngalantine	galantine de dinde	galantina di tacchino	galantina de pavo
~ goulash	Putengulasch	goulache de dinde	gulasch di tacchino	gulasch de pavo
~ kebab	Putenspieß	brochette de dinde	spiedino di tacchino	brocheta de pavo
~ leg	Putenkeule	cuisse de dinde	coscia di tacchino	muslo de pavo
~ steak	Putensteak	steak de dinde	bistecca di tacchino	bistec de pavo
~ with pomegranate sauce	Truthahn mit Granatapfelsauce	dinde à la grenade	tacchino alla melagrana	pavo con salsa de granada
vinegar chicken	Essighuhn	poulet au vinaigre	pollo all'aceto	pollo al vinagre
young pigeon; squab	junge Taube	pigeonneau	piccione novello	pichón joven
~ turkey	junger Truthahn	dindonneau	tacchino giovane	pavo joven; pavipollo

---

1) or turkey fillets - 2) oder Putenbrustfilet - 3) ou blanc de dinde, filets de dinde - 4) o filetti di tacchino

Game

Game English	Wild German	Gibier French	Selvaggina[1)] Italian	Caza Spanish
beccaficos	Feigendrosseln	becfigues	beccafichi	papafigos
black grouse; heath cock; black cock	Birkhahn	coq de bouleau; petit tétras	fagiano di monte	grigallo
blackbirds	Amseln	merles	merli	mirlos
breast of partridge	Rebhuhnbrüstchen	suprême de perdreau	petto di pernice	pechuga de perdiz
~ of quails	Wachtelbrüstchen	suprêmes de cailles	petti di quaglia	pechugas de codorniz
~ of woodcock	Schnepfenbrüstchen	suprême de bécasse	petto di beccaccia	suprema de becada
capercaillie[2)]	Auerhahn	coq de bruyère	gallo cedrone	gallo silvestre; urogallo
casserole of pheasant	geschmorter Fasan	faisan en cocotte	fagiano in casseruola	faisán en cacerola
~ of quails	geschmorte Wachteln	cailles en cocotte	quaglie in casseruola	codornices en cacerola
~ of thrushes; thrushes à la bonne femme (with diced bacon and croûtons)	Drosseln nach Hausfrauenart (mit Speckwürfeln und Croûtons); ~ im Schmortopf	grives à la bonne femme (aux lardons et croûtons); ~ en cocotte	tordi alla bonne femme (con lardo e crostini); ~ in casseruola	tordos a la bonne femme (con tocino y trocitos de pan frito); ~ en cacerola
chamois	Gämse	chamois	camoscio	gamuza
~, jugged	Gemsenpfeffer	civet de chamois	~ in salmì	~ en salmorejo
civet; game stew[3)]; salmi	Wildragout; Salmi; Civet	ragoût de gibier; salmis; civet	stufato di selvaggina; salmì; civet	estofado de caza[4)]; salmis; civet
coot	Blässhuhn	foulque noire	folaga	foja[5)]; gallina de aqua
elk	Elch; Elentier	élan	alce	anta; alce
escalope of venison	Rehschnitzel	escalope de chevreuil	scaloppina di capriolo	escalope de corzo
~ of venison with mushrooms	~ mit Champignons	~ de chevreuil aux champignons	~ di capriolo con funghi	~ de corzo con champiñones
fallow deer	Damhirsch	daim	daino	gamo
fillet of hare	Hasenfilet	filet de lièvre	filetto di lepre	lomo de liebre
game goulash	Wildgulasch	goulache de venaison	gulasch di cacciagione	gulasch de caza
~ pâté; ~ pie	Wildpastete	pâté de gibier	pâté di cacciagione	paté de caza
~ salad	Wildsalat	salade de gibier	insalata di cacciagione	ensalada de caza

1) o cacciagione - 2) also mountain cock and woodgrouse - 3) also ragout of game - 4) o ragú de caza - 5) o focha

Game

Game English	Wild German	Gibier French	Selvaggina Italian	Caza Spanish
game stew[1]; salmi; civet	Wildragout; Salmi; Civet	ragoût de gibier; salmis; civet	stufato di selvaggina; salmì; civet	estofado de caza[2]; salmis; civet
green plover; lapwing; peewit[3]	Kiebitz	vanneau	pavoncella; vanello	avefría
hare	Hase	lièvre	lepre	liebre
~ [4], jugged	Hasenpfeffer	civet de lièvre	~ in salmì	civet de liebre; liebre en salmorejo
~ pie	Hasenpastete (warm)	pâté de lièvre en croûte	pâté di lepre in crosta	paté de liebre
hazel grouse; ~ hen	Haselhuhn	gelinotte	francolino di monte	bonasa
heath cock; black grouse; ~ cock	Birkhahn	coq de bouleau; petit tétras	fagiano di monte	grigallo
hunter's kebabs	Jagdspieße	brochettes du chasseur	spiedini di caccia	brochetas de caza
lapwing; green plover; peewit[3]	Kiebitz	vanneau	pavoncella; vanello	avefría
larks	Lerchen	alouettes; mauviettes	allodole	alondras
~ with bacon	~ mit Speck	~ au lard	~ al lardo	~ con tocino
leg of rabbit	Kaninchenkeule	cuisse de lapin	coscia di coniglio	pierna de conejo
~ of venison (deer)	Hirschkeule	cuissot de cerf	cosciotto di cervo	~ de venado
~ of venison[5] (rue)	Rehkeule	~ de chevreuil[6]	~ di capriolo	~ de corzo
~ of venison with cream	~ in Sahnesauce	~ de chevreuil à la crème	~ di capriolo alla panna	~ de corzo a la crema
~ of wild boar[7]	Wildschweinskeule	~ de sanglier	~ di cinghiale	~ de jabalí
~ of wild boar in sweet-and-sour sauce	~ süß-sauer	~ de sanglier à l'aigre-doux	~ di cinghiale in agrodolce	~ de jabalí en agridulce
legs of hare	Hasenkeulen	cuisses de lièvre	cosce di lepre	~ de liebre
mallard; wild duck	Stockente; Wildente	canard sauvage	anatra selvatica[8]	pato salvaje
medallion of venison	Rehmedaillon	médaillon de chevreuil	medaglione di capriolo	medallón de corzo

---

1) also ragout of game - 2) o ragú de caza - 3) also pewit - 4) Am. hasenpfeffer - 5) also haunch of venison - 6) dit aussi gigue de chevreuil - 7) also haunch of wild boar - 8) o germano reale

Game

Game English	Wild German	Gibier French	Selvaggina Italian	Caza Spanish
medallions of venison, hunter's style (with mushrooms & tomatoes)	Rehmedaillons nach Jägerart (mit Champignons und Tomaten)	Médaillons de chevreuil chasseur (aux champignons et tomates)	medaglioni di capriolo alla cacciatora (con funghi e pomodori)	medallones de corzo a la cazadora (con champiñones y tomates)
~ of venison with chestnut purée	~ mit Maronenpüree	~ de chevreuil à la purée de marrons	~ di capriolo con purè di marroni	~ de corzo con puré de castañas
minute quails	Wachteln auf schnellste Art	cailles à la minute; ~ sautées	quaglie al minute	codornices al minuto
moorfowl; red grouse	schottisches Moorschneehuhn	grouse (lagopède d'Écosse)	lagopode; pernìce bianca di Scizia	perdiz blanca de Escocia
moorhen; waterhen	Teichhuhn; Wasserhuhn	poule d'eau	gallinella d'acqua	polla de agua; rascón
partridge; grey partridge	Rebhuhn	perdreau[1]	pernice grigia; starna	perdiz; estarna
~ terrine	Rebhuhnterrine	terrine de perdreau	terrina di pernice	terrina de perdiz
~ with apples	Rebhuhn auf normannische Art (mit Äpfeln)	perdreau à la normande (aux pommes fruits)	pernice alla normanna (con mele)	perdiz a la normanda (con manzanas)
~ with cabbage	~ mit Kohl	~ au chou	~ con cavoli	~ con coles
~ with cream sauce	~ in Rahmsauce	~ à la crème	~ alla crema	~ a la crema
peewit[2]; lapwing; green plover	Kiebitz	vanneau	pavoncella; vanello	avefría
pheasant	Fasan	faisan	fagiano	faisán
~ breast	Fasanenbrust	suprême de faisan	petto di fagiano	pechuga de faisán
~ breast in cream sauce	~ in Sahnesauce	~ de faisan à la crème	~ di fagiano alla panna	~ de faisán a la crema
~ mousse	Fasanenmousse	mousse de faisan	mousse di fagiano	mousse de faisán
~ pâté	Fasanenpastete	pâté de faisan	pâté di fagiano	paté de faisán
~, roast truffled	getrüffelter Fasan	faisan truffé	fagiano tartufato	faisán trufado
~ terrine	Fasanenterrine	terrine de faisan	terrina di fagiano	terrina de faisán
~ with mixed vegetables	Fasan Kartäuserart (mit verschiedenen Gemüsen)	faisan en chartreuse	fagiano alla certosina (con verdure miste)	faisán a la cartuja (con variedad de verduras)

---

1) perdrix - 2) also pewit

Game

Game English	Wild German	Gibier French	Selvaggina Italian	Caza Spanish
pheasant with sauerkraut	Fasan mit Sauerkraut	faisan à l'alsacienne (à la choucroute)	fagiano con crauti	faisán con chucrut
ptarmigan; snow grouse[1]	Schneehuhn	perdrix des neiges[2]	pernice bianca	perdiz blanca
quails	Wachteln	cailles	quaglie	codornices
~, broiled	~ vom Rost	~ grillées	~ alla griglia	~ a la parrilla
~ en casserole	~ in der Kasserolle	~ en cocotte	~ in casseruola	~ en cacerola
~ in nest	~ im Nestchen	~ au nid	~ nel nido	~ al nido
~ in vine leaves	~ in Weinblättern	~ aux feuilles de vigne	~ in foglia di vite	~ en hojas de vid
~ on the spit; spit-roasted quails	~ vom Spieß	~ à la broche	~ allo spiedo	~ al asador
~ Sovorov (stuffed with gooseliver & truffles)	~ Suworow (mit Gänseleber und Trüffeln gefüllt)	~ Souvarov (farcies de foie gras et truffes)	~ Suvarov (ripiene di fegato d'oca e tartufi)	~ Suvarow (rellenas de foie-gras y trufas)
~ with grapes	~ nach Winzerart (mit Weintrauben)	~ à la vigneronne (au raisin)	~ alla vignaiola (all'uva)	~ a la viñadora (con uvas)
~ with rice	~ mit Reis	~ au riz	~ al riso	~ con arroz
~ with risotto	Wachtelrisotto	risotto de cailles	risotto con le quaglie	~ con arroz
rabbit	Kaninchen	lapin (junges: lapereau)	coniglio	conejo
~ fricassee	Kaninchenfrikassee	fricassée de lapin	~ in fricassea	~ en salsa blanca
~, fried	gebackenes Kaninchen	lapin frit	~ fritto	~ frito
~ galantine	Kaninchengalantine	galantine de lapin	galantina di coniglio	galantina de conejo
~, jugged; ~ stew	Kaninchenpfeffer	lapin en civet	coniglio in salmì	civet de conejo; conejo en slamorejo
~ liver	Kaninchenleber	foie de lapin	fegato di coniglio	hígado de conejo
~ ragout	Kaninchenragout	sauté de lapin; ragoût de lapin	stufato di coniglio	estofado de conejo
~ stew; jugged rabbit	Kaninchenpfeffer	lapin en civet	coniglio in salmì	civet de conejo; conejo en slamorejo
~ terrine	Kaninchenterrine	terrine de lapin	terrina di coniglio	terrina de conejo

1) also white grouse - 2) aussi poule des neiges

Game

Game	Wild	Gibier	Selvaggina	Caza
English	German	French	Italian	Spanish
ragout of hare	Hasenragout	ragoût de lièvre	stufato di lepre	estofado de liebre
red deer[1]; venison; stag	Hirsch; Rothirsch	cerf	cervo	ciervo; venado
~ grouse; moorfowl	schottisches Moorschneehuhn	grouse (lagopède d'Écosse)	lagopode; pernìce bianca di Scizia	perdiz blanca de Escocia
red-legged partridge	Rothuhn	perdriz rouge	pernice rossa	~ roja; ~ real
reindeer	Rentier	renne	renna	reno
~ steak	Rentiersteak	steak de renne	bistecca di renna	bistec de reno
ringdove; woodpigeon	Ringeltaube; Wildtaube	palombe[2]	colombaccio; palombo	paloma torcaz
roast chamois	Gämsenbraten	rôti de chamois	arrosto di camoscio	asado de gamuza
~ hare	Hasenbraten	lièvre rôti	lepre arrosto	~ de liebre
~ ortolans	gebratene Ortolane[3]	ortolans rôtis	ortolani arrosto	hortelanos asados
~ partridge (on toast)	gebratenes Rebhuhn (auf Röstbrot)	perdreau rôti (sur canapé)	pernice arrosto (sul crostone)	perdiz asada (sobre tostada)
~ pheasant	gebratener Fasan	faisan rôti	fagiano arrosto	faisán asado
~ quails	gebratene Wachteln	cailles rôties	quaglie arrosto	codornices asadas
~ rabbit	gebratene Kaninchen	lapin rôti	coniglio arrosto	conejo asado
~ truffled pheasant	getrüffelter Fasan	faisan truffé	fagiano tartufato	faisán trufado
~ venison (deer)	Hirschbraten	cerf rôti	cervo arrosto	asado de ciervo
~ venison (rue)	Rehbraten	chevreuil rôti	capriolo arrosto	corzo asado
~ wild boar	Wildschweinbraten	sanglier rôti	arrosto di cinghiale	asado de jabalí
~ woodcock (on toast)	gebratene Schnepfe (auf Röstbrot)	bécasse rôtie (sur canapé)	beccaccia arrosto (sul crostone)	becada asada (sobre tostada)
rock partridge[4]	Steinhuhn	bartavelle; perdrix grecque	coturnice	perdiz griega
roe[5]; venison	Reh	chevreuil	capriolo	corzo
rolled roast rabbit	Kaninchenrollbraten	roulade de lapin	rotolo di coniglio	rollo de conejo asado
saddle of hare	Hasenrücken	râble de lièvre	lombo di lepre	lomo de liebre
~ of hare with juniper	~ mit Wacholdersauce	~ de lièvre au genièvre	~ di lepre al ginepro	~ de liebre al enebro
~ of rabbit	Kaninchenrücken	~ de lapin	~ di coniglio	~ de conejo

[1] also deer - [2] ou ramier - [3] auch Fettammern - [4] or greek partridge - [5] also roebuck

Game

Game English	Wild German	Gibier French	Selvaggina Italian	Caza Spanish
saddle of venison (deer)	Hirschrücken	selle de cerf	sella di cervo	lomo de venado
~ of venison (rue)	Rehrücken; Rehziemer	~ de chevreuil	~ di capriolo	silla de corzo; lomo de corzo
~ of venison creole (with fried bananas)	~ nach Kreolenart (mit gebratenen Bananen)	~ de chevreuil à la créole (aux bananes)	~ di capriolo alla creola (con banane)	lomo de corzo a la criolla (con plátanos)
~ of venison, larded	~ gespickt	~ de chevreuil piquée	~ di capriolo lardellata	~ de corzo mechado
~ of venison with cherries	~ mit Kirschen	~ de chevreuil aux cerises	~ di capriolo con ciliegie	~ de corzo con cerezas
~ of venison with morels	~ nach Försterinart (mit Morcheln)	~ de chevreuil forestière (aux morilles)	~ di capriolo alla forestale (con spugnole)	~ de corzo con colmenillas
~ of young wild boar	Frischlingsrücken	~ de marcassin	~ di cinghialetto	~ de jabato
salmi; game stew[1]; civet	Wildragout; Salmi; Civet	ragoût de gibier; salmis; civet	stufato di selvaggina; salmis; civet	estofado de caza[2]; salmis; civet
~ of partridge	Salmi von Rebhühnern	salmis de perdreau	pernice in salmì	salmis de perdiz
~ of pheasant	~ von Fasan	~ de faisan	fagiano in salmì	salmorejo de faisán
~ of wild duck	~ von Wildente	canard sauvage en salmis	anitra selvatica in salmì	~ de pato salvaje
~ of woodcock	~ von Schnepfen	salmis de bécasses	beccaccia in salmì	salmis de becada
snipe	Bekassine; Sumpfschnepfe	bécassine	beccaccino	becacina
~, broiled	~ vom Rost	~ grillée	~ alla griglia	~ a la parrilla
snow grouse[3]; ptarmigan	Schneehuhn	perdrix des neiges[4]	pernice bianca	perdiz blanca
spit-roasted quails; quails on the spit	Wachteln vom Spieß	cailles à la broche	quaglie allo spiedo	codornices al asador
~ thrushes; thrushes on the spit	Drosseln am Spieß gebraten	grives à la broche	tordi allo spiedo	tordos al asador
stag; red deer[5]; venison	Hirsch; Rothirsch	cerf	cervo	ciervo; venado
stuffed woodpigeon	gefüllte Ringeltaube	palombe farcie	colombaccio ripieno	paloma torcaz rellena
sweet-and-sour leg of wild boar	Wildschweinskeule süß-sauer	cuissot de sanglier à l'aigre-doux	cosciotto di cinghiale in agrodolce	pierna de jabalí en agridulce
teal	Krickente[6]	sarcelle	alzavola	cerceta
terrine of quails	Wachtelterrine	terrine de cailles	terrina di quaglie	terrina de codornices

1) also ragout of game - 2) o ragú de caza - 3) also white grouse - 4) aussi poule des neiges - 5) also deer - 6) auch Kriekente

Game

Game English	Wild German	Gibier French	Selvaggina Italian	Caza Spanish
thrush pâté	Drosselpastete	pâté de grives	pâté di tordi	paté de tordos
thrushes	Drosseln	grives	tordi	tordos
~ à la bonne femme (with diced bacon and croûtons); casserole of thrushes	~ nach Hausfrauenart (mit Speckwürfeln und Croûtons); im Schmortopf	~ à la bonne femme (aux lardons et croûtons); ~ en cocotte	~ alla bonne femme (con lardo e crostini); ~ in casseruola	~ a la bonne femme (con tocino y trocitos de pan frito); ~ en cacerola
~ on the spit; spit-roasted thrushes	~ am Spieß gebraten	~ à la broche	~ allo spiedo	~ al asador
~ with juniper berry sauce	~ mit Wacholdersauce	~ au genièvre	~ al ginepro	~ al enebro
venison; red deer[1]; stag venison; roe[2]	Hirsch; Rothirsch Reh	cerf chevreuil	cervo capriolo	ciervo; venado corzo
~ carpaccio (deer)	Hirschcarpaccio	carpaccio de cerf	carpaccio di cervo	carpaccio de venado
~ carpaccio (rue)	Rehcarpaccio	~ de chevreuil	~ di capriolo	~ de corzo
~ cutlet (deer)	Hirschkotelett	côtelette de cerf	costoletta di cervo	chuleta de venado
~ cutlet (rue)	Rehkotelett	~ de chevreuil	~ di capriolo	~ de corzo
~ cutlet Conti (with lentil purée)	~ Conti (mit Linsenpüree)	~ de chevreuil Conti (aux lentilles)	~ di capriolo Conti (con purè dilenticchie)	~ de corzo Conti (con puré de lentejas)
~ cutlet St. Hubert (with mushrooms and poivrade sauce)	~ St. Hubertus (mit Champignons und Pfeffersauce)	~ de chevreuil Saint-Hubert (avec champignons et sauce poivrade)	~ di capriolo Sant'Uberto (con funghi e salsa poivrade)	~ de corzo San Huberto (con champiñones y salsa poivrade)
~ cutlet with mushrooms	~ mit Pilzen	~ de chevreuil aux champignons	~ di capriolo ai funghi	~ de corzo con setas
~ fillet	Rehfilet	filet de chevreuil	filetto di capriolo	lomo de corzo
~ goulash	Rehgulasch	goulache de chevreuil	gulasch di capriolo	gulasch de corzo
~, jugged	Rehpfeffer	civet de chevreuil	civet di capriolo; capriolo in salmì	civet de corzo; salmorejo de corzo
~ noisette	Hirschmedaillon	médaillon de cerf	medaglione di cervo	medallón de ciervo
~ noisettes	Rehnüsschen	noisettes de chevreuil	nocette di capriolo	medallones de corzo

---

[1] also deer - [2] also roebuck

Game

Game English	Wild German	Gibier French	Selvaggina Italian	Caza Spanish
venison pie	Rehpastete	pâté de chevreuil	pâté di capriolo	pastel de corzo
~ ragout	Hirschragout	ragoût de cerf[1]	stufato di cervo	ragú de ciervo
~ roast	Wildbraten	rôti de venaison	arrosto di cacciagione	asado de venado
~ salad	Hirschfleischsalat	cerf à la vinaigrette	cervo in insalata	venado a la vinagreta
~ sausages	Rehwürstchen	saucisses de chevreuil	salsicce di capriolo	salchichas de corzo
~ steak (deer)	Hirschsteak	steak de cerf	bistecca di cervo	bistec de venado
~ steak (rue)	Rehsteak	~ de chevreuil	~ di capriolo	~ de corzo
~ stew	Rehragout	ragoût de chevreuil[2]	stufato di capriolo	estofado de corzo
~ tartare	Rehtatar	tartare de chevreuil	tartara di capriolo	corzo a la tártara
waterhen; moorhen	Teichhuhn; Wasserhuhn	poule d'eau	gallinella d'acqua	polla de agua; rascón
wild boar	Wildschwein	sanglier	cinghiale	jabalí
~ boar cutlet	Wildschweinkotelett	côtelette de sanglier	costoletta di cinghiale	chuleta de jabalí
~ boar, jugged	Wildschweinpfeffer	sanglier en civet	cinghiale in salmì	civet de jabalí
~ boar sausage	Wildschweinwurst	saucisson de sanglier	salsiccia di cinghiale	salchichón de jabalí
~ duck; mallard	Stockente; Wildente	canard sauvage	anatra selvatica[3]	pato salvaje
~ duck with orange sauce	Wildente mit Orangensauce	~ sauvage à la bigarade	~ selvatica all'arancia	~ silvestre a la naranja
~ rabbit	Wildkaninchen	lapin de garenne	coniglio selvatico	conejo de monte; ~ salvaje
woodcock	Schnepfe; Waldschnepfe	bécasse	beccaccia	becada; chocha
~ flambé	flambierte Schnepfe	~ flambée	~ alla fiamma	~ flameada
~, grilled; broiled woodcock	gegrillte Schnepfe	~ grillée	~ alla griglia	~ a la parrilla
~ pâté	Schnepfenpastete	pâté de bécasses	pâté di beccaccia	paté de becada
woodpigeon; ringdove	Ringeltaube; Wildtaube	palombe[4]	colombaccio; palombo	paloma torcaz
~, stuffed	gefüllte Ringeltaube	~ farcie	~ ripieno	~ torcaz rellena
young wild boar	Frischling	marcassin	cinghialetto	jabato

---

1) ou sauté de cerf - 2) ou sauté de chevreuil - 3) o germano reale - 4) ou ramier

Vegetables

Vegetables English	**Gemüse** German	**Légumes** French	**Verdure** Italian	**Verduras** Spanish
artichokes	Artischocken	artichauts	carciofi	alcachofas
artichoke bottoms	Artischockenböden	fonds d'artichauts	fondi di carciofo	fondos de alcachofas
~ bottoms, stuffed	gefüllte Artischockenböden	~ d'artichauts farcis	~ di carciofo ripieni	~ de alcachofas rellenos
~ hearts	Artischockenherzen	cœurs d'artichauts	cuori di carciofo	corazones de alcachofas
artichokes, fried	gebackene Artischocken	artichauts frits	carciofi fritti	alcachofas fritas
~ tartare sauce	Artischocken mit Tatarensauce	~ sauce tartare	~ con salsa tartara	~ con salsa tártara
~ vinaigrette sauce	~ in Vinaigrette	~ à la vinaigrette	~ in insalata	~ a la vinagreta
asparagus	Spargel	asperges	asparagi	espárragos
~ au gratin	überbackener Spargel	~ au gratin	~ gratinati	~ al gratén
~ sauce hollandaise	Spargel mit Sauce Hollandaise	~ sauce hollandaise	~ con salsa olandese	~ en salsa holandesa
~ soufflé	Spargelsoufflé	soufflé aux asperges	soufflé di asparagi	soufflé de espárragos
~ tips	Spargelspitzen	pointes d'asperges	punte d'asparagi	puntas de espárragos
~ tips in cream	~ in Rahmsauce	~ d'asperges à la crème	~ d'asparagi alla panna	espárragos a la crema
~ vinaigrette sauce	Spargel mit Vinaigrette	asperges à la vinaigrette[1]	asparagi con salsa vinaigrette[2]	~ a la vinagreta
~ with a fried egg	~ auf Mailänder Art (mit Spiegelei)	~ à la milanaise (garnies œuf poêlé)	~ alla milanese (con un uovo al burro)	~ a la milanesa (con huevo al plato)
~ with fried breadcrumbs	~ auf polnische Art (mit Butterbröseln)	~ à la polonaise (à la mie de pain frite)	~ alla polacca (con pan grattato rosolato)	~ a la polaca (con pan rallado frito)
~ with melted butter	~ mit zerlassener Butter	~ au beurre fondu	~ al burro fuso	~ con mantequilla fundida
assorted vegetables	Gemüseplatte	assiette de légumes variés	piatto di verdure miste; verdure assortite	surtido de legumbres; legumbres variadas
~ vegetables with fried egg	~ mit Ei	légumes variés à l'œuf	verdure assortite con uovo al tegame	legumbres variadas con huevo al plato
aubergines[3]	Auberginen; Eierfrüchte	aubergines	melanzane	berenjenas
~, fried	frittierte Auberginen	~ frites	~ fritte	~ fritas

---

1) dites aussi asperges à L'huile - 2) asparagi all'olio - 3) Am. eggplants

Vegetables

Vegetables English	Gemüse German	Légumes French	Verdure Italian	Verduras Spanish
aubergines, stuffed	gefüllte Auberginen	aubergines farcies	melanzane ripiene	berenjenas rellenas
baked tomatoes Provençal (filled with breadcrumbs & garlic)	Tomaten auf provenzalische Art (mit Bröseln und Knoblauch gratinierte Tomaten)	tomates à la provençale (tomates gratinées, farcies mie de pain, ail et persil haché)	pomodori alla provenzale (pomodori gratinati ripieni di pangrattato e aglio)	tomates a la provenzal (tomates al gratén rellenos de miga de pan y ajo)
bamboo shoots	Bambussprossen	germes de bambou	germogli di bambù	brotes de bambú
beans; haricots	Bohnen	haricots	fagioli	judías; alubias
bean purée	Bohnenpüree	purée de haricots	purè di fagioli	~ en puré
beans and bacon	Speckbohnen	haricots blancs au lard	fagioli con pancetta	~ blancas con tocino
béchamel beans	grüne Bohnen mit Béchamel	~ verts à la béchamel	fagiolini alla besciamella	~ verdes con bechamel
beetroots; red beets	rote Bete[1)	betteraves	barbabietole; rape rosse	remolachas
black popular mushrooms	Stockschwämmchen	albarelles	pioppareli; pioppini	setas de chopo
~ truffles	schwarze Trüffeln	truffes noires	tartufi neri	trufas negras
Boston baked beans (with salt pork and molasses)	Bostoner Bohnen (mit Speck und Melasse im Ofen geschmort)	haricots à la bostonienne (cuits au four avec petit sali et mélasse)	fagioli al forno alla bostoniana (con pancetta e melassa)	judías al estilo de Boston (cocidos al horno con tocino y melaza)
broad beans[2)	dicke Bohnen; Saubohnen[3)	fèves	fave	habas
broccoli	Brokkoli[4)	brocolis	broccoli	bróculis; brécoles
~ florets	Brokkoliröschen	bouquets de brocolis	cimette di broccoli	ramitos de bróculis
Brunswick asparagus	Braunschweiger Spargel	asperges de Brunswick	asparagi di Brunswick	espárragos de Brunswick
Brussels sprouts	Rosenkohl	choux de Bruxelles	cavolini di Bruxelles	coles de Bruselas
~ sprouts au gratin	überbackener Rosenkohl	~ de Bruxelles gratinés	~ di Bruxelles gratinati	~ de Bruselas gratinadas
~ sprouts, sautéed	Rosenkohl in Butter	~ de Bruxelles sautés	cavoletti di Bruxelles al burro	~ de Bruselas salteadas
buttered peas	Buttererbsen	petits pois au beurre	piselli al burro	guisantes salteados
cabbage	Kohl; Kraut	chou	cavolo	col; berza; repollo
~, braised	geschmorter Weißkohl	~ blanc braisé	~ brasato	repollo estofado
~, stuffed	Kohlroulade	paupiette de choux	involtino di cavolo	col rellena

---
1) auch rote Rüben - 2) Am. also fava beans - 3) auch Puffbohnen - 4) oder Spargelkohl

Vegetables

Vegetables English	**Gemüse** German	**Légumes** French	**Verdure** Italian	**Verduras** Spanish
cabbage, stuffed	gefüllter Weißkohl	chou blanc farci	cavolo ripieno	repollo relleno
cardoons	Kardonen	cardons	cardi; cardoni	cardos
~ in cream	~ in Rahmsauce	~ à la crème	~ alla crema	~ a la crema
~ with marrow sauce	~ mit Marksauce	~ à la moelle	~ al midollo	~ con tuétano
carrots	Karotten; Möhren	carottes	carote	zanahorias
~, glazed	glasierte Karotten	~ glacées	~ glassate	~ glaseadas
~ in cream	Karotten in Sahnesauce	~ à la crème	~ alla panna	~ a la crema
cauliflower	Blumenkohl	chou-fleur	cavolfiore	coliflor
~, boiled	~ englisch	~ à l'anglaise	~ lessato	~ a la inglesa
~ cheese	gratinierter Blumenkohl	~ Mornay (au gratin)	~ gratinato	~ al gratén
~ mould[1]	Blumenkohlflan; Blumenkohlauflauf	flan de chou-fleur[2]	sformato di cavolfiore	flan de coliflor; budín de coliflor
~, sautéed	sautierter Blumenkohl	chou-fleur sauté	cavolfiore saltato	coliflor salteada
~ with fried breadcrumbs	Blumenkohl auf polnische Art (mit Butterbröseln)	~ à la polonaise (à la mie de pain frite)	~ alla polacca (con pan grattato rosolato)	~ a la polaca (con pan rallado frito)
celeriac	Knollensellerie	céleri-rave	sedano rapa	apio nabo[3]
celery	Sellerie	céleris	sedani	apio
~ au gratin	gratinierter Sellerie	~ gratinés	~ al gratin	~ gratinado
~, braised	gedünsteter Sellerie	~ braisés	~ brasati	~ estofado
~, creamed	Sellerie in Rahmsauce	~ à la crème	~ alla besciamella	~ a la crema
~ in gravy	~ in Jus	~ au jus	~ al sugo di carne	~ con jugo de carne
~ rémoulade	~ mit Remouladensauce	céleri rémoulade	sedano con maionese	~ nabo con mayonesa
ceps	Steinpilze	cèpes	porcini	setas; boletos; rodellones
~, grilled	gegrillte Steinpilze	~ grillés	~ alla griglia	~ a la parrilla
~ in shallot sauce	Steinpilze in Schalottensauce	~ à la bordelaise	~ allo scalogno	~ con escalonias
champignons	Champignons	champignons de Paris[4]	funghi (coltivati)[5]	champiñones
chanterelles	Pfifferlinge; Eierschwämme	girolles; chanterelles	finferli; gallinacci; cantarelli	rebozuelos

---

1) also cauliflower pudding - 2) dit aussi pain de chou-fleur ou gâteau de chou-fleur - 3) o apio rábano - 4) ou champignons de couche - 5) o champignon

Vegetables

Vegetables English	Gemüse German	Légumes French	Verdure Italian	Verduras Spanish
chards; Swiss chards[1]	Mangold	bettes; blettes; poirées	bietole	acelgas
~, buttered	~ in Butter	~ au beurre	~ al burro	~ salteadas
cherry tomatoes	Kirschtomaten	tomates cerises	pomodorini ciliegia	tomates cereza[2]
marron chestnuts; Spanish chestnut	Maronen	marrons	marroni	castañas
chestnut purée	Püree von Maronen	purée de marrons	purè di marroni	puré de castañas
~, Spanish; marron chestnuts	Maronen	marrons	marroni	castañas
chestnuts, glazed	glasierte Kastanien	châtaignes glacées	castagne glassate	~ glaseadas
chickpeas	Kichererbsen	pois chiches	ceci	garbanzos
chicory[3]	Chicorée	endives	indivia belga[4]	endibias; endivias
~, braised	geschmorter Chicorée	~ braisées	~ belga brasata	~ braseadas
~ fried in butter	Chicorée Müllerinart	~ à la meunière	~ belga al burro	~ de Bruselas a la molinera
~ in cream	~ in Rahm	~ à la crème	~ belga alla crema	endibia a la crema
chinese cabbage	Chinakohl	chou chinois	cavolo cinese	col de China
chives	Schnittlauch	ciboulette	erba cipollina	cebollino
corn on the cob	Maiskolben	épis de maïs	pannocchia di granturco	mazorca de maíz
~ on the cob, grilled	~ vom Grill	~ de maïs grillé	~ di granturco alla griglia	~ de maíz asada
~ salad; lamb's lettuce	Feldsalat	mâche; doucette	valerianella; soncino	hierba de canónigos[5]
cos lettuce; romaine	Römersalat	romaine; laitue romaine	lattuga romana	lechuga romana
courgettes[6]	Zucchini	courgettes	zucchini ; zucchine	calabacines
~, fried	frittierte Zucchini	~ frites	~ fritti	~ fritos
~ gratin	Zucchinigratin	gratin de courgettes	gratin di zucchine	gratén de calabacines
~, stewed	geschmorte Zucchini	courgettes à l'étouffée	zucchini stufati	calabacines estofados
~, stuffed	gefüllte Zucchini	~ farcies	~ ripieni	~ rellenos
cress; watercress	Kresse; Brunnenkresse	cresson[7]	crescione	berro
crudités (raw vegetables)	Rohkostplatte	assiette de crudités	crudità (verdure crude)	crudités (legumbres crudas)

[1] also spinach beets - [2] o tomatitos - [3] also witloof, Am. endive or French endive - [4] o insalata belga - [5] o milamores - [6] Am. zucchini(s) - [7] aussi cresson de fontaine

Vegetables

Vegetables English	**Gemüse** German	**Légumes** French	**Verdure** Italian	**Verduras** Spanish
crudités in season	Rohkost der Saison	crudités de saison	crudità di stagione	crudités del tiempo
cucumbers	Gurken	concombres	cetrioli	pepinos
~, stewed	geschmorte Gurken	~ braisés	~ stufati	~ estofados
~, stuffed	gefüllte Gurken	~ farcis	~ ripieni	~ rellenos
dandelion	Löwenzahn	pissenlit; dent-de-lion	tarassaco; dente di leone	diente de león
early vegetables	Frühgemüse	primeurs	primizie	primicias; verduras tempranas
endive[1]; frisée	Endivie; Frisée	chicorée frisée	indivia riccia	escarola; endibia
fennel	Fenchel; Fenchelknollen	fenouils	finocchi	hinojos
~ au gratin	überbackener Fenchel	~ au gratin	~ gratinati	~ al gratén
~, fried	gebackener Fenchel	~ frits	~ fritti	~ fritos
flageolet beans (green kidney beans)	Flageoletbohnen[2] (unreife Bohnenkerne)	flageolets	fagioli verdi	semillas verdes de judías
french beans; green beans; string beans	grüne Bohnen	haricots verts	fagiolini	judías verdes
~ beans, buttered	~ Bohnen mit Butter	~ verts à l'anglaise (au beurre)	~ al burro	~ verdes a la inglesa (salteadas)
frisée; endive[1]	Endivie; Frisée	chicorée frisée	indivia riccia	escarola; endibia
garden cress	Gartenkresse	cresson alénois	crescione d'orto	mastuerzo
gherkins; pickles	Gewürzgurken; Cornichons	cornichons	cetriolini sott'aceto	pepinillos en vinagre
green asparagus	grüner Spargel	asperges vertes	asparagi verdi	espárragos verdes
~ beans; french beans; string beans	grüne Bohnen	haricots verts	fagiolini	judías verdes
~ peas, French style (stewed with small onions & lettuce)	Erbsen auf französische Art (mit Zwiebelchen und Kopfsalat gedünstet)	petits pois à la française (cuits avec petits oignons et laitue)	piselli alla francese (stufati con cipolline e lattuga)	guisantes a la francesa (cocidos con lechuga y cebollitas)
~ peas with bacon	~ mit Speck	~ pois au lard	~ con la pancetta	~ con tocino
~ peas with ham	~ mit Schinken	~ pois au jambon	~ al prosciutto	~ con jamón

---

1) Am. chicory - 2) oder grüne Bohnen

Vegetables

Vegetables English	**Gemüse** German	**Légumes** French	**Verdure** Italian	**Verduras** Spanish
green peppers	grüne Paprikaschoten	poivrons verts	peperoni verdi	pimientos verdes
~ peppers, stuffed	gefüllte Paprikaschoten	~ farcis	~ ripieni	~ rellenos
gumbos; okra pods	Okraschoten; Gombos	gombos	gombi	gombos
haricots; beans	Bohnen	haricots	fagioli	judías; alubias
honey mushrooms	Hallimasche; Honigpilze	armillaires	chiodini	armilarias
hop sprouts	Hopfensprossen	jets de houblon	cime di luppolo	retoños de lúpulo
horns of plenty mushrooms	Totentrompeten	trompettes-des-morts	trombette dei morti	trompetas de la muerte
horseradish	Meerrettich; Kren	raifort	rafano; cren	rábano picante
~, creamed	Meerrettichsahne	~ à la crème	~ alla panna	~ picante a la crema
imperial mushrooms	Kaiserlinge; Kaiserpilze	oronges	ovoli	oronjas
Japanese artichokes	Knollenziest	crosnes	tuberine[1]	stachys
~ artichokes sauté	sautierter Knollenziest	~ sautés	tuberi del Giappone al burro	~ salteados
Jerusalem artichokes	Topinamburs	topinambours	topinambur	aguaturmas[2]; tupinambos
kale	Grünkohl; Blattkohl	chou vert	cavolo verde	col verde
kidney beans; red beans	rote Bohnen	haricots rouges	fagioli rossi	judías pintas
kohlrabi	Kohlrabi	chou-rave	cavolo rapa	colinabo
lamb's lettuce; corn salad	Feldsalat	mâche; doucette	valerianella; soncino	hierba de canónigos[3]
leek	Porree; Lauch	poireaux	porri	puerros
~ au gratin	überbackener Porree	~ au gratin	~ gratinati	~ gratinados
lentils	Linsen	lentilles	lenticchie	lentejas
lentil purée	Püree von Linsen	purée de lentilles[4]	purè di lenticchie	puré de lentejas
lentils with bacon	Linsen mit Speck; Specklinsen	lentilles au lard	lenticchie con pancetta	lentejas con tocino
lettuce	Kopfsalat	laitues	lattughe	lechugas
~, braised	geschmorter Kopfsalat	~ braisées	~ brasate	~ braseadas
Lima beans	Limabohnen; Mondbohnen	haricots de Lima	fagioli di Lima	judías
maize; sweetcorn	Mais	maïs doux	mais	maíz
mashed turnips	Püree von weißen Rüben	purée de navets	purè di rape	puré de nabos

---

[1] o tuberi del Giappone - [2] llamadas también cotufas y patacas - [3] o milamores - [4] aussi purée Ésaü

Vegetables

Vegetables English	Gemüse German	Légumes French	Verdure Italian	Verduras Spanish
meadow mushrooms	Maipilze; Mairitterlinge	mousserons	funghi prugnoli	mucerones; mojardones
mixed vegetables	Mischgemüse	macédoine de légumes[1]	macedonia di verdure	macedonia de verduras
morels	Morcheln	morilles	spugnole; morchelle	colmenillas; cagarrias; morillas
morel tart	Morcheltorte	tourte aux morilles	torta di spugnole	torta de colmenillas
morels in cream sauce	Morcheln in Sahnesauce	morilles à la crème	spugnole alla panna	colmenillas a la crema
mushrooms	Pilze	champignons	funghi	setas; hongos
mushroom caps	Steinpilzköpfe	chapeaux de cèpes	cappelle di porcini	sombreros de setas
~ caps, broiled	gegrillte Steinpilzköpfe	~ de cèpes grillés	capelle di porcini alla griglia	~ de setas a la parrilla
~ purée	Püree von Champignons	purée de champignons	purè di funghi	puré de champiñones
mushrooms, broiled	gegrillte Champignons	champignons grillés	funghi in gratella	champiñones a la parrilla
~, creamed	Champignons in Rahmsauce	~ de Paris à la crème	~ alla panna	~ a la crema
~, sauté	sautierte Champignons	~ sautés	~ al burro	~ salteados
~, stuffed	gefüllte Champignons	~ farcis	~ ripieni	~ rellenos
nettle	Brennnessel	ortie	ortica	ortiga
okra pods; gumbos	Okraschoten; Gombos	gombos	gombi	gombos
onions	Zwiebeln	oignons	cipolle	cebollas
onion purée	Püree von Zwiebeln	purée Soubise	purè di cipolle	puré de cebollas
~ rings, fried	gebackene Zwiebeln	oignons frits	cipolle fritte	cebollas fritas
~ tart	Zwiebeltorte	tarte à l'oignon	torta di cipolle	tarta de cebolla
onions, glazed	glasierte Zwiebeln	oignons glacés	cipolle glassate	cebollas glaseadas
~, stewed	geschmorte Zwiebeln	~ braisés	~ brasate	~ estofadas
~, stuffed	gefüllte Zwiebeln	~ farcis	~ ripiene	~ rellenas
oyster mushrooms	Austernpilze	pleurotes	pleuroti[2]	setas de cardo; pleurotos
palm hearts	Palmherzen	cœurs de palmier	cuori di palma	palmitos
parasol mushrooms	Parasolpilze; Schirmpilze	coulemelles	mazze di tamburo	parasoles; apagadores
parsnip	Pastinake	panais	pastinaca	chirivías
peas; green peas	Erbsen	petits pois	piselli	guisantes

---

1) ou jardinière (de légumes) - 2) detti anche orecchiette e geloni

Vegetables

Vegetables English	Gemüse German	Légumes French	Verdure Italian	Verduras Spanish
pea purée[1]	Püree von Erbsen	purée Saint-Germain; ~ de pois cassés	purea di piselli[2]; passato di piselli	puré de guisantes
pearl onions	Perlzwiebeln; Silberzwiebeln	petits oignons	cipolline	cebollitas
peas in potato nests	Erbsen im Nestchen	~ pois au nid	nidi di patate con piselli	guisantes en nidos de patatas
~, minted	~ mit Minze	~ pois à la menthe	piselli alla menta	~ con menta
peppers; pimientos	Paprikaschoten	poivrons	peperoni	pimientos
~, grilled	gegrillte Paprikaschoten	~ grillés	~ grigliati	~ a la parrilla
pickles; gherkins	Gewürzgurken; Cornichons	cornichons	cetriolini sott'aceto	pepinillos en vinagre
pineapple sauerkraut	Ananaskraut	choucroute à l'ananas	crauti all'ananas	chucrut con piña
pumpkin; squash	Kürbis	potiron; citrouille	zucca	calabaza
purée	Püree	purée	purè; purea	puré
purslane	Portulak	pourpier	portulaca	verdolaga
radicchio[3]	Radicchio	trévise; chicorée rouge	radicchio rosso di Treviso	achicoria[4]
~, grilled	~ vom Grill	~ grillée	~ alla griglia	~ a la parrilla
radish	Rettich	radis (noir)	rafano; ravanello	rábano
radishes	Radieschen	~ roses	ravanelli	rabanitos
ratatouille niçoise (Provençal stew of vegetables)	Ratatouille niçoise (provenzalisches Gemüseragout)	ratatouille niçoise (ragoût de leégumes variés)	peperonata nizzarda (con zucchini, pomodori, melanzane, peperoni)	ratatouille (estofado de verduras variadas)
red beans; kidney beans	rote Bohnen	haricots rouges	fagioli rossi	judías pintas
~ beets; beetroots	~ Bete[5]	betteraves	barbabietole; rape rosse	remolachas
~ cabbage	Rotkohl; Blaukraut	chou rouge	cavolo rosso	lombarda; col lombarda
~ cabbage Flemish style (with apples)	~ auf flämische Art (mit Äpfeln)	~ rouge à la flamande (aux pommes fruits)	~ rosso alla fiamminga (con mele)	~ a la flamenca (con manzanas)
~ cabbage with chestnuts	~ mit Maronen	~ rouge à la limousine (aux marrons)	~ rosso alla limosina (con marroni)	~ a la lemosina (con castañas)

---

1) also pease pudding - 2) o purè di piselli - 3) a red-leaved chicory - 4) o achicoria de Treviso - 5) auch rote Rüben

Vegetables

Vegetables English	Gemüse German	Légumes French	Verdure Italian	Verduras Spanish
red peppers	rote Paprikaschoten	poivrons rouges	peperoni rossi	pimientos rojos; ~ encarnados
rice-filled tomatoes	Tomaten mit Reis gefüllt	tomates farcies au riz	pomodori ripieni di riso	tomates rellenos de arroz
rocket	Rauke; Rucola	roquette	rucola; ruchetta	oruga; ruqueta
romaine; cos lettuce	Römersalat	romaine; laitue romaine	lattuga romana	lechuga romana
russulas	Täublinge	russules	russole; colombine	carboneras[1]
saffron milk caps	Reizker	lactaires	lattari; lattaioli	níscalos; robellones
salsify[2]; scorzonera	Schwarzwurzeln	salsifis; scorsonères	scorzonera	salsifí[3]
~, fried	frittierte Schwarzwurzeln	~ frits	~ fritta	~ frito
~, sautéed	Schwarzwurzeln in Butter	~ sautés	~ al burro	salsifi salteadas
sauerkraut	Sauerkraut	choucroute	crauti	chucrut
~, garnished	garniertes Sauerkraut	~ à l'alsacienne	~ all'alsaziana	chucruta a la alsaciana
savoy[4]	Wirsing	chou frisé; ~ de Milan	verza	col rizada; berza
~ cabbage parcels	Wirsing-Päckchen	paquets de chou frisé	fagottini di verza	bolsitas de col rizada
~ cabbage strudel	Wirsingstrudel	strudel au chou frisé	strudel di verza	strudel de col rizada
scorzonera; salsify[2]	Schwarzwurzeln	salsifis; scorsonères	scorzonera	salsifí[3]
seakale	Meerkohl	chou marin	cavolo marittimo	col marina
seaweeds	Algen	algues	alghe	algas
shallots	Schalotten	échalotes	scalogni	chalotes; ascalonias
~ in red wine	~ in Rotwein	~ au vin rouge	~ al vino rosso	~ en vino tinto
shoots; sprouts	Sprossen	pousses; germes	germogli	brotes; retoños
sorrel	Sauerampfer	oseille	acetosella; acetosa	acedera
soy-bean sprouts	Sojabohnensprossen	germes de soja	germogli di soia	brotes de soja
spinach	Spinat	épinards	spinaci	espinacas
~ au gratin	überbackener Spinat	~ au gratin	~ gratinati	~ al gratén
~, buttered	Spinat in Butter (Blattspinat)	~ à l'anglaise[5] (au beurre)	~ al burro	~ con mantequilla
~, creamed	Rahmspinat; Spinat mit Sahne	~ à la crème	~ alla panna	~ a la crema

---

1) o setas de cura - 2) also black salsify - 3) también salsifíes negros o de España - 4) also savoy cabbage - 5) ou épinards en branches

Vegetables

Vegetables English	Gemüse German	Légumes French	Verdure Italian	Verduras Spanish
spinach pudding	Spinatflan; Spinatauflauf	flan d'épinards[1]	sformato di spinaci	flan de espinacas; budín de espinacas
~ purée	Spinatpüree	purée d'épinards	spinaci passati	puré de espinacas
~ roll	Spinatroulade	roulade d'épinards	rotolo di spinaci	rollo de espinacas
~ with fried egg	Spinat mit Spiegelei	épinards à l'œuf	spinaci all'uovo	espinacas con huevo
spring onions	Frühlingszwiebeln; Lauchzwiebeln	oignons nouveaux	cipollotti	cebolletas
sprouts; shoots	Sprossen	pousses; germes	germogli	brotes; retoños
squash; pumpkin	Kürbis	potiron; citrouille	zucca	calabaza
~ blossoms, fried	gebackene Zucchiniblüten	fleurs de courge frites	fiori di zucca fritti	flores de calabacines fritas
string beans; french beans; green beans	grüne Bohnen	haricots verts	fagiolini	judías verdes
succotash (maize and beans boiled together)	Succotash (Eintopf aus Mais und Bohnen)	succotash (mélange de maïs et de haricots bouillis)	succotash (granturco e fagioli bolliti insieme)	succotash (mezcla de maíz y de judías cocidos juntos)
sugar peas[2]	Zuckerschoten	pois gourmands[3]	taccole; piselli mangiatutto	tirabeques[4]
swedes[5]	Steckrüben; Kohlrüben	choux-navets; rutabagas	rape	nabos
~, glazed	glasierte Steckrüben	~ glacés	~ glassate	~ glaseados
sweet potatoes[6]	Süßkartoffeln; Bataten	patates douces	patate americane; batate	batatas; boniatos
sweetcorn; maize	Mais	maïs doux	mais	maíz
swiss chards in cream	Mangold in Sahnesauce	bettes à la crème	bietole alla panna	acelgas a la crema
tabbouleh (bulgur salad)	Taboulé (Salat aus Bulgur)	taboulé (salade de boulgour)	taboulé (insalata di bulghur)	taboulé (ensalada de boulgour)
tomatoes	Tomaten	tomates	pomodori	tomates
~ au gratin	überbackene Tomaten	~ au gratin	~ gratinati	~ al gratén
~, dried	getrocknete Tomaten	~ séchées	~ secchi	~ secados
~, grilled	gegrillte Tomaten	~ grillées	~ alla griglia	~ a la parrilla
~, stuffed	gefüllte Tomaten	~ farcies	~ ripieni	~ rellenos
truffles	Trüffeln	truffes	tartufi	trufas

1) aussi pain d'épinards - 2) or mangetout peas - 3) ou pois mange-tout - 4) o guisantes mollares - 5) also swedish turnips, Am. rutabagas - 6) Am. yams

Vegetables

Vegetables English	**Gemüse** German	**Légumes** French	**Verdure** Italian	**Verduras** Spanish
truffles baked in ashes	Trüffeln in Asche gegart	truffes sous la cendre	tartufi sotto la cenere	trufas a la brasa
~ in napkin	~ in der Serviette	~ à la serviette	~ in salvietta	~ en servilleta
turnips	Mairüben; weiße Rüben	navets	rape	nabos
~, glazed	glasierte Rüben	~ glacés	~ glassate	~ glaseados
vegetable quiche	Gemüsequiche	quiche aux légumes	quiche di verdura	quiche de verdura
~ strudel	Gemüsestrudel	strudel aux légumes	strudel di verdura	strudel de verdura
~ tart	Gemüsetarte	tarte aux légumes	torta di verdura	torta de verdura
~ terrine	Gemüseterrine	terrine de légumes	terrina di verdure	terrina de verdura
vegetables, grilled	Grillgemüse	légumes grillés	verdure grigliate	parrillada de verduras
~ in season	Gemüse der Saison	~ de saison	~ di stagione	verduras de temporada
~, steamed	gedämpftes Gemüse	~ à la vapeur	~ al vapore	~ al vapor
vegetarian cakes	Vegetarier-Frikadellen	fricadelles de légumes	polpette di verdura	albóndigas de verdura
watercress; cress	Kresse; Brunnenkresse	cresson[1]	crescione	berro
white bean purée	Püree von weißen Bohnen	purée soissonnaise	purè di fagioli bianchi	puré de judías blancas
~ beans; ~ haricots	weiße Bohnen	haricots blancs	fagioli bianchi	judías blancas
~ cabbage	Weißkohl[2]	chou blanc; ~ pommé	cavolo bianco	repollo; col blanca
~ truffles	weiße Trüffeln	truffes blanches	tartufi bianchi	trufas blancas
wild asparagus	wilder Spargel	asperges sauvages	asparagi selvatici	espárragos trigueros; ~ silvestres
~ endive; ~ chicory	Zichorie	chicorée sauvage	cicoria selvatica	achicoria silvestre
~ herbs	Wildkräuter	herbes sauvages	erbe di campo	hierbas espontáneas
~ mushrooms	Waldpilze	champignons sauvages	funghi di bosco	setas silvestres
winter vegetables	Wintergemüse	légumes d'hiver	verdura invernale	verduras de invierno

---

1) aussi cresson de fontaine - 2) auch Weißkraut

Potatoes

Potatoes English	Kartoffeln German	Pommes de terre French	Patate Italian	Patatas Spanish
bacon potatoes	Speckkartoffeln	pommes au lard	patate al lardo	patatas con tocino
baked jacket potatoes[1] (baked in their skins)	Ofenkartoffeln (in der Schale gebacken)	~ au four (cuites telles quelles)	~ al forno in camicia	~ asadas con su piel
~ potatoes; roast potatoes	Bratkartoffeln; Röstkartoffeln; geröstete Kartoffeln	~ rôties	~ arrostite; ~ arrosto; crocchette arrosto	croquetas asadas
béchamel potatoes	Béchamelkartoffeln	~ à la béchamel	~ alla besciamella	patatas con bechamel
boiled potatoes	Salzkartoffeln	~ à l'anglaise; ~ nature	~ lesse	~ hervidas; ~ vapor; ~ cocidas
bouillon potatoes	Bouillon-Kartoffeln	~ au bouillon	~ cotte nel brodo	~ caldosas
boulangère potatoes (baked with onions)	Bäckerin-Kartoffeln (mit Zwiebeln überbacken)	~ boulangère (cuites au four avec oignons)	~ alla fornaia (cotte in forno con cipolle)	~ a la panadera (asadas al horno con cebollas)
caraway potatoes	Kümmelkartoffeln	~ au cumin	~ al comino	~ al comino
château potatoes (olive-shaped fried potatoes); olive potatoes	Schlosskartoffeln (olivenförmig geschnitten und in Butter gebraten); Olivenkartoffeln	~ château (tournées en grosses olives et sautées au beurre)	~ château (tagliate in forma di grosse olive e rosolate nel burro)	~ castillo (patatas salteadas en forma de gruesas aceitunas)
chips; potato chips[2]	Kartoffelchips; Chips	~ chips	~ chips; patatine	~ chips; croquetas fritas (a la inglesa)
creamed potatoes	Rahmkartoffeln	~ à la crème	~ alla panna; ~ alla crema	~ a la crema
croquette potatoes amandine	Berny-Kartoffeln (Kartoffelkroketten mit Mandeln paniert); Mandelkroketten	~ Berny (pommes croquettes aux amandes); ~ amandines; ~ de terre amandines	~ Berny (crocchette di patate involte in mandorle)	croquetas empanadas con almendras; ~ de patatas con almendras
dauphine potatoes (potato croquettes)	Dauphine-Kartoffeln (Kartoffelkroketten)	~ dauphine (croquettes en forme de boulette)	~ dauphine (crocchette di patate)	~ a la delfina (croquetas en forma de tapón)
dill potatoes	Dillkartoffeln	~ à l'aneth	~ all'aneto	~ con eneldo

---

[1] or potatoes baked in their jackets - [2] also saratoga chips

Potatoes

Potatoes English	Kartoffeln German	Pommes de terre French	Patate Italian	Patatas Spanish
duchesse potatoes (croquette potatoes browned in the oven)	Duchesse-Kartoffeln (überbackene Kartoffelkroketten); Herzogin-Kartoffeln	pommes duchesse (croquettes dorées au four)	patate duchesse (crocchette di patate cotte in forno)	croquetas duquesa (croquetas cocidas al horno)
fondant potatoes	Schmelzkartoffeln	~ fondantes	~ fondenti	patatas fundientes
french fried potatoes[1]; Pont-Neuf potatoes	Pont-Neuf-Kartoffeln (gebackene Stäbchenkartoffeln); Pommes frites	~ pont-neuf (pommes frites en bâtonnets); ~ frites	~ Pont-Neuf (patate fritte a bastoncini); ~ fritte	~ Pont-Neuf (patatas fritas en forma de bastoncillos); ~ fritas
fried potatoes; sauté potatoes	Schwenkkartoffeln; Bratkartoffeln	~ sautées; ~ rissolées	~ saltate; ~ sauté; ~ rosolate	~ salteadas
grilled potatoes	Grillkartoffeln	~ grillées	~ grigliate	croquetas a la parrilla
jacket potatoes[2]	Pellkartoffeln; Kartoffeln in der Schale	~ en robe des champs[3]	~ in camicia	patatas hervidas con su piel
~ potatoes[4], baked (baked in their skins)	Ofenkartoffeln (in der Schale gebacken)	~ au four (cuites telles quelles)	~ al forno in camicia	~ asadas con su piel
lorette potatoes (cheesy potato croquettes)	Lorette-Kartoffeln (Käse-Kroketten)	~ Lorette (pommes croquettes au fromage)	~ Lorette (crocchette al formaggio)	~ Lorette (croquetas con queso)
lyonnaise potatoes (fried with onions)	Lyoner Kartoffeln (mit Zwiebeln gebraten)	~ à la lyonnaise (sautées aux oignons)	~ alla lionese (rosolate con cipolle)	~ a la lionesa (salteadas con cebolla)
macaire potatoes (potato cake fried in butter)	Macaire-Kartoffeln (Kartoffelfladen in der Pfanne gebräunt)	~ Macaire (galette de pommes rissolée à la poêle)	~ Macaire (tortino di patate rosolato in padella)	~ Macaire (pastel de patatas dorado en mantequilla)
maître d'hôtel potatoes (with parsley butter)	Maître d'hôtel-Kartoffeln (mit Petersilienbutter)	~ maître d'hôtel (au beurre et persillé)	~ maître d'hôtel (patate con burro al prezzemolo)	~ a la maître d'hôtel (con mantequilla de perejil)
mashed potatoes	Kartoffelpüree; Kartoffelbrei	~ en purée[5]	purè di patate	puré de patatas
mousseline potatoes (mashed potatoes with whipped cream)	Schaumkartoffeln (Kartoffelpüree mit Schlagsahne vermischt)	~ mousseline[6] (purée de pommes à la crème)	patate mousseline (purè di patate con panna montata)	patatas mousseline (puré de patatas adicionado de nata batida)

1) also chips, Am. french fries - 2) or potatoes in their jackets - 3) ou pommes en chemise - 4) or potatoes baked in their jackets - 5) ou mousseline - 6) ou mousse Parmentier

Potatoes

Potatoes English	Kartoffeln German	Pommes de terre French	Patate Italian	Patatas Spanish
new potatoes	Frühkartoffeln; neue Kartoffeln	pommes nouvelles	patate novelle	croquetas tempranas; patatas nuevas
noisette potatoes (nut-shaped fried potatoes)	Nusskartoffeln (haselnussgroße Bratkartoffeln)	~ noisettes (rissolées en forme de noisette)	~ nocciola (patate in forma di nocciola)	patatas salteadas (en forma de avellana)
olive potatoes; château potatoes (olive-shaped fried potatoes)	Schlosskartoffeln (olivenförmig geschnitten und in Butter gebraten); Olivenkartoffeln	~ château (tournées en grosses olives et sáutées au beurre)	~ château (tagliate in forma di grosse olive e rosolate nel burro)	~ castillo (patatas salteadas en forma de gruesas aceitunas)
onion potatoes	Zwiebelkartoffeln	~ aux oignons	~ con cipolle	~ con cebolla
parisienne potatoes (noisette potatoes rolled in meat-glaze)	Pariser Kartoffeln (Nusskartoffeln in Fleischglace gerollt)	~ à la parisienne (pommes noisettes à la glace de viande)	~ alla parigina (patate nocciola al sugo di carne)	~ a la parisiense (patatas en forma de avellana salteadas al jugo de carne)
parmentier potatoes (cube-shaped and fried)	Parmentier-Kartoffeln (gebratene Kartoffelwürfel)	~ Parmentier (pommes en dés, sautées au beurre)	~ Parmentier (patate a dadi rosolate nel burro)	~ Parmentier (salteadas en forma de dado)
parsley potatoes	Petersilienkartoffeln	~ persillées	~ al prezzemolo	~ al perejil
Pont-Neuf potatoes; french fried potatoes[1]	Pont-Neuf-Kartoffeln (gebackene Stäbchenkartoffeln); Pommes frites	~ pont-neuf (pommes frites en bâtonnets); ~ frites	~ Pont-Neuf (patate fritte a bastoncini); ~ fritte	~ Pont-Neuf (patatas fritas en forma de bastoncillos); ~ fritas
potato cakes	Kartoffelpuffer; Reibekuchen	galettes de pommes	frittelle di patate	pastelitos de patata
~ chips[2]; chips	Kartoffelchips; Chips	pommes chips	patate chips; patatine	patatas chips; croquetas fritas (a la inglesa)
~ croquettes[3]	Kartoffelkroketten	~ croquettes[4]	crocchette di patate	croquetas de patata
~ gnocchi; ~ dumplings	Kartoffelgnocchi; Kartoffelklößchen	gnocchi de pommes; gnocchis à la piémontaise	gnocchi di patate	ñoquis de patatas
~ gratin	Kartoffelgratin	gratin dauphinois	gratin di patate	gratén de patatas

1) also chips, Am. french fries - 2) also saratoga chips - 3) or croquette potatoes - 4) ou croquettes de pommes de terre

Potatoes

Potatoes English	Kartoffeln German	Pommes de terre French	Patate Italian	Patatas Spanish
potato nests	Kartoffelnest	nids de pommes paille	nidi di patate	nidos de patatas
~ salad	Kartoffelsalat	pommes à l'huile (en salade)	patate in insalata	patatas en ensalada
~ soufflé	Kartoffelauflauf	soufflé de pommes	soufflé di patate	soufflé de patatas
~ straws; straw potatoes	Strohkartoffeln	pommes paille	patate fritte; ~ paglia	patatas paja
potatoes Anna (potato cake)	Anna-Kartoffeln (Kartoffelfladen)	~ Anna (galette de pommes de terre)	~ Anna (tortino di patate)	~ Ana (pastel de patatas)
~ au gratin	überbackene Kartoffeln	~ au gratin	~ gratinate	~ al gratén
~, baked; roast potatoes	Bratkartoffeln; Röstkartoffeln; geröstete Kartoffeln	~ rôties	~ arrostite; ~ arrosto; crocchette arrosto	croquetas asadas
~, boiled	Salzkartoffeln	~ à l'anglaise; ~ nature	~ lesse	patatas hervidas; ~ vapor; ~ cocidas
~, creamed	Rahmkartoffeln	~ à la crème	~ alla panna; ~ alla crema	~ a la crema
~ en papillote	Folienkartoffeln	~ en papillotes	~ al cartoccio	croquetas en papillote
~, fried; sauté potatoes	Schwenkkartoffeln; Bratkartoffeln	~ sautées; ~ rissolées	~ saltate; ~ sauté; ~ rosolate	patatas salteadas
~, grilled	Grillkartoffeln	~ grillées	~ grigliate	croquetas a la parrilla
~, mashed	Kartoffelpüree; Kartoffelbrei	~ en purée[1]	purè di patate	puré de patatas
~, steamed	Dampfkartoffeln	~ vapeur	patate al vapore	croquetas al vapor
~, stewed	Schmorkartoffeln	~ à l'étuvée	~ in umido	patatas guisadas
~, stuffed	gefüllte Kartoffeln	~ farcies	~ ripiene	croquetas rellenas
~, truffled	Trüffelkartoffeln	~ aux truffes	~ tartufate	patatas trufadas
roast potatoes; baked potatoes	Bratkartoffeln; Röstkartoffeln; geröstete Kartoffeln	~ rôties	~ arrostite; ~ arrosto; crocchette arrosto	croquetas asadas
rosemary potatoes	Rosmarinkartoffeln	~ au romarin	~ al rosmarino	patatas al romero
Rösti (fried pancake of grated potatoes)	Rösti (geraspelte Bratkartoffeln)	Roesti (pommes rapées et rissolées à la poêle)	Rösti (tortino di patate grattugiate)	Rosti (patatas ralladas gruesas y fritas)

---

[1] ou mousseline

Potatoes

Potatoes English	Kartoffeln German	Pommes de terre French	Patate Italian	Patatas Spanish
sauté potatoes; fried potatoes	Schwenkkartoffeln; Bratkartoffeln	pommes sautées; ~ rissolées	patate saltate; ~ sauté; ~ rosolate	patatas salteadas
savoy potatoes (potatoes gratinated with broth & cheese)	Savoyer Kartoffelgratin (mit Käse und Bouillon überbacken)	gratin savoyard (gratin de pommes au bouillon et fromage)	~ alla savoiarda (gratinate con brodo e formaggio)	~ a la saboyarda (gratinadas con caldo y queso)
sesame potatoes	Sesamkartoffeln	pommes au sésame	~ al sesamo	~ al sésamo
shoestring potatoes[1]	Pommes allumettes; Streichholzkartoffeln	~ allumettes	~ fritte (a forma di fiammifero)	~ cerilla
soufflé potatoes (twice-fried in deep fat)	~ soufflées (zweimal frittiert)	~ soufflées (replongées dans la friture)	~ soffiate (fritte due volte)	~ soufflées (patatas fritas dos veces)
steamed potatoes	Dampfkartoffeln	~ vapeur	~ al vapore	croquetas al vapor
stewed potatoes	Schmorkartoffeln	~ à l'étuvée	~ in umido	patatas guisadas
straw potatoes; potato straws	Strohkartoffeln	~ paille	~ fritte; ~ paglia	~ paja
stuffed potatoes	gefüllte Kartoffeln	~ farcies	~ ripiene	croquetas rellenas
surprise potatoes	Überraschungskartoffeln	~ surprise	~ a sorpresa	patatas sorpresa
sweet potatoes[2]	Süßkartoffeln; Bataten	patates douces	~ americane; batate	batatas; boniatos
thyme potatoes	Thymiankartoffeln	pommes au thym	~ al timo	patatas al tomillo
truffled potatoes	Trüffelkartoffeln	~ aux truffes	~ tartufate	~ trufadas
Voisin potatoes (cake of potato, butter and cheese)	Voisin-Kartoffeln (Kartoffeltörtchen mit Butter und Käse)	~ Voisin (galette de pommes au beurre et fromage)	~ Voisin (tortino di patate, burro e formaggio)	~ Voisin (pastel hecho de patatas, mantequilla y queso)
waffle potatoes[3]	Waffelkartoffeln	~ gaufrettes	~ fritte	~ fritas (en forma de barquillos)

---

1) or julienne potatoes - 2) also batatas of Spanish potatoes, Am. yams - 3) also lattice French fried potatoes

Farinaceous dishes

Farinaceous dishes English	Teigwaren und Reis German	Pâtes et riz French	Pasta e riso Italian	Pastas italianas; arroz Spanish
asparagus risotto	Spargelrisotto	risotto aux asperges	risotto agli asparagi	arroz con espárragos
bacon dumplings	Speckknödel	boulettes au lard	canederli allo speck	albóndigas con tocino
baked noodles	Nudelgratin	pâtes au gratin	pasta al forno	pasta al gratén
Barley risotto	Graupenrisotto	risotto d'orge	risotto d'orzo	risotto de cebada
beetroot gnocchi	Rote-Bete-Gnocchi	gnocchis aux betteraves	gnocchi di barbabietola	ñoquis de remolacha
~ ravioli	Rote-Bete-Ravioli	raviolis aux betteraves	ravioli di barbabietola	raviolis de remolacha
bread dumplings	Semmelknödel	boulettes de pain	canederli di pane	albóndigas de pan
brown rice	Vollreis	riz complet	riso integrale	arroz integral[1)
buckwheat crêpes	Buchweizencrêpes	crêpes de sarrasin	crêpes di grano saraceno	crepes de trigo sarraceno
~ polenta	Buchweizenpolenta	polenta de sarrasin	polenta nera	polenta de trigo sarraceno
butter noodles	Butternudeln	nouilles au beurre	tagliatelle al burro	tallarines con mantequilla
~ rice	Butterreis	riz blanc; ~ au beurre	riso in bianco; ~ al burro	arroz blanco
cannelloni (stuffed rolls of noodle dough)	Cannelloni (gefüllte Nudelteigrollen)	cannelloni (sorte de gros macaroni farci)	cannelloni	canelones[2) (rollos de pasta rellenos)
~ à la niçoise	~ auf Nizzaer Art	~ à la niçoise	~ alla nizzarda	~ a la nizarda
~ florentine	~ mit Spinatfüllung; ~ auf Florentiner Art	~ à la florentine	~ con gli spinaci; ~ alla fiorentina	~ con espinacas; ~ a la florentina
chanterelle risotto	Pfifferlingrisotto	risotto aux girolles	risotto con i finferli	risotto de rebozuelos
cheese dumplings	Käsenockerln	noques au fromage	gnocchi al formaggio	albóndigas de queso
cheese-filled ravioli	Ravioli mit Quarkfüllung	raviolis au fromage blanc	ravioli di ricotta	raviolis de requesón
chicken liver risotto	Risotto mit Geflügelleber	risotto aux foies de volaille	risotto con fegatini	risotto con higadillos de ave
chinese noodles	Glasnudeln	vermicelles chinois	vermicelli cinesi	fideos de arroz
couscous	Kuskus; Couscous	couscous	cuscus	cuscús; cuzcuz
creole rice	Kreolenreis	riz créole	riso alla creola	arroz a la criolla
crêpes with ham	Crêpes mit Schinken	crêpes au jambon	crespelle al prosciutto	crepes con jamón
~ with spinach	~ mit Spinat	~ à la florentine	~ con spinaci	~ con espinacas
curried rice	Curryreis	riz au curry	riso al curry	arroz al curry

---

1) o arroz con cáscara - 2) o canalones

Farinaceous dishes

Farinaceous dishes English	Teigwaren und Reis German	Pâtes et riz French	Pasta e riso Italian	Pastas italianas; arroz Spanish
cuttlefish risotto	Risotto mit Tintenfisch; Tintenfischrisotto	risotto à l'encre de seiche	risotto al nero di seppia	risotto negro
egg noodles	Eiernudeln	pâtes aux œufs	pasta all'uovo	pasta de huevo
fish ravioli	Fischravioli	raviolis de poisson	ravioli di pesce	raviolis de pescado
~ risotto	Fischrisotto	risotto de poisson	risotto di pesce	risotto de pescado
fresh noodles	frische Nudeln	pâtes fraîches	pasta fresca	pasta fresca
ginger rice	Ingwerreis	riz au gingembre	riso allo zenzero	arroz con jengibre
gnocchi (dumplings)	Gnocchi	gnocchis; gnocchi	gnocchi	ñoquis
~ à la parisienne (baked dumplings of choux pastry)	Pariser Gnocchi (gratinierte Klößchen aus Brandteig)	~ à la parisienne (gnocchi de pâte à choux fromagée)	~ alla parigina (gnocchi di farina gratinati)	~ a la parisiense (ñouis de harina al gratén)
~ à la romaine (semolina dumplings)	römische Gnocchi (gratinierte Grießklößchen)	gnocchi à la romaine (à la semoule)	~ alla romana (gnocchi di semolino)	~ a la romana (ñoquis de sémola)
Greek rice	Reis auf griechische Art	riz à la grecque	riso alla greca	arroz a la griega
green noodles	grüne Bandnudeln	nouilles vertes	tagliatelle verdi	tallarines verdes
hominy (crushed maize cooked with water or milk)	Maisgrießbrei (in Wasser oder Milch gekocht)	hominy (bouillie de maïs à l'eau on au lait)	hominy (farina grossa di granturco cotta in acqua o latte)	hominy (gachas de maiz cocidas en agua o leche)
lasagne	Lasagne	lasagnes	lasagne	lasaña
lenten ravioli; meatless ravioli	Fastenravioli	ravioli au maigre[1]	ravioli di magro	ravioles de vigilia
liver dumplings	Leberknödel	boulettes de foie	canederli di fegato	albóndigas de hígado
macaroni	Makkaroni	macaronis	maccheroni	macarrones
~ cheese; ~ mornay	gratinierte Makkaroni	~ au gratin	~ gratinati	~ gratinados
~ timbale	Makkaroni-Timbale; Makkaroni-Pastete	timbale de macaronis	timballo di maccheroni	timbal de macarrones
~ with butter	Makkaroni mit Butter	macaroni au beurre	maccheroni al burro	macarrones con mantequilla

---

[1] aussi ravioli farcis au maigre

Farinaceous dishes

Farinaceous dishes English	Teigwaren und Reis German	Pâtes et riz French	Pasta e riso Italian	Pastas italianas; arroz Spanish
macaroni with tomato sauce	Makkaroni mit Tomatensauce	macaronis sauce tomate; ~ à la napolitaine	maccheroni al pomodoro	macarrones con salsa de tomate
meatless ravioli; lenten ravioli	Fastenravioli	ravioli au maigre[1]	ravioli di magro	ravioles de vigilia
mushroom ravioli	Pilzravioli	raviolis aux champignons	~ di funghi	raviolis de setas
~ risotto	Steinpilzrisotto	risotto aux cèpes	risotto ai funghi porcini	risotto de setas
noodles; tagliatelle	Bandnudeln; Tagliatelle	nouilles; tagliatelles	tagliatelle	tallarines
noodles; pasta	Nudeln	nouilles; pâtes	pasta	pasta
~, baked	Nudelgratin	pâtes au gratin	~ al forno	~ al gratén
~ in cream sauce	Bandnudeln in Sahnesauce	nouilles à la crème	tagliatelle alla panna	tallarines a la crema
pasta; noodles	Nudeln	nouilles; pâtes	pasta	pasta
pilaf rice; pilaw rice[2]	Pilawreis	riz pilaf	riso pilaf	arroz pilaf
polenta (maize porridge)	Polenta (Maisbrei)	polenta	polenta	polenta (gachas de maíz)
potato gnocchi; ~ dumplings	Kartoffelgnocchi; Kartoffelklößchen	gnocchi de pommes; gnocchis à la piémontaise	gnocchi di patate	ñoquis de patatas
pumpkin gnocchi	Kürbisgnocchi	gnocchis au potiron	~ di zucca	~ de calabaza
radicchio ravioli	Radicchioravioli	raviolis à la trévise	ravioli al radicchio	raviolis de achicoria
~ risotto	Risotto mit Radicchio	risotto à la trévise	risotto al radicchio	risotto con achicoria
ravioli	Ravioli	raviolis; ravioli	ravioli	raviolis; ravioles
rice	Reis	riz	riso	arroz
~ croquettes	Reiskroketten	croquettes de riz	crocchette di riso	croquetas de arroz
~, curried	Curryreis	riz au curry	riso al curry	arroz al curry
~ ring	Reisring	bordure de riz[3]	corona di riso	corona de arroz
~ ring with mushrooms	~ mit Pilzen	~ de riz aux champignons	~ di riso con funghi	~ de arroz con setas
~ timbale; ~ pie	Reis-Timbale; Reis-Pastete	timbale de riz	timballo di riso	timbal de arroz
~ with mushrooms	Reis mit Steinpilzen	riz aux cèpes	riso con funghi porcini	arroz de setas
risotto	Risotto	risotto	risotto	risotto

1) aussi ravioli farcis au maigre - 2) also pilau rice - 3) ou couronne de riz

Farinaceous dishes

Farinaceous dishes English	Teigwaren und Reis German	Pâtes et riz French	Pasta e riso Italian	Pastas italianas; arroz Spanish
saffran risotto	Risotto auf Mailänder Art (mit Safran gewürzt)	risotto à la milanaise (risotto safrané)	risotto alla milanese (con zafferano)	risotto a la milanesa (con azafrán)
saffron rice	Safranreis	riz au safran	riso allo zafferano	arroz al azafrán
seafood risotto	Risotto mit Meeresfrüchten	risotto aux fruits de mer	risotto coi frutti di mare	risotto de mariscos
spaghetti	Spaghetti	spaghettis; spaghetti	spaghetti	espaguetis
~ Bolognese (with minced meat sauce)	~ auf Bologneser Art (mit Hackfleischsauce)	~ à la bolonaise (avec petit ragoût de bœuf)	~ alla bolognese (al ragù)	~ a la boloñesa (con salsa de carne)
~ with anchovies	~ mit Sardellen	~ aux anchois	~ con le acciughe	~ con anchoas
~ with tomato sauce	~ mit Tomatensauce	~ sauce tomate	~ al pomodoro	~ con salsa de tomate
spätzle (small flour dumplings)	Spätzle	spätzle (petits gnocchi de farine)	spätzle (gnocchetti di farina)	spätzle (ñoquis pequeños de harina)
spelt noodles	Dinkelnudeln	tagliatelles d'épeautre	tagliatelle di farro	tallarines de espelta
~ risotto	Dinkelrisotto	risotto d'épeautre	risotto di farro	risotto de espelta
spinach dumplings	Spinatknödel	boulettes aux épinards	canederli di spinaci	albóndigas de espinacas
~ ravioli	Spinatravioli	raviolis aux épinards	ravioli di spinaci	raviolis de espinacas
tagliatelle; noodles	Bandnudeln; Tagliatelle	nouilles; tagliatelles	tagliatelle	tallarines
tomato risotto	Risotto mit Tomaten	risotto à la tomate	risotto al pomodoro	risotto de tomate
tortilla (thin flat maize cake)	Tortilla (Maisfladen)	tortilla (galette ou crêpe de maïs)	tortilla sottile (focaccia di mais)	tortilla (torta de maíz)
truffle risotto	Risotto mit Trüffeln	risotto aux truffes	risotto al tartufo	risotto con trufas
tyrolean dumplings	Tiroler Knödel	boulettes à la tyrolienne	canederli tirolesi	albóndigas tirolesas
vegetable crêpes	Crêpes mit Gemüse	crêpes aux legumes	crespelle[1] con verdura	crepes con verdura
vermicelli	Vermicelli; Fadennudeln	vermicelles	vermicelli	fideos
wild garlic gnocchi	Bärlauchgnocchi	gnocchis à l'ail sauvage	gnocchi all'aglio orsino	ñoquis de ajo de oso
~ rice	Wildreis	riz sauvage	riso selvatico	arroz salvaje

---

[1] o crêpes

Salads

Salads English	**Salate** German	**Salades** French	**Insalate** Italian	**Ensaladas** Spanish
Plain salads	*Einfache Salate*	*Salades simples*	*Insalate semplici*	*Ensaladas sencillas*
asparagus salad	Spargelsalat	salade d'asperges	insalata d'asparagi	ensalada de espárragos
bean salad	Bohnensalat	~ de haricots	~ di fagioli	~ de judías
beetroot salad	Rote-Bete-Salat	~ de betterave	~ di barbabietole	~ de remolacha
cabbage salad; coleslaw	Krautsalat	~ de chou	~ di cavolo	~ de coles
cauliflower salad	Blumenkohlsalat	~ de chou-fleur	~ di cavolfiore	~ de coliflor
celeriac salad	Selleriesalat (aus Knollensellerie)	~ de céleri-rave	~ di sedano rapa	~ de apio-nabo
celery salad	Selleriesalat	~ de céleri	~ di sedano	~ de apio
chanterelle salad	Pfifferlingsalat	~ de girolles	~ di gallinacci	~ de rebozuelos
chicory salad	Chicoréesalat	~ d'endives	~ d'indivia belga	~ de endibia
coleslaw; cabbage salad	Krautsalat	~ de chou	~ di cavolo	~ de coles
corn salad; lamb's lettuce salad	Feldsalat	~ de mâche; ~ de doucette	~ di soncino[1]; ~ di valerianella	~ de hierba de canónigo
cos lettuce salad[2]	Römersalat; Sommerendivien-Salat	~ romaine	~ di lattuga romana	~ de lechuga romana
courgette salad	Zucchinisalat	~ de courgettes	~ di zucchine	~ de calabacines
cucumber salad	Gurkensalat	~ de concombres	~ di cetrioli	~ de pepino
dandelion salad	Löwenzahnsalat	~ de pissenlits	~ di dente di leone	~ de diente de león
endive salad; frisée salad	Endiviensalat; Friséesalat	~ (de chicorée) frisée	~ d'indivia riccia	~ de escarola
~ salad; escarole salad	Winterendivien-Salat; Eskariolsalat	~ de scarole	~ di scarola	~ de escarola
fennel salad	Fenchelsalat	~ de fenouil	~ di finocchi	~ de hinojo
french bean salad	Bohnensalat (grün)	~ de haricots verts	~ di fagiolini	~ de judías verdes
frisée salad; endive salad	Endiviensalat; Friséesalat	~ (de chicorée) frisée	~ d'indivia riccia	~ de escarola
garden cress salad	Gartenkresse-Salat	~ de cresson alénois	~ di crescione d'orto	~ de mastuerzo
green salad	grüner Salat	~ verte	~ verde	~ verde

---

1) o insalata di dolcetta, insalata di gallinelle - 2) also romaine salad

Salads

Salads English	**Salate** German	**Salades** French	**Insalate** Italian	**Ensaladas** Spanish
lamb's lettuce salad; corn salad	Feldsalat	salade de mâche; ~ de doucette	insalata di soncino[1]; ~ di valerianella	ensalada de hierba de canónigo
leaf salad	Blattsalat	~ verte	~ verde	~ verde
lentil salad	Linsensalat	~ de lentilles	~ di lenticchie	~ de lentejas
lettuce salad	Kopfsalat	~ de laitue	~ di lattuga	~ de lechuga
mushroom salad (with champignons)	Champignonsalat	~ de champignons	~ di champignon	~ de champiñones
~ salad	Pilzsalat	~ de champignons	~ di funghi	~ de setas
~ salad (with ceps)	Steinpilzsalat	~ de cèpes	~ di porcini	~ de setas
palm heart salad	Palmherzensalat	~ de cœurs de palmier	~ di cuori di palma	~ de palmitos
pepper salad	Paprikasalat	~ de poivrons	~ di peperoni	~ de pimientos
potato salad	Kartoffelsalat	~ de pommes (de terre)	~ di patate	~ de patatas
~ salad, lukewarm	warmer Kartoffelsalat	~ tiède de pommes de terre	~ tiepida di patate	~ tibia de patatas
radicchio salad	Radicchiosalat	~ de trévise	~ di radicchio	~ de achicoria
radish salad	Radieschensalat	~ de radis (roses)	~ di ravanelli	~ de rabanitos
red cabbage salad	Rotkohlsalat	~ de chou rouge	~ di cavolo rosso	~ de lombarda
rocket salad	Raukesalat	~ de roquette	~ di rucola	~ de oruga
salad in season	Salat der Saison	~ de saison	~ di stagione	~ del tiempo
~ with bacon	~ mit Speckwürfeln	~ aux lardons	~ al lardo	~ con tocino
salsify salad	Schwarzwurzelsalat	~ de salsifis	~ di scorzonera	~ de salsifí
sauerkraut salad	Sauerkrautsalat	~ de choucroute	~ di crauti	~ de chucrut
spinach beet salad	Mangoldsalat	~ de bettes	~ di bietole	~ de acelgas
~ salad (raw)	Spinatsalat (roh)	~ d'épinards (crus)	~ di spinaci (crudi)	~ de espinacas (crudas)
sprout salad	Sprossensalat	~ de pousses	~ di germogli	~ de brotes
tomato salad	Tomatensalat	~ de tomate	~ di pomodori	~ de tomate
vegetable salad	Gemüsesalat	~ de légumes	~ di verdura	~ de verdura
watercress salad	Brunnenkressesalat	~ de cresson (de fontaine)	~ di crescione	~ de berros
wheat salad	Weizensalat	~ de blé	~ di grano	~ de trigo

[1] o insalata di dolcetta, insalata di gallinelle

Salads

Salads	**Salate**	**Salades**	**Insalate**	**Ensaladas**
English	German	French	Italian	Spanish

Compound salads | *Zusammengesetzte Salate* | *Salades composées* | *Insalate composte* | *Ensaladas compuestas*

English	German	French	Italian	Spanish
autumn salad	Herbstsalat	salade d'automne	insalata autunnale	ensalada de otoño
black and white salad (potatoes & truffles)	Schwarzweißer Salat (Kartoffeln und Trüffeln)	~ demi-deuil (pommes de terre et truffes noires)	~ bianca e nera (patate e tartufi neri)	~ medio luto (ensalada de patatas y trufas negras)
Caesar salad (cos lettuce, anchovies, egg)	Cäsarsalat (römischer Salat, Sardellen, Ei)	~ césar (romaine, anchois, œuf)	~ alla Cesare (lattuga romana, acciughe, uovo)	~ César (lechuga romana, anchoas, huevo)
Carmen salad (red peppers, breast of chicken, peas & rice)	Carmen-Salat (rote Paprikaschoten, Hühnerfleisch, Erbsen, Reis)	~ Carmen (poivrons rouges, blanc de poule, petits pois, riz)	~ Carmen (peperoni rossi, petto di pollo, piselli e riso)	~ Carmen (carne de ave, pimientos, arroz, guisantes)
exotic salad	exotischer Salat	~ exotique	~ esotica	~ exótica
fancy salad	Bunter Salat	~ mêlée	~ capricciosa	~ ilustrada
fish salad	Fischsalat	~ de poisson	~ di pesce	~ de pescado
Francillon salad (potatoes, mussels, truffles)	Francillon-Salat (Kartoffeln, Miesmuscheln, Trüffeln)	~ Francillon (pommes de terre, moules, truffes)	~ Francillon (patate, cozze, tartufi)	~ Francillon (patatas, mejillones, trufas)
lettuce-tomato salad	Tomaten-Kopfsalat	~ de tomate et laitue	~ di pomodori e lattuga	~ de lechuga y tomate
Lorette salad (lamb's lettuce, celery, beetroot, French dressing)	Lorette-Salat (Rapunzel, Staudensellerie, rote Rüben)	~ Lorette (mâche, céleri, betteraves, vinaigrette)	~ Lorette (valerianella, sedano, barbabietole, olio e aceto)	~ Lorette (hierba de los canónigos, apio y remolacha)
mixed salad	gemischter Salat	~ panachée; ~ variée; ~ mêlée	~ mista	~ variada
Ninon salad (lettuce & orange salad)	Ninon-Salat (Kopfsalat und Orangenspalten)	~ Ninon (salade de laitue à l'orange)	~ Ninon (lattuga e spicchi d'arance)	~ Ninon (lechuga y naranja)
pasta salad; noodle salad	Nudelsalat	~ de pâtes	~ di pasta	~ de pasta
Rachel salad (celery, artichoke bottoms, potatoes, asparagus tips)	Rachel-Salat (Sellerie, Artischockenböden, Kartoffeln und Spargelspitzen)	~ Rachel (céleri, pommes de terre, fonds d'artichauts, pointes d'asperges)	~ Rachel (sedano, patate, fondi di carciofo, punte d'asparagi, maionese)	~ Rachel (apio, patatas, fondos de alcachofas, puntas de espárragos, mayonesa)

Salads

Salads English	Salate German	Salades French	Insalate Italian	Ensaladas Spanish
raw vegetable salad	Rohkostsalat	salade crue	insalata di verdure crude	ensalada de verdura cruda
rice salad	Reissalat	~ de riz	~ di riso	~ de arroz
russian salad (mixed vegetable salad dressed with mayonnaise)	russischer Salat (Gemüsesalat mit Mayonnaise angemacht)	~ russe (salade de légumes divers liée à la mayonnaise)	~ russa (insalata di verdure miste legata con maionese)	~ rusa[1] (ensalada de hortalizas variadas adrezada con mayonesa)
salad niçoise (tomatoes, anchovies, black olives, potatoes, french beans, capers)	Nizzaer Salat (Tomaten, Sardellen, schwarze Oliven, Kartoffeln, grüne Bohnen und Kapern)	~ niçoise (tomates, filets d'anchois, olives noires, pommes de terre, haricots verts, câpres)	~ nizzarda (pomodori, acciughe, olive nere, patate, fagiolini, capperi)	~ nizarda (tomates, anchoas, aceitunas negras, patatas, judías verdes, alcaparras)
springtime salad	Frühlingssalat	~ de printemps	~ primaverile	~ de primavera
summer salad	Sommersalat	~ d'été	~ estiva	~ de verano
tomato and cucumber salad	Gurken-Tomaten-Salat	~ de concombres et tomates	~ di pomodori e cetrioli	~ de tomate y pepino
~ and mozzarella salad	Tomaten-Mozzarella-Salat; Caprese	~ de tomates à la mozzarella	~ caprese (di pomodori e mozzarella)	~ de tomate y mozzarella
Tosca salad (celery, poultry, truffles, Parmesan, mayonnaise)	Tosca-Salat (Sellerie, Geflügel, Trüffeln, Parmesan, Mayonnaise)	~ Tosca (céleri, volaille, truffes parmesan, mayonnaise)	~ Tosca (sedano, pollo, tartufi, parmigiano, maionese con senape)	~ Tosca (apio, carne de ave, trufas blancas, parmesano)
Waldorf salad (apples, celeriac & walnuts, mayonnaise)	Waldorfsalat (Äpfel, Knollensellerie, Walnüsse, Mayonnaise)	~ Waldorf (pommes fruits, céleri-rave, noix, mayonnaise)	~ Waldorf (sedano rapa, mele e noci, maionese)	~ Waldorf (apio-nabo, manzanas y nueces, mayonesa)

---

[1] o ensaladilla rusa

Cheese

Cheese English	**Käse** German	**Fromages** French	**Formaggi** Italian	**Quesos** Spanish
blue cheese	Blauschimmelkäse; Edelpilzkäse	fromage persillé[1]	formaggio erborinato	queso azul
buffalo mozzarella	Büffel-Mozzarella	mozzarella de bufflonne	mozzarella di bufala	mozzarella de búfala
caraway cheese	Kümmelkäse	fromage au cumin	formaggio al comino	queso de comino
cheese croquettes	Käsekroketten	croquettes au fromage	crocchette al formaggio	croquetas de queso
~, grated	geriebener Käse	fromage râpé	formaggio grattugiato	queso rallado
cheese-puffs; chou buns with cheese	Käsewindbeutel	choux au fromage	bignè al formaggio	lionesas de queso
cheese quiche	Käsequiche	quiche au fromage	torta al formaggio	quiche de queso
~ soufflé	Käsesoufflé	soufflé au fromage	soufflé di formaggio	soufflé de queso
~ spread	Streichkäse	fromage à tartiner	formaggio da spalmare	queso para untar
~ straws	Käsestangen	paillettes au fromage	bastoncini al formaggio	barritas de queso
~ tartlet	Käsetörtchen	ramequin	tartelletta al formaggio	tartaleta de queso
cheeseboard	Käseplatte	plateau de fromages	formaggi assortiti	surtido de quesos
chèvre; goat cheese	Ziegenkäse	chèvre	formaggio di capra[2]	queso de cabra
choice of cheese; selection of cheese	Käseauswahl	assortiment de fromages	assortimento di formaggi	tabla de quesos
chou buns with cheese; cheese-puffs	Käsewindbeutel	choux au fromage	bignè al formaggio	lionesas de queso
cottage cheese; curd cheese[3]	Quark; Topfen	fromage blanc	ricotta	requesón; queso fresco
cream cheese	Rahmkäse	~ à la crème	formaggio alla panna	queso de crema
curd cheese[3]; cottage cheese	Quark; Topfen	~ blanc	ricotta	requesón; queso fresco
Dutch cheese[4]	Holländer Käse; Edamer	hollande	olandese	queso de Holanda
emmenthal; Swiss cheese	Emmentaler	emmenthal; emmental	emmental	emmenthal
ewe's cheese[5]	Schafkäse	fromage de brebis	pecorino	queso de oveja
fondue; Swiss fondue	Fondue; Käsefondue	fondue au fromage	fondue; fonduta	fondue de queso

1) dit aussi bleu - 2) o formaggio di caprino - 3) also curd(s) - 4) Am. édam - 5) also sheep's cheese

Cheese

Cheese English	**Käse** German	**Fromages** French	**Formaggi** Italian	**Quesos** Spanish
fresh cheese	Frischkäse	fromage frais	formaggio fresco	queso fresco
goat cheese; chèvre	Ziegenkäse	chèvre	~ di capra[1]	~ de cabra
gorgonzola (blue cheese)	Gorgonzola (Blauschimmelkäse)	gorgonzola (fromage persillé)	gorgonzola (formaggio erborinato)	gorgonzola (queso azul)
grated cheese	geriebener Käse	fromage râpé	formaggio grattugiato	queso rallado
gruyère	Greyerzer; Gruyère; Schweizer Käse	gruyère	groviera; gruviera	~ gruyère
herb cheese	Kräuterkäse	fromage aux herbes	formaggio alle erbe	~ de hierbas
Liptauer (soft, white cheese of ewe's milk with paprika & caraway-seeds)	Liptauer (Frischkäse aus Schafmilch, mit Paprika und Kümmel)	Liptauer (fromage blanc de brebis, additionné de paprika et cumin)	Liptauer (formaggio fresco di latte di pecora mista con paprica e comino)	Liptauer (queso blanco de leche de oveja con pimentón y comino)
mascarpone (white cheese of full-cream)	Mascarpone (Doppelrahm-Frischkäse)	mascarpone (fromage frais double-crème)	mascarpone (formaggio fresco di tutta panna)	mascarpone (queso fresco de nata doble)
matured cheese	reifer Käse	fromage affiné; ~ fait	formaggio stagionato	queso curado
mozzarella	Mozzarella	mozzarella	mozzarella	mozzarella
parmesan	Parmesan	parmesan	parmigiano	parmesano
petit-suisse (soft full-cream cheese)	Petit-suisse (milder frischer Rahmkäse)	petit-suisse (fromage frais très gras)	petit-suisse (formaggio ricco di panna)	petit-suisse (queso fresco de nata)
roquefort (blue cheese of ewe's milk)	Roquefort (Blauschimmel-käse aus Schafmilch)	roquefort (fromage persillé de lait de brebis)	roquefort (formaggio erborinato di latte di pecora)	roquefort (queso azul de leche de oveja)
selection of cheese; choice of cheese	Käseauswahl	assortiment de fromages	assortimento di formaggi	tabla de quesos
smoked cheese	Räucherkäse	fromage fumé	formaggio affumicato	queso ahumado
soft cheese	Weichkäse	~ mou	~ morbido	~ blando
Swiss cheese; emmenthal	Emmentaler	emmenthal; emmental	emmental	emmenthal
~ fondue; fondue	Fondue; Käsefondue	fondue au fromage	fondue; fonduta	fondue de queso
tofu (curd from soybeans)	Tofu (Bohnenquark)	tofu (fromage de soja)	tofu (formaggio di soia)	tofu (requesón de soja)

---

[1] o formaggio di caprino

Sweets

Sweets English	**Süßspeisen** German	**Entremets** French	**Dolci** Italian	**Postres** Spanish
almond brittle	Mandelkrokant	praliné-amandes	croccante di mandorle	crocante de almendras
~ cake	Mandeltorte	gâteau aux amandes	torta di mandorle	tarta de almendras
~ creme	Mandelcreme	crème frangipane	crema alle mandorle	crema de almendras
~ soufflé	Mandelauflauf	soufflé aux amandes	soufflé alle mandorle	soufflé de almendras
angel cake[1]	Engelskuchen (leichtes Biskuit)	biscuit mousseline	pan degli angeli	bizcocho
apple, caramelized	karamellisierter Apfel	pomme caramélisée	mela caramellata	manzana acaramelada
~ charlotte (stewed apples enclosed in bread slices)	Apfelcharlotte (Apfelmus in Brotscheibenhülle)	charlotte aux pommes (marmelade de pommes dans enveloppe de tranches de pain)	charlotte di mele (passato di mele in involucro di fette di pane)	charlota de manzana (puré de manzanas en envoltura de rebanadas de pan)
~ crêpes; Norman pancakes (with apples)	Crêpes auf normannische Art (mit Äpfeln)	crêpes à la normande (aux pommes fruits)	crêpes alla normanna (con mele)	crepes a la normanda (con manzanas)
~ crumble	Apfel-Crumble (Apfel mit Streuseln)	crumble aux pommes[2]	gratin di mele	gratén de manzana
~ dumpling (apple baked in pastry)	Apfel im Schlafrock	pomme en robe; ~ en surprise	mela in camicia; ~ in gabbia	manzana vestida
~ fritters	Apfelbeignets; gebackene Apfelringe	beignets de pommes	frittelle di mele	buñuelos de manzana
~ mousse	Apfelschaum	mousse aux pommes	mousse di mele	espuma de manzana
~ pie	Apfelpie	pie aux pommes	pie di mele; torta di mele	pastel de manzana; tarta de manzana
~ strudel	Apfelstrudel	strudel aux pommes	strudel di mele	strudel de manzana
~ tart	Apfeltorte	tarte aux pommes	torta di mele	tarta de manzana
~ turnover	Apfeltasche	chausson aux pommes	fagottino di mele	bolsita de manzana; pastelillo de manzana
apples, stewed	Apfelkompott	compote de pommes	mele cotte	compota de manzanas
apricot dumplings	Marillenknödel	boulettes aux abricots	gnocchi alle albicocche	albóndigas de albaricoques

---

1) also angel foodcake - 2) ou gratin de pommes

Sweets

Sweets English	**Süßspeisen** German	**Entremets** French	**Dolci** Italian	**Postres** Spanish
apricot soufflé	Aprikosensoufflé	soufflé aux abricots	soufflé di albicocche	soufflé de albaricoques
~ tart	Aprikosenkuchen	tarte aux abricots	torta di albicocche	tarta de albaricoques
aspic of wild berries	Waldfrüchte in Aspik	aspic de fruits des bois	aspic di frutti di bosco	aspic de frutas silvestres
assorted pastries	Auswahl an Backwerk	pâtisserie assortie	pasticceria assortita	pastelería fina
avocado pear cream	Avocadocreme	crème à l'avocat	crema all'avocado	crema de aguacate
baba; rum baba (small yeast-raised cake soaked in rum syrup)	Baba mit Rum; Rum-Baba	baba au rhum	babà al rum	babá al ron
baked Alaska[1] (ice-cream covered with meringue and baked)	Omelett norwegisch (Eis mit Baiserhaube); Überraschungs-Omelette (Eis mit Eierschnee bedeckt und gebacken); Eisomelette	omelette norvégienne (glace meringuée, colorée au four); ~ surprise	omelette a sorpresa (gelato meringato al forno); gelato al forno	sierra Nevada[2] (helado merengado al horno)
~ apples	Bratäpfel	pommes au four	mele al forno	manzanas asadas
~ filled apples (filled with butter and sugar)	gefüllte Bratäpfel[3] (mit Butter und Zucker gefüllt)	~ à la bonne femme (pomme au four remplie beurre et sucre)	~ ripiene al forno[4] (ripiene di burro e zucchero)	~ rellenas al horno (rellenas de mantequilla y azucar)
banana fritters	Bananenbeignets	beignets de bananes	frittelle di banane	buñuelos de plátanos
~ split (split bananas with ice-cream and whipped cream)	Banana split (aufgeschnittene Banane mit Eis und Schlagsahne)	bananesplit (banane fendue garnie de glace et de Chantilly)	banane split (banane tagliata longetudinalmente con gelato e panna)	banana split (banana cortada longitudinalmente con helado y nata)
bananas flambé	flambierte Bananen	bananes flambées	~ alla fiamma	plátanos flameados
bavarois[5] (custard with gelatine & whipped cream added)	Bavarois[6] (kalte Süßspeise aus Eiercreme und Schlagsahne)	bavarois[7] (entremets froid à base de crème anglaise et Chantilly)	bavarese (dolce freddo a base di crema inglese e panna montata)	bavarois[8] (crema inglesa mezclada con gelatina y nata batida)
beignets; fritters	Beignets; Krapfen; Küchel	beignets	frittelle	buñuelos
biscuits[9]	Kekse; Biskuits	gâteaux secs; biscuits	biscotti	galletas; bizcochos

---

[1] Am. - [2] o tortilla Alaska - [3] auch Äpfel nach Hausfrauenart - [4] o mele alla bonne femme - [5] also Bavarian cream - [6] oder Bayerische Creme - [7] ou bavaroise, appelé aussi «Moscovite» - [8] o bavaroise - [9] Am. cookies

Sweets

Sweets English	**Süßspeisen** German	**Entremets** French	**Dolci** Italian	**Postres** Spanish
black cherry dessert	Clafoutis (Kirschauflauf)	clafoutis aux cerises	clafoutis (dolce di ciliege)	pastel lemosín de cerezas
~ forest gateau (with morello cherries)	Schwarzwälder Kirschtorte	gâteau de la Forêt-Noire (aux cerises)	torta della Selva Nera (torta di ciliege)	tarta de la Selva Negra (con cerezas)
blancmange (almondmilk & gelatine)	Blancmanger (Mandelmilch mit Gelatine)	blanc-manger (lait d'amande et gélatine)	biancomangiare (latte di mandorle e gelatina)	manjar blanco (leche de almendras y gelatina)
blueberry cake	Heidelbeertorte	gâteau aux myrtilles	torta di mirtilli	tarta de arándanos
bombe (cone-shaped ice-cream)	Eisbombe (zwei Eissorten in Halbkugelform)	bombe glacée (glace composée)	bomba (gelato a due sapori, in forma di cono)	bomba helada (helado de dos sabores, hecho en molde)
~ Nesselrode (chestnut and vanilla ice-cream)	~ Nesselrode (außen Kastanien-, innen Vanilleeis)	~ Nesselrode (glace marrons-vanille)	~ Nesselrode (gelato di marroni e vaniglia)	~ Nesselrode (helado de castaña y vainilla)
brioche; bun	Brioche	brioche	brioche	brioche
brittle ice-cream	Krokanteis	glace pralinée	gelato al croccante	helado de crocante
buckwheat cake	Buchweizentorte	gâteau au sarrasin	torta di grano saraceno	tarta de trigo sarraceno
~ crêpe	Buchweizencrêpe	crêpe de sarrasin	crêpe di grano saraceno	crepe de trigo sarraceno
bun; brioche	Brioche	brioche	brioche	brioche
butter-cream cake	Buttercremetorte	gâteau à la crème au beurre	torta di crema al burro	tarta de crema
cabinet pudding (custard, sponge biscuits, candied fruit)	Diplomatenpudding (aus Eiercreme, Löffelbiskuits, kandierten Früchten)	pouding diplomate (fait de crème anglaise, biscuits et fruits confits)	budino diplomatico (fatto di crema inglese, savoiardi e canditi)	budín diplomático (hecho de natillas, bizochos y fruta confitada)
cake; gateau; tart	Torte; Kuchen; Tarte	gâteau; tarte	torta; dolche	tarta; pastel
candied fruit; glacé fruit	kandierte Früchte	fruits confits	frutta candita	fruta confitada[1]
caramel custard[2]	Karamelcreme	crème renversée au caramel[3]	crème caramel	flan (al caramelo)
~ ice-cream	Karamelleis	glace au caramel	gelato al caramello	helado al caramelo
~ sauce	Karamellsauce	sauce au caramel	salsa al caramello	salsa de caramelo
carrot cake	Karottentorte	gâteau aux carottes	torta di carote	tarta de zanahorias

1) o fruta escarchada - 2) or baked custard - 3) dite aussi flan au caramel

Sweets

Sweets English	**Süßspeisen** German	**Entremets** French	**Dolci** Italian	**Postres** Spanish
cassata (ice-cream slice with candied fruit)	Cassata (Sahneeisschnitte mit kandierten Früchten)	cassate (glace composée aux fruits confits)	cassata (gelato di panna con frutta candita)	cassata (mantecado con fruta confitada)
catalan cream[1]	katalanische Creme	crème catalane	crema catalana	crema catalana
champagne sabayon	Champagner-Zabaione	sabayon au champagne	zabaione allo champagne	sabayón de champañ
~ sorbet[2]	Champagner-Sorbet	sorbet au champagne	sorbetto allo champagne	sorbete al champaña
Chantilly; whipped cream	Schlagsahne	crème Chantilly[3]	panna montata	nata batida; ~ montada; chantillí
charlotte russe (custard with a casing of sponge fingers)	Charlotte russe (Vanillecreme in Biskuithülle)	charlotte russe (bavarois à la vanille dans enveloppe de biscuits)	charlotte alla russa (crema alla vaniglia in involucro di savoiardi)	charlota rusa (crema de vainilla en envoltura de bizcocho)
cheese dumplings	Quarkknödel	boulettes au fromage blanc	gnocchi di ricotta	albóndigas de queso
cheese-filled pancakes	Topfenpalatschinken	pannequets au fromage blanc	crêpes alla ricotta	crepes con queso fresco
cheese strudel (filled with sweet curds)	Topfenstrudel	strudel au fromage blanc	strudel di ricotta	strudel de queso
cheesecake	Käsekuchen; Quarkkuchen; Topfenkuchen	gâteau au fromage blanc	torta di ricotta	tarta de queso
cherries in red wine	Rotweinkirschen	cerises au vin rouge	ciliege al vino rosso	cerezas al vino tinto
~ jubilee (flaming cherries)	flambierte Kirschen	~ jubilé (flambées au kirsch)	~ giubileo (ciliege flambé)	~ jubileo (cerezas flameadas)
cherry omelette; omelette with cherries	Omelett mit Kirschen; Kirschenomelett	omelette Montmorency	omelette con ciliege	tortilla de cerezas
~ sauce	Kirschsauce	sauce aux cerises	salsa di ciliege	salsa de cerezas
~ strudel	Kirschstrudel	strudel aux cerises	strudel di ciliege	strudel de cerezas
~ tart; ~ flan	Kirschtorte	tarte aux cerises	torta di ciliege	tarta de cerezas
~ tartlet	Kirschtörtchen	tartelette aux cerises	tartelletta con ciliege	tartaleta de cerezas
chestnut cake	Kastanientorte	gâteau aux marrons	torta di castagne	tarta de castaña
~ log	Kastanienbaumstamm	bûche aux marrons	tronco alle castagne	tronco de castañas

[1] also burnt cream - [2] also champagne sherbet - [3] ou crème fouettée

Sweets

Sweets English	Süßspeisen German	Entremets French	Dolci Italian	Postres Spanish
chocolate bavarois	Schokoladenbavarois	bavarois au chocolat	bavarese al cioccolato	bavarois de chocolate
~ cream	Schokoladencreme	crème au chocolat	crema al cioccolato	crema de chocolate
~ éclairs	Schokoladeneclairs	éclairs au chocolat	bignè al cioccolato; éclairs al cioccolato	lionesa de chocolate; éclairs de chocolate
~ gateau	Schokoladentorte	gâteau au chocolat	torta al cioccolato	tarta de chocolate
~ ice-cream	Schokoladeneis	glace au chocolat	gelato di cioccolato	helado de chocolate
~ log	Schokoladenbaumstamm	bûche au chocolat	tronco al cioccolato	tronco de chocolate
~ mousse	Schokoladenschaum	mousse au chocolat	mousse al cioccolato	mousse de chocolate
~ pudding	Schokoladenpudding	pudding au chocolat	budino di cioccolato	pudín de chocolate
~ roulade	Schoko-Biskuitrolle	biscuit roulé au chocolat	rotolo al cioccolato	brazo de chocolate
~ sauce	Schokoladensauce	sauce au chocolat	salsa di cioccolato	salsa de chocolate
~ soufflé	Schokoladensoufflé	soufflé au chocolat	soufflé al cioccolato	soufflé de chocolate
~ truffles	Schokoladentrüffeln	truffes au chocolat	tartufi di cioccolato	trufas de chocolate
chou bun; cream puff	Windbeutel	chou	bignè; bignola; chou	lionesa; chou
~ bun with cream	~ mit Sahne	~ à la crème	~ alla crema	~ con crema
Christmas cake; yule log	Weihnachtsbaumstamm	bûche de Noël	tronco di Natale	tronco de Navidad
~ pudding (boiled pudding with raisins, currants, spices)	Weihnachtspudding (aus Rosinen, Zitronat, Gewürzen)	Christmas pudding (à base de raisins secs, de farine, de fruits confits, d'épices)	budino natalizio (con uva passa, canditi e spezie)	budín de Navidad (con pasas, fruta confitada, especias)
cinnamon ice-cream	Zimteis	glace à la cannelle	gelato alla cannella	helado de canela
citrus fruit parfait	Zitrusfrüchte-Parfait	parfait aux agrumes	parfait di agrumi	parfait de cítricos
coconut cake	Kokosnusstorte	gâteau à la noix de coco	torta alla noce di cocco	tarta de coco
coffee cream	Mokkacreme	crème au café	crema al caffè	natillas de café
~ cream sundae (iced coffee with whipped cream)	Eiskaffee	café liégeois	caffè con gelato e panna	blanco y negro (café frío con helado y nata)
~ éclairs	Mokkaeclairs	éclairs au café	bignè al caffè	lionesa de café
~ granita	Mokkagranita	granité au café	granita al caffè	granizado de café

Sweets

Sweets English	**Süßspeisen** German	**Entremets** French	**Dolci** Italian	**Postres** Spanish
coffee ice-cream	Kaffee-Eis; Mokkaeis	glace au café	gelato al caffè	helado de café
~ parfait	Mokkaparfait	parfait au café	parfait al caffè	parfait de café
~ soufflé	Mokkasoufflé	soufflé au café	soufflé al caffè	soufflé de café
compote; stewed fruit	Kompott	compote	frutta cotta; composta	compota; fruta cocida
cottage cheese cream	Quarkcreme	crème au fromage blanc	crema di ricotta	crema de queso fresco
country cake	Bauerntorte	tarte paysanne	torta rustica	tarta campesina
coupe; sundae	Eisbecher	coupe glacée	coppa di gelato	copa de helado
~ Jacques (ice cream with fruit salad)	~ mit Früchten	~ Jacques (macédoine garnie de glace)	~ Jacques (macedonia al gelato)	~ Jacques (helado con ensalada de fruta)
cream cake; ~ gateau	Sahnetorte; Cremetorte	gâteau à la crème	torta alla crema	tarta de crema
~ horn[1)]; ~ cornet; ~ roll	Schillerlocke; Schaumrolle	cornet à la crème	cannolo alla panna[2)]	canutillo a la crema
~ puff; chou bun	Windbeutel	chou	bignè; bignola; chou	lionesa; chou
~ slice[3)]	Cremeschnitte	tranche de mille-feuille; ~ de millefeuille	millefoglie alla crema	milhojas de crema
crème Beau rivage (custard with whipped cream)	Creme Beau-Rivage (Vanillecreme mit Schlagsahne)	crème Beau rivage (crème renversée à la vanille, décorée de Chantilly)	crema Beau rivage (crema alla vaniglia con panna montata)	crema Beau-rivage (flan adornado de nata batida)
~ brûlée[4)]	Crème brûlée	~ brûlée	~ bruciata	~ catalana
~ caramel[5)]	Karamellpudding	~ caramel[6)]	crème caramel	flan (al caramelo)
crêpe bundles	Crêpebeutelchen	aumônières de crêpes	fagottini di crêpes	bolsitas de crepe
crêpes (French pancakes)	Crêpes	crêpes	crêpes[7)]	crepes
~ flambé	flambierte Crêpes	~ flambées	~ alla fiamma	~ flameadas
~ Georgette (with slices of pineapple)	Crêpes Georgette (mit Ananasscheiben)	~ Georgette (fourrées tranches d'ananas)	~ Georgette (con fettine d'ananas)	crêpes Georgette (crêpes con piña)
~ suzette (with flaming orange liqueur)	~ Suzette (mit Orangenlikör flambiert)	~ suzette	~ suzette (crêpes flambé all'arancia)	crepes suzette (flameadas a la naranja)
custard; vanilla cream	englische Creme; Vanillecreme; Eiercreme	crème anglaise[8)]	crema inglese; ~ alla vaniglia	crema inglesa; natillas de vainilla

---

1) Am. cornucopia - 2) o cannoncino alla panna - 3) also millefeuille, Am. napoleon - 4) or burnt cream - 5) also caramel custard - 6) dite aussi flan au caramel et crème renversée - 7) o crespelle - 8) ou crème à la vanille

Sweets

Sweets English	Süßspeisen German	Entremets French	Dolci Italian	Postres Spanish
custard (sauce)	Vanillesauce	sauce vanille[1]	salsa alla vaniglia	salsa de vainilla
doughnuts; krapfen	Berliner; ~ Pfannkuchen; Faschingskrapfen	beignets viennois[2]	krapfen; bomboloni	bollos de Berlín
dried fruit salad	Trockenfrüchtesalat	salade de fruits secs	macedonia di frutta secca	macedonia de frutas secas
éclairs (small cakes of choux pastry filled with cream & iced)	Eclairs (längliches Gebäck mit Cremefüllung u. Glasur oder Schokoladenüberzug)	éclairs (gâteau à la crème de forme allongée)	bignè (pasticcino alla crema di forma allungata); éclairs	lionesa (pastel a la crema de forma alargada); éclairs
elderberry parfait	Holunderparfait	parfait au sureau	parfait al sambuco	parfait de saúco
~ sauce	Holundersauce	sauce au sureau	salsa di sambuco	salsa de saúco
exotic fruit salad	exotischer Obstsalat	salade de fruits exotiques	macedonia di frutta esotica	ensalada de frutas exóticas
fancy biscuits; petits fours	Petits fours; Teegebäck	petits fours	petits-fours; pasticcini da tè	pastas de té; ~ secas
filbert soufflé	Haselnussauflauf	soufflé aux noisettes	soufflé di nocciole	soufflé de avellanas
flan; tart; pie	Kuchen (Mürbeteig)	tarte; flan	crostata	tarta
floating island (meringue shells in custard sauce)	schwimmende Insel (eierförmige Meringen auf Vanillesauce); Schnee-Eier	île flottante (meringues en forme d'œuf sur sauce vanille); œufs à la neige	uova alla neve (meringhe a forma d'uovo su salsa alla vaniglia)	isla flotante (huevos de merengue sobra salsa de vainilla); huevos de nieve
flummery of semolina and fruit sauce	Flammeri[3] mit Fruchtsaft	flamri[4] sauce aux fruits	budino di semolino con salsa di frutta	pudín de sémola con salsa de fruta
fool (fruit puree mixed with cream)	Fool (Art Mousse aus Obstpüree und Schlagsahne)	fool (mousse fait d'une purée de fruits et de crème fouettée)	fool (purè di frutta mescolata con panna montata)	fool (puré de fruta mezclado con nata batida)
french toast	Arme Ritter	pain perdu; ~ doré	pan dorato; ~ perduto	torrijas
fritters; beignets	Beignets; Krapfen; Küchel	beignets	frittelle	buñuelos
frozen soufflé	Eissoufflé	soufflé glacé	soufflé gelato	soufflé helado
fruit crumble	Obst mit Streuseln	gratin de fruits; crumble aux fruits	gratin di frutta	gratén de fruta

---

[1] ou sauce anglaise - [2] appelés aussi berlines - [3] Grießflammeri - [4] flan de semoule

Sweets

Sweets English	Süßspeisen German	Entremets French	Dolci Italian	Postres Spanish
fruit ice-cream	Fruchteis	glace aux fruits	gelato di frutta; sorbetto	helado de fruta; sorbete
~ jelly	Obstgelee	gelée de fruits	gelatina di frutta	jalea de fruta
~ meringue pie	Obsttorte mit Baiserhaube	gâteau meringué aux fruits	torta di frutta meringata	tarta de fruta amerengada
~ salad	Obstsalat	salade de fruits; macédoine; fruits rafraîchis	macedonia di frutta; insalata di frutta	ensalada de frutas; macedonia de frutas
~ salad with champagne	~ mit Schaumwein	~ de fruits au champagne	~ di frutta allo champagne	~ de frutas al champán
~ savarin; savarin with fruits	Savarin mit Früchten	savarin aux fruits	savarin alla frutta	savarín con fruta
~, stewed; compote	Kompott	compote	frutta cotta; composta	compota; fruta cocida
~ tart; ~ pie	Obsttorte	tarte aux fruits	torta di frutta	tarta de fruta
~ tartlet	Obsttörtchen	tartelette aux fruits	tartelletta di frutta	tartaleta de fruta
fruitcake; plum-cake	englischer Kuchen; Königskuchen	cake aux fruits confits	plum cake	cake; plum-cake
gateau; cake; tart	Torte; Kuchen; Tarte	gâteau; tarte	torta; dolche	tarta; pastel
~ St Honoré[1] (rich cream cake bordered with small puffs)	Saint-Honoré-Torte (Cremetorte mit Windbeutelchen garniert)	Saint-Honoré (gâteau à la crème avec bordure de petits choux)	Saint-Honoré (torta alla crema guarnita tutt'intorno di bignè)	sanhonorato (tarta de crema guarnecida de pequeñas lionesas)
gingerbread	Lebkuchen; Pfefferkuchen	pain d'épice	panpepato	pan de especias; alajú
~ ice-cream	Lebkucheneis	glace au pain d'épice	gelato al panpepato	helado de pan de especias
glacé fruit; candied fruit	kandierte Früchte	fruits confits	frutta candita	fruta confitada[2]
gooseberry fool	Stachelbeer-Mousse	mousse aux groseilles à maquereau	mousse di uva spina	espuma di uva espina
~ tart; ~ pie	Stachelbeertorte	tarte aux groseilles à maquereau	torta di uva spina	tarta de uva espina
granita	Granita; Gramolata	granité	granita; gramolata	granizado
grapefruit sorbet	Pampelmusensorbet; Grapefruitsorbet	sorbet au pamplemousse	sorbetto al pompelmo	sorbete de pomelo
grenadine parfait	Grenadinen-Parfait	parfait à la grenadine	parfait di granatina	parfait de granadina

---

[1] also Saint-Honoré - [2] o fruta escarchada

Sweets

Sweets English	**Süßspeisen** German	**Entremets** French	**Dolci** Italian	**Postres** Spanish
gugelhupf (yeast cake with raisins)	Gugelhupf	kouglof; kugelhopf	kugelhupf (dolce di pasta lievitata)	kugelhupf (pastel de molde alto)
harlequin soufflé (half vanilla, half chocolate)	Harlekinsoufflé (Vanille und Schokolade)	soufflé Arlequin (moitié vanille, moitié chocolat)	soufflé Arlecchino (vaniglia e cioccolato)	soufflé arlequín (vanilla y chocolate)
hazelnut brittle	Haselnusskrokant	praliné-noisettes	croccante di nocciole	crocante de avellanas
~ cream	Haselnusscreme	crème aux noisettes	crema di nocciole	crema de avellanas
~ ice-cream	Haselnusseis	glace aux noisettes	gelato di nocciola	helado de avellanas
honey parfait	Honig-Halbgefrorenes	parfait au miel	semifreddo al miele	semifrío de miel
ice-cream	Eis (Eiscreme)	glace	gelato	helado; sorbete
~ cake	Eistorte	biscuit glacé	torta gelato	tarta helada
~ meringue	Baiser mit Eiscreme; Eisbaiser	meringue glacée	meringa col gelato	merengue con helado
~, mixed	gemischtes Eis	glace panachée	gelato misto	helado variado
ice-soufflé	Eisauflauf	soufflé glacé	soufflé gelato	soufflé helado
jam omelette	Omelett mit Konfitüre	omelette à la confiture	omelette con marmellata	tortilla de mermelada
jamaica coupe	Eisbecher Jamaika	coupe Jamaïque	coppa Giamaica	copa Jamaica
kaiserschmarren (raisin omelet cut up into pieces)	Kaiserschmarren (Rosinen-Omelette in Stücke zerteilt)	kaiserschmarren (omelette aux raisins coupée en morceaux)	kaiserschmarren (omelette spezzettata all'uvetta)	tortilla a la vienesa (tortilla de pasas cortada en trozos)
key lime pie; lime tart	Limettentorte	tarte au citron vert	torta alla limetta; ~ al limone verde	tarta de lima
kirsch cake	Zuger Kirschtorte	gâteau zougoise au kirsch	~ al kirsch di Zug	~ al kirsch
~ soufflé	Kirschwasserauflauf	soufflé au kirsch	soufflé al kirsch	soufflé al kirsch
krapfen; doughnuts	Berliner; ~ Pfannkuchen; Faschingskrapfen	beignets viennois[1]	krapfen; bomboloni	bollos de Berlín
lavender ice-cream	Lavendeleis	glace à la lavande	gelato di lavanda	helado de lavanda
lemon cream	Zitronencreme	crème au citron	crema al limone	crema de limón
~ granita	Zitronengranita	granité au citron	granita al limone	granizado de limón

---

[1] appelés aussi berlines

Sweets

Sweets English	Süßspeisen German	Entremets French	Dolci Italian	Postres Spanish
lemon ice-cream	Zitroneneis	glace au citron	gelato di limone	helado de limón
~ meringue pie	Zitronentorte mit Baiser	tarte meringuée au citron	torta meringata al limone	tarta de limón amerengada
~ sorbet	Zitronensorbet	sorbet au citron	sorbetto al limone	sorbete de limón
~ soufflé	Zitronensoufflé	soufflé au citron	soufflé al limone	soufflé de limón
~ tart; ~ pie	Zitronentorte	tarte au citron	torta al limone	tarta de limón
lemongrass ice-cream	Zitronengras-Eis	glace à la citronnelle	gelato di citronella	helado de citronela
lime tart; key lime pie	Limettentorte	tarte au citron vert	torta alla limetta; ~ al limone verde	tarta de lima
linzertorte (latticed tart made of short pastry with nuts and cinnamon, jam filling)	Linzer Torte (Mürbeteig mit Zimt und Nüssen, mit Marmelade bestrichen)	linzertarte (tarte en pâte sablée à la cannelle, garnie de confiture)	~ di Linz (torta di pasta frolla profumata con cannella e coperta di marmellata)	~ de Linz (tarta de mermelada hecha de pastaflora con nueces y canela)
macaroons	Makronen[1]; Amaretti	macarons	amaretti	mostachones; macarrones
madeira cake; pound cake	Sandkuchen	quatre-quarts	torta paradiso[2]	cuatro cuartos
maple syrup	Ahornsirup	sirop d'érable	sciroppo d'acero	sirope de arce
marble cake	Marmorkuchen	gâteau marbré	dolce marmorizzato	pastel veteado
marzipan	Marzipan	massepain	marzapane	mazapán
mascarpone cream	Mascarponecreme	crème au mascarpone	crema al mascarpone	crema de mascarpone
melon ice-cream	Meloneneis	glace au melon	gelato di melone	helado de melón
meringue (a mixture of beaten egg whites and sugar pâtisserie)	Meringe (Gebäck aus gesüßtem Eischnee)	meringue (fait d'un mélange de blanc d'œufs sucrés)	meringa (dolce a base di bianchi d'uovo zuccherati e montati a neve)	merengue (dulce hecho con claras dehuevo y azúcar)
~ apple	Apfel mit Baiserhaube	pomme meringuée	mela meringata	manzana amerengada
~ cake; vacherin (rounds of meringue alternated with whipped cream)	Vacherin (Schichttorte aus Meringeböden und Schlagsahne); Baisertorte	vacherin Chantilly (cercles de meringue superposés, garnis de Chantilly); gâteau meringué	vacherin (dischi di meringa alternati con panna montata); torta di meringa	vacherin (tarta hecha de capas alternadas de merengue y nata); postre de merengue

---

[1] Mandelmakronen - [2] o quattro quarti

Sweets

Sweets English	**Süßspeisen** German	**Entremets** French	**Dolci** Italian	**Postres** Spanish
meringue Chantilly	Baiser mit Schlagsahne; Sahnebaiser	meringue Chantilly	meringa con la panna	merengue con nata
~ pie	Baisertorte	gâteau meringué	torta meringata	tarta amerengada
milk rice	Milchreis	riz au lait	riso al latte	arroz con leche
millefeuille (cake of puff pastry)	Blätterteigtorte; Tausendblätterkuchen	gâteau feuilleté	millefoglie (torta di pasta sfoglia); sfogliata	tarta de hojaldre
mince pie (pie filled with raisins, spices, candied peel)	Mince pie (Törtchen gefüllt mit Rosinen, Orangeat, Gewürzen)	mince pie (tartelette garnie de raisins secs, fruits confits, épices)	mince pie (tarteletta ripiena d'un trito di uva passa, canditi e spezie)	mince pie (tarteleta relleña de pasas, fruta confitada y especias)
mixed berry au gratin	Waldfrüchtegratin	gratin de fruits des bois	gratin di frutti di bosco	gratén de frutas silvestres
~ berry tart	Beerentorte	tarte aux baies rouges	torta ai frutti di bosco	tarta de bayas
mocha cake	Mokkatorte	moka; gâteau moka	~ al caffè	~ de café
montblanc (mashed chestnuts with cream)	Montblanc (Kastanienpüree mit Schlagsahne)	mont-blanc (purée de marrons à la Chantilly)	montebianco (passato di castagne con panna)	negro en camisa (puré de castañas con nata)
mousse (frozen whipped cream mixture)	Mousse (gefrorene aromatisierte Schlagsahne)	mousse (glacée)	mousse (gelato a base di panna montata)	mousse (helado a base de nata batida)
mousse; parfait	Parfait; Halbgefrorenes	parfait; biscuit glacé	~ parfait; semifreddo	parfait; semifrío
napfkuchen (yeast cake with raisins)	Napfkuchen	napfkuchen (baba allemand)	napfkuchen (dolce di pasta lievitata)	napfkuchen (dulce de pasta levada)
neapolitan ice-cream (ice-cream made in layers of three different flavours)	Neapolitaner Eisschnitte (Eisschnitte aus drei verschiedenfarbigen Lagen)	tranche napolitaine (glace à trois parfums disposée en couches)	gelato alla napoletana (gelato a tri strati di differente sapore)	helado napolitano (tajada de helado hecho de tres diferentes sabores); mantecado de tres gustos
nesselrode pudding (chestnut pudding)	Pudding Nesselrode (Maronenpudding)	pouding Nesselrode (pudding aux marrons)	budino Nesselrode (budino di marroni)	pudín Nesselrode (budín de castañas)
Norman pancakes (with apples); apple crêpes	Crêpes auf normannische Art (mit Äpfeln)	crêpes à la normande (aux pommes fruits)	crêpes alla normanna (con mele)	crepes a la normanda (con manzanas)

Sweets

Sweets English	**Süßspeisen** German	**Entremets** French	**Dolci** Italian	**Postres** Spanish
nougat ice-cream	Nougateis	glace au nougat	gelato al torrone	helado de turrón
nut cake	Nusstorte	gâteau aux noix	torta alle noci	tarta de nueces
~ ring cake	Nusskranz	couronne aux noix	ciambella alle noci	roscón de nueces
oat cakes	Hafergebäck	galettes d'avoine	biscotti all'avena	galletas de avena
omelette; omelet	Omelett	omelette	omelette	tortilla
~ flambé	flambiertes Omelett	~ flambée	~ alla fiamma; ~ flambé	~ flameada
~ with cherries; cherry omelette	Omelett mit Kirschen; Kirschenomelett	~ Montmorency	~ con ciliege	~ de cerezas
orange salad	Orangensalat	salade d'oranges	insalata d'arance	ensalada de naranja
~ sauce	Orangensauce	sauce à l'orange	salsa all'arancia	salsa de naranja
~ tart	Orangentorte	tarte à l'orange	torta all'arancia	tarta de naranja
palmiers	Schweinsohren	palmiers	ventagli	palmeras
pancake	Pfannkuchen	pannequet; crêpe	crêpe[1]; crespella	crepe
pancakes with jam	Crêpes mit Konfitüre; Palatschinken; Pfannkuchen mit Konfitüre	crêpes à la confiture; pannequets à la confiture	crêpes alla marmellata	crepes con mermelada
parfait; mousse	Parfait; Halbgefrorenes	parfait; biscuit glacé	mousse parfait; semifreddo	parfait; semifrío
pastry	Gebäck	pâtisserie; petit gâteau	pasta	pasta
peach Alexandra (on vanilla ice-cream, with strawberry purée)	Pfirsich Alexandra (auf Vanilleeis, mit Erdbeerpüree)	pêche alexandra (sur glace vanille, avec purée de fraises)	pesca Alessandra (con gelato di vaniglia e purè di fragole)	melocotón Alejandra (con mantecado y puré de fresas)
~ cardinal (with raspberry sauce and slivered almonds)	~ Kardinalsart (mit Himbeerpüree und Mandelsplittern)	~ cardinal (à la purée de framboises et amandes effilées)	~ alla cardinale (con sciroppo di lampone e mandorle a filetti)	~ a la cardenal (con puré de frambuesas y almendras)
~ flambé	flambierte Pfirsich	~ flambée	~ alla fiamma	~ flameado

---

1) o crêpe frittatina

Sweets

Sweets English	**Süßspeisen** German	**Entremets** French	**Dolci** Italian	**Postres** Spanish
peach Melba (with vanilla ice-cream and raspberry sauce)	Pfirsich Melba (Pfirsich auf Vanilleeis mit Himbeerpüree)	pêche Melba (sur glace vanille avec coulis de framboises)	pesca Melba (con gelato di vaniglia e salsa di lampone)	melocotón Melba (con helado de vainilla y salsa de frambuesas)
pear Alma (stewed in port wine, decorated with whipped cream)	Birne Alma (in Portwein pochiert, mit Schlagsahne verziert)	poire Alma (pochée au porto, décorée de crème Chantilly)	pera Alma (cotta nel vino di Porto, decorata con panna montata)	pera Alma (cocida en vino de Oporto, decorada con nata)
~ Helena (pear on vanilla ice-cream with hot chocolate sauce)	~ Helene (mit Vanilleeis und heißer Schokoladensauce)	~ Belle-Hélène (sur glace vanille avec sauce chocolat chaude)	~ Elena (con gelato di vaniglia e salsa di cioccolato calda)	~ Elena (con helado de vainilla y salsa de chocolate caliente)
pears, caramelized	karamellisierte Birnen	poires caramelisées	pere caramellate	peras acarameladas
~ in red wine	Birnen in Rotwein; Rotweinbirnen	~ au vin rouge	~ al vino rosso	~ al vino tinto
pecan pie	Pecannusstorte	tarte à la noix de pacane	torta di noci pecan	tarta de pacana
petits fours; fancy biscuits	Petits fours; Teegebäck	petits fours	petits-fours; pasticcini da tè	pastas de té; ~ secas
pie; tart; flan	Kuchen (Mürbeteig)	tarte; flan	crostata	tarta
pineapple fritters	Ananasbeignets	beignets d'ananas	frittelle d'ananas	buñuelos de piña
~ tart	Ananastorte	tarte à l'ananas	torta all'ananas	tarta de piña
~ tartlet	Ananastörtchen	tartelette à l'ananas	tartelletta all'ananas	tartaleta de piña
~ with kirsch	Ananas mit Kirschwasser	ananas au kirsch	ananas al kirsch	piña al kirsch
~ with whipped cream	~ mit Schlagsahne	~ à la Chantilly	~ con panna	~ con nata
pistachio ice-cream	Pistazieneis	glace aux pistaches	gelato al pistacchio	helado de pistachos
plum-cake; fruitcake	englischer Kuchen; Königskuchen	cake aux fruits confits	plum cake	cake; plum-cake
plum dumplings	Zwetschgenknödel	boulettes aux prunes	gnocchi alle prugne	albóndigas de ciruelas
~ pudding	Plumpudding	plum-pudding	plum pudding	plum pudding
~ sauce	Zwetschgensauce	sauce aux quetsches	salsa di prugne	salsa de ciruelas
~ tart; ~ flan	Pflaumenkuchen; Zwetschgenkuchen	tarte aux prunes; ~ aux quetsches	torta di prugne; ~ di susine	tarta de ciruelas

Sweets

Sweets English	**Süßspeisen** German	**Entremets** French	**Dolci** Italian	**Postres** Spanish
plums, stewed	Zwetschgenröster	compote de quetsches	composta di prugne	compota de ciruelas
poppy-seed cake	Mohntorte	gâteau au pavot	torta al papavero	tarta de adormidera
~ strudel	Mohnstrudel	strudel au pavot	strudel al papavero	strudel de adormidera
pound cake; madeira cake	Sandkuchen	quatre-quarts	torta paradiso[1]	cuatro cuartos
Prince Pückler ice-cream (vanilla, strawberry & chocolate ice-cream)	Fürst-Pückler-Eis (Vanille-, Erdbeer- und Schokoladeeis)	glace prince Pückler (glace vanille, fraise et chocolat)	gelato alla Pückler (gelato di vaniglia, fragola e cioccolato)	helado Pückler (de vainilla, fresas y chocolate)
profiteroles[2] with chocolate sauce	Windbeutel mit Schokoladensauce	profiteroles au chocolat (choux à la crème nappés de sauce chocolat)	profiteroles al cioccolato (bignè alla crema con salsa di cioccolato)	profiteroles al chocolate (lionesas de crema con salsa de chocolate)
pudding	Pudding	pouding; pudding	budino	pudín[3]
pumpkin pie	Kürbistorte	tarte au potiron	torta di zucca	tarta de calabaza
punch cake	Punschtorte	gâteau au punch	~ al punch	~ de ponche
quince marmalade	Quittenpaste	pâte de coings; cotignac	cotognata	carne de membrillo[4]
raspberry ice-cream	Himbeereis	glace aux framboises	gelato di lampone	helado de frambuesas
~ jelly	Himbeergelee	gelée de framboises	gelatina di lamponi	jalea de frambuesas
~ sauce[5]	Himbeersauce	sauce aux framboises	salsa di lamponi	salsa de frambuesas
red fruit charlotte	Rote-Früchte-Charlotte	charlotte aux fruits rouges	charlotte ai frutti rossi	charlota de frutas rojas
~ fruit jelly	rote Grütze	gelée de fruits rouges	gelatina di frutti rossi	jalea de frutas rojas
redcurrant jelly	Johannisbeer-Gelee	~ de groseilles	~ di ribes	~ de grosellas
~ tart	Johannisbeer-Torte	tarte aux groseilles	torta di ribes	tarta de grosellas
rhubarb mousse	Rhabarberschaum	mousse de rhubarbe	spuma di rabarbaro	espuma de ruibarbo
~ tart	Rhabarbertorte	tarte à la rhubarbe	torta al rabarbaro	tarta de ruibarbo
~ tartlet	Rhabarbertörtchen	tartelette à la rhubarbe	tarteletta al rabarbaro	tartaleta de ruibarbo
ribboned Bavarian cream	bayerische Schichtcreme	bavarois rubané	bavarese variegata	crema bávara tricolor
rice pudding	Reisauflauf	gâteau de riz	dolce di riso	pudín de arroz

---

1) o quattro quarti - 2) small cream-puffs - 3) o budin - 4) o codoñate - 5) also melba sauce

Sweets

Sweets English	**Süßspeisen** German	**Entremets** French	**Dolci** Italian	**Postres** Spanish
rice pudding with candied fruit	Reis Kaiserinart (Milchreis mit kandierten Früchten)	riz à l'impératrice (gâteau de riz aux fruits confits)	riso all'imperatrice (riso al latte con canditi)	arroz a la emperatriz (arroz con leche y fruta confitada)
~ Trauttmansdorff (rice pudding mixed with cream, gelatine, and candied fruits)	~ Trauttmansdorff (Milchreis mit Schlagsahne, Gelatine und kandierten Früchten vermischt)	~ à l'impératrice (riz au lait additionné de crème fouettée, gélatine et fruits confits)	~ all'imperatrice (riso al latte con aggiunta di panna, gelatina e canditi)	~ a la emperatriz (arroz con leche aficionado de nata, gelatina y fruta confitada)
ring cake	Kranzkuchen	couronne	ciambella	roscón
rum baba (small yeast-raised cake soaked in rum syrup); baba	Baba mit Rum; Rum-Baba	baba au rhum	babà al rum	babá al ron
~ coffee parfait	Mokkaparfait mit Rum	parfait martiniquais	parfait al caffè e rum	parfait de café al rón
~ omelette	Omelett mit Rum	omelette au rhum	omelette al rum	tortilla al ron
sabayon (foamy wine sauce of egg-yolk, sugar & wine); zabaglione	Zabaione (schaumige Creme aus Eigelb, Zucker und Wein); Sabayon; Weinschaumcreme	sabayon (crème mousseuse de jaunes d'œufs, sucre et vin)	zabaione (crema di tuorli d'uovo, zucchero e vino)	sabayón (hecha de yemas, azucar y vino)
~, iced	gefrorene Zabaione	~ glacé	~ gelato	crema sabayon helada
Sachertorte (chocolate cake from Vienna)	Sachertorte (Wiener Schokoladenkuchen)	Sachertorte (gâteau viennois au chocolat)	torta Sacher (torta viennese di cioccolato)	Sachertorte (tarta de chocolate originaria de Vienna)
Salzburg sweet dumplings	Salzburger Nockerln	noques à la viennoise	gnocchi di Salisburgo	ñoquis de Salzburgo
savarin (ring-shaped yeast cake soaked in liqueur)	Savarin (Hefekranz, mit Likör getränkt)	savarin (variété de baba)	savarin (varietà di babà a forma di ciambella)	savarín (pastel en forma de corona mojado en licor)
~ with fruits; fruit savarin	~ mit Früchten	~ aux fruits	~ alla frutta	~ con fruta
~ with whipped cream	~ mit Schlagsahne	~ Chantilly	~ alla panna	~ con nata
semolina pudding	Grießpudding	pudding de semoule	budino di semolino	pudín de sémola

Sweets

Sweets English	**Süßspeisen** German	**Entremets** French	**Dolci** Italian	**Postres** Spanish
shortbread	Mürbegebäck	sablés; biscuits sablés	frollini	galletas de pastaflora
silvester bombe	Silvester-Eisbombe	bombe Saint-Sylvestre	bomba San Silvestro	bomba San Silvestre
silvester-eve gateau	Silvester-Torte	gâteau de la Saint-Sylvestre	torta San Silvestro	tarta San Silvestre
sorbet[1]	Sorbet[2]	sorbet	sorbetto	sorbete
soufflé omelette	Omelette soufflée	omelette soufflée	omelette soufflée	tortilla soufflée
~ Rothschild (vanilla soufflé with candied fruit)	Rothschild-Soufflé (Vanilleauflauf mit kandierten Früchten)	soufflé Rothschild (soufflé vanille aux fruits confits)	soufflé Rothschild (soufflé alla vaniglia con canditi)	soufflé Rothschild (soufflé de vainilla con fruta confitada)
sponge cake	Biskuitkuchen	biscuit de Savoie	pan di Spagna	bizcocho; tarta de bizcocho
~ fingers[3]	Löffelbiskuits	biscuits à la cuillère	savoiardi	soletillas; bizcochos
Stephanie omelette (with strawberries)	Omelette Stephanie (mit Erdbeeren)	omelette Stéphanie (aux fraises)	omelette Stefania (con fragole)	tortilla Estefanía (con fresas)
strawberries with cream	Erdbeeren mit Sahne	fraises à la Chantilly	fragole con la panna	fresas con nata
~ with sabayon	~ mit Weinschaumsauce	~ au sabayon	~ allo zabaione	~ con sabayón
strawberry bavarois	Erdbeerbavarois	bavarois aux fraises	bavarese alle fragole	bavarois de fresas
~ cream	Erdbeercreme	crème aux fraises	crema di fragole	crema de fresas
~ ice-cream	Erdbeereis	glace aux fraises	gelato di fragola	helado de fresa
~ mousse	Erdbeermousse	mousse aux fraises	mousse di fragole	mousse de fresas
~ parfait	Erdbeerparfait	parfait aux fraises	semifreddo alle fragole	parfait de fresas
~ roulade[4]	Erdbeerrolle	roulé aux fraises	rotolo alle fragole	brazo de gitano de fresas
~ shortcake	Erdbeer-Biskuittorte	biscuit mousseline aux fraises	pan di Spagna alle fragole	bizcocho con fresas
~ tart	Erdbeertorte	tarte aux fraises	torta di fragole	tarta de fresas
sundae; coupe	Eisbecher	coupe glacée	coppa di gelato	copa de helado
surprise melon (filled with fruit salad)	Überraschungs-Melone (mit Obstsalat gefüllt)	melon aux fruits	melone a sorpresa (ripieno di macedonia)	melón sorpresa (relleno de ensalada de fruta)

---

1) Am. sherbet - 2) auch Sorbett - 3) also sponge biscuits and ladyfingers - 4) also strawberry roll

Sweets

Sweets English	**Süßspeisen** German	**Entremets** French	**Dolci** Italian	**Postres** Spanish
surprise oranges (filled with orange ice-cream)	Überraschungs-Orangen (mit Orangeneis gefüllt)	oranges en surprise (remplies de glace à l'orange)	arance a sorpresa (ripiene di gelato d'arancia)	naranjas sorpresa (rellenas de sorbete de naranja)
sweets from the trolley	Nachspeisen vom Wagen	chariot des desserts	dolci dal carrello	carrito de postres
swiss roll[1] (baked jam roll)	Biskuitrolle	roulé; biscuit roulé	rotolo con marmellata[2]	brazo de gitano
syllabub (dessert of cream or milk whipped with wine and sugar)	Syllabub (schaumige Creme aus Milch oder Sahne, Wein, Zucker)	syllabub (sorte de sabayon fait de créme ou lait, vin et sucre)	syllabub (sorta di zabaione a base di panna o latte, vino, zucchero)	syllabub (espuma hecha de nata o leche, vino y azucar)
tangerine ice-cream	Mandarineneis	glace aux mandarines	gelato di mandarino	helado de mandarinas
tart; cake; gateau	Torte; Kuchen; Tarte	gâteau; tarte	torta; dolche	tarta; pastel
tart; flan; pie	Kuchen (Mürbeteig)	tarte; flan	crostata	tarta
tartlet	Törtchen[3]	tartelette	torteletta	tartaleta
tipsy cake; trifle (sponge cake soaked in liqueur and topped with custard)	Trifle (kalte Süßspeise aus likörgetränktem Biskuit und Creme)	trifle (entremets froid fait de génoise imlibée de liqueur et de crème pâtissière)	zuppa inglese (dolce fatto di strati di crema e di savoiardi intrisi di liquore)	trifle (dulca frío hecho de bizcochos mojados en licor y de natillas)
tiramisu (coffee-flavoured mascarpone dessert)	Tiramisu (Mascarpone-Dessert mit Kaffeearoma)	tiramisu (entremets de mascarpone au café)	tiramisù (dolce di mascarpone al caffè)	tiramisù (postre de mascarpone al café)
treacle tart	Melassekuchen	tarte à la mélasse	torta alla melassa	tarta de melaza
trifle (sponge cake soaked in liqueur and topped with custard); tipsy cake	Trifle (kalte Süßspeise aus likörgetränktem Biskuit und Creme)	trifle (entremets froid fait de génoise imlibée de liqueur et de crème pâtissière)	zuppa inglese (dolce fatto di strati di crema e di savoiardi intrisi di liquore)	trifle (dulca frío hecho de bizcochos mojados en licor y de natillas)
twelfth-night cake	Dreikönigskuchen	galette des rois	torta dell'Epifania	torta de Reyes
upside-down cake	Tarte Tatin (gestürzter Apfelkuchen)	tarte Tatin (tarte aux pommes renversée)	tarte Tatin (torta di mele rovesciata)	tarta Tatín (tarta volteada de manzana)

---

1) Am. jelly roll - 2) o salame inglese - 3) auch Tortelett

Sweets

Sweets English	Süßspeisen German	Entremets French	Dolci Italian	Postres Spanish
vacherin (rounds of meringue alternated with whipped cream); meringue cake	Vacherin (Schichttorte aus Meringeböden und Schlagsahne); Baisertorte	vacherin Chantilly (cercles de meringue superposés, garnis de Chantilly); gâteau meringué	vacherin (dischi di meringa alternati con panna montata); torta di meringa	vacherin (tarta hecha de capas alternadas de merengue y nata); postre de merengue
vanilla bavarois	Vanillebavarois	bavarois à la vanille	bavarese alla vaniglia	bavarois de vainilla
~ cream; custard	englische Creme; Vanillecreme; Eiercreme	crème anglaise[1]	crema inglese; ~ alla vaniglia	crema inglesa; natillas de vainilla
~ ice-cream	Vanilleeis	glace à la vanille	gelato di vaniglia	helado de vainilla; mantecado
~ parfait	Vanilleparfait	parfait à la vanille	parfait alla vaniglia	parfait de vainilla
~ pudding	Vanillepudding	pudding à la vanille	budino alla vaniglia	budín de vainilla
~ soufflé	Vanillesoufflé	soufflé à la vanille	soufflé alla vaniglia	soufflé de vainilla
variety of pies and cakes	verschiedene Torten; Auswahl an Torten	gâteaux variés	torte assortite; assortimento di torte	surtido de postres; tartas diversas
waffles	Waffeln	gaufres	cialde	barquillos
wedding cake	Hochzeitstorte	gâteau de mariagetorta nuziale	torta nuziale	pastel de boda
whipped cream; Chantilly	Schlagsahne	crème Chantilly[2]	panna montata	nata batida; ~ montada; chantillí
white chocolate mousse	Mousse von weißer Schokolade	mousse au chocolat blanc	mousse di cioccolato bianco	mousse de chocolate blanco
~ lady coupe	Eisbecher Weiße Dame	coupe dame blanche	coppa dama bianca	copa dama blanca
yogurt ice-cream	Joghurteis	glace au yaourt	gelato allo yogurt	helado de yogur
yule log; Christmas cake	Weihnachtsbaumstamm	bûche de Noël	tronco di Natale	tronco de Navidad
zabaglione; sabayon (foamy wine sauce of egg-yolk, sugar & wine)	Zabaione (schaumige Creme aus Eigelb, Zucker und Wein); Sabayon; Weinschaumcreme	sabayon (crème mousseuse de jaunes d'œufs, sucre et vin)	zabaione (crema di tuorli d'uovo, zucchero e vino)	sabayón (hecha de yemas, azucar y vino)

1) ou crème à la vanille - 2) ou crème fouettée

Fruit

Fruit	**Obst**	**Fruits**	**Frutta**	**Frutas**
English	German	French	Italian	Spanish
almond	Mandel	amande	mandorla	almendra
American cranberry; cranberry	Moosbeere	canneberge	mirtillo palustre	arándano rojo
apple	Apfel	pomme	mela	manzana
apples, stewed	Apfelkompott	compote de pommes	mele cotte	compota de manzanas
apricot	Aprikose	abricot	albicocca	albaricoque
avocado; ~ pear	Avocado	avocat	avocado	aguacate
banana	Banane	banane	banana	plátano
berries; wild berries	Waldfrüchte; Waldbeeren	fruits des bois	frutti di bosco	frutos del bosque
bilberry; blueberry	Blaubeere; Heidelbeere; Schwarzbeere	myrtille	mirtillo	arándano
black grapes	blaue Trauben	raisin noir	uva nera	uvas negras
blackberry; bramble	Brombeere	mûre sauvage[1]	mora di rovo	mora; zarzamora
blackcurrant	schwarze Johannisbeere	cassis; groseille noire	ribes nero	grosella negra; casis
blood orange	Blutorange	orange sanguine	arancia sanguigna	naranja sanguina
blueberry; bilberry	Blaubeere; Heidelbeere; Schwarzbeere	myrtille	mirtillo	arándano
bramble; blackberry	Brombeere	mûre sauvage[1]	mora di rovo	mora; zarzamora
Brazil nut	Paranuss	noix du Brésil	noce del Brasile	nuez de Pará
cantaloup melon[2]	Cantaloupe	cantaloup	melone cantalupo	melón cantalupo
cape gooseberry[3]	Kapstachelbeere; Blasenkirsche; Alkekengi; Physalis	alkékenge	alchechengi	alquequenje
carambola; star fruit	Sternfrucht; Karambole	carambole	carambola	carambola
carob	Johannisbrot	caroube	carruba	algarroba
cashew nut	Cashewnuss	noix de cajou	anacardio	anacardo
cherries, stewed	Kirschkompott	compote de cerises	composta di ciliege	compota de cerezas
cherry	Kirsche	cerise	ciliegia	cereza

1) ou mûre de ronce - 2) also cantaloupe melon - 3) also winter cherry, Am. ground-cherry

Fruit

Fruit English	**Obst** German	**Fruits** French	**Frutta** Italian	**Frutas** Spanish
chestnut	Kastanie	châtaigne	castagna	castaña
~, Spanish; marron chestnut	Marone	marron	marrone	castaña
citron	Zitronatzitrone	cédrat	cedro	cidra
citrus fruits	Zitrusfrüchte	agrumes	agrumi	cítricos; agrios
clementine	Klementine	clémentine	mandarancio; clementina	clementina
coconut	Kokosnuss	noix de coco	noce di cocco	coco
compote; stewed fruit	Kompott	compote	frutta cotta; composta	compota; fruta cocida
cowberries[1], stewed	Preiselbeerkompott	~ d'airelles	composta di mirtillo rosso	~ de arándano rojo
cowberry; mountain cranberry	Preiselbeere	airelle[2]	mirtillo rosso	arándano rojo
cranberry; American cranberry	Moosbeere	canneberge	~ palustre	~ rojo
currant	Johannisbeere	groseille	ribes	grosella
currants	Korinthen	raisins de Corinthe	uvetta di Corinto	pasas de Corinto
custard apple	Zimtapfel; Chirimoya	anone; chérimole	cerimolia; anona	chirimoya; anona
damson	Damaszenerpflaume	prune de Damas	susina damaschina	ciruela damascena
date	Dattel	datte	dattero	dátil
dried fruit	Dörrobst; Trockenobst[3]	fruits secs	frutta secca	frutos secos
early fruit	Frühobst	primeurs	primizie	~ primeros; primicias; fruta temprana
elderberry	Holunder	sureau	sambuco	saúco
exotic fruit	exotische Früchte	fruits exotiques	frutta esotica	fruta exótica
fig	Feige	figue	fico	higo
filbert; hazelnut	Haselnuss	noisette; aveline	nocciola	avellana
forced fruit; hothouse fruit	Treibhausobst	fruits de serre	frutta di serra	fruta de invernadero
fresh fruit	frisches Obst	~ frais	~ fresca	~ fresca
~ fruit basket	Früchtekorb	corbeille de fruits	cesto di frutta	cesta de frutas
fruit, candied; glacé fruit	kandierte Früchte	fruits confits	frutta candita	fruta confitada[4]

1) also stewed cranberries - 2) ou airelle rouge - 3) oder Trockenfrüchte - 4) o fruta escarchada

Fruit

Fruit English	**Obst** German	**Fruits** French	**Frutta** Italian	**Frutas** Spanish
fruit in season	Obst der Saison	fruits de saison	frutta di stagione	fruta de temporada
~ in syrup	~ in Sirup	~ au sirop	~ sciroppata	~ en almíbar
~ salad	Obstsalat	salade de fruits; macédoine; fruits rafraîchis	macedonia di frutta; insalata di frutta	ensalada de frutas; macedonia de frutas
~, stewed; compote	Kompott	compote	frutta cotta; composta	compota; fruta cocida
glacé fruit; candied fruit	kandierte Früchte	fruits confits	~ candita	fruta confitada[1]
gooseberry	Stachelbeere	groseille à maquereau	uva spina	uva espina[2]
grapes	Trauben; Weintrauben	raisin	uva	uvas
grapefruit	Grapefruit; Pampelmuse	pamplemousse[3]	pompelmo	pomelo; toronja
greengage	Reineclaude[4]	reine-claude	prugna regina Claudia	ciruela claudia
guava	Guave[5]	goyave	guaiava; guava	guayaba
hazelnut; filbert	Haselnuss	noisette; aveline	nocciola	avellana
hothouse fruit; forced fruit	Treibhausobst	fruits de serre	frutta di serra	fruta de invernadero
Japanese medlar; loquat	japanische Mispel	nèfle du Japon	nespola del Giappone	níspero del Japón
jujube	Jujube; Brustbeere	jujube	giuggiola	azufaifa
kiwi; ~ fruit	Kiwi	kiwi	kiwi; kivi	kiwi
kumquat	Kumquat; Zwergorange	kumquat	kumquat; mandarino cinese	naranja china
lemon	Zitrone	citron	limone	limón
lime	Limone; Limette	~ vert; lime	limetta; lime	lima
litchi; lychee	Litschi	litchi	litchi (prugna cinese)	lichi
loquat; Japanese medlar	japanische Mispel	nèfle du Japon	nespola del Giappone	níspero del Japón
mandarin (orange)[6]	Mandarine	mandarine	mandarino	mandarina
mango	Mango	mangue	mango	mango
marron chestnut; Spanish chestnut	Marone	marron	marrone	castaña
medlar	Mispel	nèfle	nespola	níspero; níspola
melon	Melone	melon	melone	melón
mirabelle; yellow plum	Mirabelle	mirabelle	mirabella (sorta di susina)	ciruela amarilla

---

1) o fruta escarchada - 2) o grosella espinosa - 3) ou grape-fruit - 4) auch Reneklode - 5) auch Guajave - 6) also tangerine

Fruit

Fruit English	**Obst** German	**Fruits** French	**Frutta** Italian	**Frutas** Spanish
mixed fruit	gemischtes Obst	fruits assortis	frutta mista	fruta variada
~ stewed fruit	~ Kompott	compote assortie	composta mista	compota variada
morello[1]; sour cherry	Sauerkirsche; Weichselkirsche	griotte	amarena; visciola; marasca	guinda
mountain cranberry; cowberry	Preiselbeere	airelle[2]	mirtillo rosso	arándano rojo
mulberry	Maulbeere	mûre	mora di gelso	mora
muscat grapes; muscatel	Muskatellertrauben	muscat; raisin muscat	uva moscata	uvas moscatel
nectarine	Nektarine	brugnon; nectarine	nettarina; pesca noce	nectarina[3]
nut; walnut	Walnuss	noix	noce	nuez
orange	Apfelsine; Orange	orange	arancia; arancio	naranja
~, candied	kandierte Orange	~ confite	~ candita	~ confitada
~ salad	Orangensalat	salade d'oranges	insalata d'arance	ensalada de naranja
papaya	Papaya	papaye	papaia; papaya	papaya
passion fruit	Maracuja; Passionsfrucht	fruit de la passion	frutto della passione[4]	maracuyá; fruta de la pasión; granadilla
peach	Pfirsich	pêche	pesca	melocotón
peanut	Erdnuss	cacahuète; arachide	arachide[5]	cacahuete[6]
pear	Birne	poire	pera	pera
pears, stewed	Birnenkompott	compote de poires	composta di pere	compota de peras
pecan; ~ nut	Pecannuss	pacane; noix de pacane	pecan; noce pecan	pacana
persimmon	Kaki[7]	kaki	cachi; caco	caqui
pineapple	Ananas	ananas	ananas	piña[8]
plum	Pflaume; Zwetschge[9]	prune; quetsche	prugna; susina	ciruela
pomegranate	Granatapfel	grenade	melagrana	granada
prickly pear	Kaktusfeige	figue de Barbarie	fico d'India	higo chumbo
prune	Dörrpflaume; Backpflaume	pruneau	prugna secca	ciruela pasa
prunes, stewed	Backpflaumenkompott	compote de pruneaux	prugne cotte	compota de ciruelas

---

1) or morello cherry - 2) ou airelle rouge - 3) también griñón y briñón - 4) o maracuja - 5) o nocciolina americana - 6) Am. maní - 7) auch Kakipflaume - 8) Am. ananás - 9) oder Zwetsche

Fruit

Fruit English	**Obst** German	**Fruits** French	**Frutta** Italian	**Frutas** Spanish
quince	Quitte	coing	cotogna; mela cotogna	membrillo
quinces, stewed	Quittenkompott	compote de coings	composta di cotogne	compota de membrillo
raisins	Rosinen	raisins secs	uvetta; uva passa	pasas; uvas pasas
raspberry	Himbeere	framboise	lampone	frambuesa
red berries	rote Beeren	baies rouges	bacche rosse	bayas rojas
~ fruit	~ Früchte	fruits rouges	frutti rossi	frutas rojas
redcurrant	~ Johannisbeere	groseille rouge	ribes rosso	grosella roja
reinette; rennet	Renette; Reinette	pomme reinette	mela renetta	manzana reineta
rhubarb	Rhabarber	rhubarbe	rabarbaro	ruibarbo
rose-hip	Hagebutte	églantine	rosa canina	escaramujo
rowanberry	Vogelbeere (Ebereschenfrucht)	sorbe sauvage	sorba selvatica	serba silvestre
sour cherry; morello[1]	Sauerkirsche; Weichselkirsche	griotte	amarena; visciola; marasca	guinda
star fruit; carambola	Sternfrucht; Karambole	carambole	carambola	carambola
strawberry	Erdbeere	fraise	fragola	fresón; fresa
sultanas	Sultaninen	raisins secs de Smyrne	uva sultanina	pasas sultanas[2]
tropical fruit	Tropenfrüchte	fruits tropicaux	frutti tropicali	frutas tropicales
walnut; nut	Walnuss	noix	noce	nuez
watermelon	Wassermelone	melon d'eau; pastèque	anguria; cocomero	sandía; melón de agua
white grapes	weiße Trauben	raisin blanc	uva bianca	uvas blancas
wild berries; berries	Waldfrüchte; Waldbeeren	fruits des bois	frutti di bosco	frutos del bosque
~ strawberry	Walderdbeere	fraise des bois	fragola di bosco	fresa silvestre
williams pear[3]	Williams Christbirne	poire williams	pera William	pera williams
yellow plum; mirabelle	Mirabelle	mirabelle	mirabella (sorta di susina)	ciruela amarilla

---

[1] or morello cherry - [2] o pasas de esmirna - [3] Am. Bartlett pear

Bread and pizzas

Bread and pizzas English	Brot und Pizzas German	Pain et pizzas French	Pane e pizze Italian	Pan y pizzas Spanish
bagel (round roll with a hole in the middle)	Bagel (Brötchen mit Loch in der Mitte)	bagel (petit pain en forme d'anneau)	bagel (panino a forma di ciambella)	bagel (panecillo en forma de rosca)
baguette	Baguette	baguette	baguette	baguette; barra
biological bread	Bio-Brot	pain biologique	pane biologico	pan biológico
black bread; brown bread	Schwarzbrot	~ noir	~ nero	~ moreno; ~ negro
breadcrumbs	Paniermehl; Semmelbrösel[1]	chapelure	pan grattato[2]	~ rallado
bretzel; pretzel (crisp knot-shaped biscuit)	Brezel	bretzel	brezel	rosquilla
brown bread; black bread	Schwarzbrot	pain noir	pane nero	pan moreno; ~ negro
bun	Rosinenbrötchen	petit pain aux raisins secs	panino all'uvetta	panecillo con pasas
buttered toast	Toast mit Butter	toast beurré	fetta di pane tostato con burro	toast con mantequilla
caraway roll	Kümmelbrötchen	petit pain au cumin	panino al comino	panecillo al comino
cheese sandwich	Käsebrot	sandwich au fromage	~ al formaggio	bocadillo de queso
corn bread	Maisbrot	pain de maïs	pane di granturco	pan de maíz
crispbread[3] (Swedish wholemeal crackers)	Knäckebrot (knusprige Scheiben Vollkornbrot)	knäckebrot (galettes de farine non blutée)	knäckebrot (gallette sottili di farina integrale)	knäckebrot (especie de pan integral sueco)
croissant; crescent [4]	Croissant; Hörnchen; Kipfel	croissant	cornetto; croissant	medialuna; croissant; cuerno
croûtons	Croûtons (geröstete Brotwürfel)	croûtons	crostini	costrones (trocitos de pan frito)
double-decker	Doppeldecker	double-decker	sandwich doppio	emparedado doble
five-cereals bread	Fünfkornbrot	pain aux cinq cereals	pane ai cinque cereali	pan de cinco cereales
flat bread; focaccia	Fladenbrot	fougasse; fouace; galette	focaccia	torta
folded-over pizza	Pizzatasche	pizza en chausson	calzone	pizza rellena
four-season pizza	Pizza Vier Jahreszeiten	~ quatre saisons	pizza quattro stagioni	~ cuatro estaciones
French roll; roll	Brötchen; Semmel	petit pain	panino	panecillo; bollo; mollete
fresh bread; new bread	frisches Brot	pain-frais	pane fresco	pan fresco

1) oder Brösel - 2) pangrattato - 3) Am. rye crisps - 4) or crescent roll

Bread and pizzas

Bread and pizzas English	Brot und Pizzas German	Pain et pizzas French	Pane e pizze Italian	Pan y pizzas Spanish
Graham bread[1]	Grahambrot	pain Graham	pane Graham	pan Graham
grissini (crisp bread in long thin sticks)	Grissini (knuspriges Stangenbrot)	gressins (pain en forme de bâtonnet sec)	grissini	grissini (pan en forma de barritas)
ham sandwich	Schinkenbrot	sandwich au jambon	panino al prosciutto	bocadillo de jamón
home-baked bread	selbst gebackenes Brot	pain maison	pane casereccio	pan casero
loaf; large loaf	Landbrot	~ de campagne	pagnotta; grossa pagnotta	~ de payés; hogaza
marinara pizza	Pizza Matrosenart	pizza à la marinière	pizza alla marinara	pizza a la marinera
milk roll	Milchbrötchen	petit pain au lait	panino al latte	bollo de leche; mollete
minipizzas	Mini-Pizzas	mini-pizzas	pizzette	pizzetas
mushroom pizza	Pizza mit Pilzen	pizza aux champignons	pizza ai funghi	pizza de setas
Neapolitan-style pizza	~ neapolitanisch	~ napolitaine	~ napoletana	~ napolitana
new bread; fresh bread	frisches Brot	pain-frais	pane fresco	pan fresco
onion pizza	Pizza mit Zwiebeln	pizza aux oignons	pizza alle cipolle	pizza de cebolla
pizza, folded-over	Pizzatasche	~ en chausson	calzone	~ rellena
~, four-season	Pizza Vier Jahreszeiten	~ quatre saisons	pizza quattro stagioni	~ cuatro estaciones
~, Margherita (tomato and mozzarella)	~ Margherita (Tomate und Mozzarella)	~ Margherita (tomate et mozzarella)	~ Margherita (pomodoro e mozzarella)	~ Margherita (tomate y mozzarella)
~, marinara	~ Matrosenart	~ à la marinière	~ alla marinara	~ a la marinera
~, mushroom	~ mit Pilzen	~ aux champignons	~ ai funghi	~ de setas
~, Neapolitan-style	~ neapolitanisch	~ napolitaine	~ napoletana	~ napolitana
~, onion	~ mit Zwiebeln	~ aux oignons	~ alle cipolle	~ de cebolla
~, seafood	~ mit Meeresfrüchten	~ aux fruits de mer	~ ai frutti di mare	~ de mariscos
~, vegetarian	~ mit Gemüse	~ végétarienne	~ alle verdure	~ de verduras
~, wholemeal	Vollkornpizza	~ au blé complet	~ integrale	~ integral
~, wood-stove baked	Holzofen-Pizza	~ cuite au bois	~ cotta a legna	~ al horno de leña
pretzel (crisp knot-shaped biscuit); bretzel	Brezel	bretzel	brezel	rosquilla

---

[1] Am. whole wheat bread

Bread and pizzas

Bread and pizzas English	Brot und Pizzas German	Pain et pizzas French	Pane e pizze Italian	Pan y pizzas Spanish
pumpernickel (wholemeal rye-bread)	Pumpernickel	pumpernickel (pain noir de seigle broyé)	pane di segale (molto scuro)	pumpernickel (pan negro de centeno)
roll; French roll	Brötchen; Semmel	petit pain	panino	panecillo; bollo; mollete
rusks[1]; zwieback	Zwieback	biscottes	fette biscottate; pane biscottato	biscotes
rye-bread	Roggenbrot	pan de seigle	pane di segale	pan de centeno
sandwich	belegtes Brot[2]; Sandwich	sandwich	sandwich; panino	bocadillo; emparedado
~ loaf	Kastenbrot; Toastbrot	pain de mie; ~ anglais	pane a cassetta; pan carrè	pan de molde; ~ inglés
~ toast (toasted ham and cheese sandwich)	Croque-monsieur (getoasteter Schinken-Käse-Sandwich); Sandwich-Toast	croque-monsieur[3] (sandwich grillé au jambon et fromage)	toast (coppia di fette di pane tostate con formaggio e prosciutto)	bikini (emparedado caliente de jamón y queso)
seafood pizza	Pizza mit Meeresfrüchten	pizza aux fruits de mer	pizza ai frutti di mare	pizza de mariscos
seed roll	Mohnbrötchen	petit pain au pavot	panino al papavero	panecillo con adormidera
sesame roll	Sesambrötchen	~ pan au sésame	~ al sesamo	~ de sésamo
slice of bread	Brotschnitte[4]	tranche de pain	fetta di pane	rebanada de pan
soy bread	Sojabrot	pain de soja	pane di soia	pan de soja
toast	Röstbrot; Scheibe Toast	toast; tranche de pain grillé	toast; fetta di pane tostato	tostada
~, buttered	Toast mit Butter	~ beurré	fetta di pane tostato con burro	toast con mantequilla
unleavened bread	ungesäuertes Brot	pain azyme	pane azzimo	pan ázimo
vegetarian pizza	Pizza mit Gemüse	pizza végétarienne	pizza alle verdure	pizza de verduras
white bread; wheat bread	Weißbrot	pain blanc	pane bianco	pan blanco
wholemeal bread	Vollkornbrot; Schrotbrot	~ complet	~ integrale	~ completo; ~ integral
~ pizza	Vollkornpizza	pizza au blé complet	pizza integrale	pizza integral
wood-stove baked bread	Holzofen-Brot	pain cuit au bois	pane cotto a legna	pan de leña
~ baked pizza	Holzofen-Pizza	pizza cuite au bois	pizza cotta a legna	pizza al horno de leña
zwieback; rusks[1]	Zwieback	biscottes	fette biscottate; pane biscottato	biscotes

1) or biscuit rusks - 2) oder belegtes Brötchen - 3) ou croque-madame - 4) auch Schnitte oder Scheibe Brot

Spices & condiments

Spices & condiments English	Gewürze German	Épices et condiments French	Spezie e condimenti Italian	Especias y condimentos Spanish
allspice; pimento; Jamaica pepper	Piment; Nelkenpfeffer; Jamaikapfeffer	piment; poivre de la Jamaïque	pimento; pepe della Giamaica	pimienta de Jamaica
Angelica	Angelika; Engelwurz	Angélique	Angelica	Angélica
anise; aniseed	Anis	anis	anice	anís
aromatic herbs; herbs	Kräuter; Gewürzkräuter	herbes aromatiques	erbe aromatiche	hierbas aromáticas
basil	Basilikum	basilic	basilico	albahaca
bay	Lorbeer	laurier	alloro	laurel
~ leaf	Lorbeerblatt	feuille de laurier	foglia d'alloro	hoja de laurel
borage	Borretsch	bourrache	borragine	borraja
burnet	Pimpinelle; Bibernelle	pimprenelle	salvastrella; pimpinella	pimpinela; sanguisorba
candied citron peel	Zitronat	cédrat confit	cedro candito	cidra confitada
capers	Kapern	câpres	capperi	alcaparras
caraway	Kümmel	cumin des prés; carvi	comino tedesco; carvi	comino
cardamom	Kardamom	cardamome	cardamomo	cardamomo
cayenne pepper; red pepper	Cayennepfeffer	poivre de Cayenne	pepe di Caienna	pimienta de Cayena
chervil	Kerbel	cerfeuil	cerfoglio	perifollo
chilli[1]; hot pepper	Chili[2]; Pfefferschote	piment rouge; ~ fort	peperoncino rosso	guindilla; chile
chives	Schnittlauch	ciboulette	erba cipollina	cebollino
cinnamon	Zimt	cannelle	cannella	canela
clove	Nelke; Gewürznelke	clou de girofle	chiodo di garofano	clavo (de olor)
coriander	Koriander	coriandre	coriandolo	cilantro
cumin	Kreuzkümmel	cumin	cumino; comino	comino
curry[3]	Curry	curry; cari; cary	curry	curry
dill	Dill	aneth	aneto	eneldo
fennel	Fenchel	fenouil	finocchio	hinojo
garlic	Knoblauch	ail	aglio	ajo
~ clove	Knoblauchzehe	gousse d'ail	spicchio d'aglio	diente de ajo
gherkins; pickles	Gewürzgurken; Cornichons	cornichons	cetriolini sott'aceto	pepinillos en vinagre

---

1) Am. chili - 2) oder Shilischote - 3) or curry-powder

Spices & condiments

Spices & condiments English	Gewürze German	Épices et condiments French	Spezie e condimenti Italian	Especias y condimentos Spanish
ginger	Ingwer	gingembre	zenzero	jengibre
green pepper	grüner Pfeffer	poivre vert	pepe verde	pimienta verde
herbs; aromatic herbs	Kräuter; Gewürzkräuter	herbes aromatiques	erbe aromatiche	hierbas aromáticas
horseradish	Meerrettich; Kren	raifort	rafano; cren	rábano picante
hot pepper; chilli[1]	Chili[2]; Pfefferschote	piment rouge; ~ fort	peperoncino rosso	guindilla; chile
indian cress; nasturtium	Kapuzinerkresse	capucine	nasturzio; cappuccina	capuchina
Jamaica pepper; pimento; allspice	Piment; Nelkenpfeffer; Jamaikapfeffer	piment; poivre de la Jamaïque	pimento; pepe della Giamaica	pimienta de Jamaica
juniper	Wacholder	genièvre	ginepro	enebro
~ berries	Wacholderbeeren	baies de genièvre	bacche di ginepro	bayas de enebro
lavender	Lavendel	lavande	lavanda	lavanda
lemon balm	Melisse; Zitronenmelisse	mélisse; citronnelle	melissa; citronella	melisa; toronjil
lemongrass	Zitronengras	verveine des Indes	erba limone	hierba de Limón
lovage	Liebstöckel	livèche	levistico; sedano di monte	levístico; apio de montaña
mace	Muskatblüte	macis	macis	macis; macia
marjoram	Majoran	marjolaine	maggiorana	mejorana
mild spices	milde Gewürze	épices douces	spezie dolci	especias dulces
mint	Minze	menthe	menta	menta; hierbabuena
mixed pickles	Mixed Pickles	mixed pickles[3]	sottaceti	encurtidos (en vinagre)
mugwort	Beifuß	armoise	artemisia	artemisa
mustard	Senf	moutarde	senape; mostarda	mostaza
nasturtium; indian cress	Kapuzinerkresse	capucine	nasturzio; cappuccina	capuchina
nutmeg	Muskatnuss	muscade; noix de muscade	noce moscata	nuez moscada
oregano; wild marjoram	Oregano	origan	origano	orégano
paprika	Paprika; Paprikapulver	paprika	paprica; paprika	pimentón
parsley	Petersilie	persil	prezzemolo	perejil
pepper	Pfeffer	poivre	pepe	pimienta
peppercorns	Pfefferkörner	~ en grains	~ in grani	~ en granos

1) Am. chili - 2) oder Shilischote - 3) ou pickles

Spices & condiments

Spices & condiments English	Gewürze German	Épices et condiments French	Spezie e condimenti Italian	Especias y condimentos Spanish
pickles; gherkins	Gewürzgurken; Cornichons	cornichons	cetriolini sott'aceto	pepinillos en vinagre
pimento; allspice; Jamaica pepper	Piment; Nelkenpfeffer; Jamaikapfeffer	piment; poivre de la Jamaïque	pimento; pepe della Giamaica	pimienta de Jamaica
pine nuts	Pinienkerne; Pignolen	pignons	pinoli	piñones
pink pepper	rosa Pfeffer	poivre rose	pepe rosa	pimienta rosa
pistachio[1]	Pistazie	pistache	pistacchio	pistacho
poppy-seed	Mohn	pavot	papavero	adormidera
pumpkin seeds	Kürbiskerne	graines de courge	semi di zucca	semillas de calabaza
ramson; wild garlic	Bärlauch	ail sauvage	aglio orsino	ajo de oso
red pepper; cayenne pepper	Cayennepfeffer	poivre de Cayenne	pepe di Caienna	pimienta de Cayena
rosemary	Rosmarin	romarin	rosmarino	romero
rue	Weinraute	rue	ruta	ruda
saffron	Safran	safran	zafferano	azafrán
~ stigmas	Safranfäden	pistils de safran	pistilli di zafferano	hebras de azafrán
sage	Salbei	sauge	salvia	salvia
savory; summer savory	Bohnenkraut	sarriette	santoreggia	ajedrea
sesame	Sesam	sésame	sesamo	sésamo
~ seeds	Sesamsamen	graines de sésame	semi di sesamo	semillas de sésamo
shallot	Schalotte	échalote	scalogno	chalote; ascalonia
star anise	Sternanis	anis étoilé; badiane	anice stellato; badiana	anís estrellado; badiana
sunflower seeds	Sonnenblumenkerne	graines de tournesol	semi di girasole	pipas de girasol
tarragon	Estragon	estragon	dragoncello; estragone	estragón; dragoncillo
thyme	Thymian	thym	timo	tomillo
turmeric	Kurkuma; Gelbwurz	curcuma	curcuma	cúrcuma
vanilla	Vanille	vanille	vaniglia	vainilla
wild garlic; ramson	Bärlauch	ail sauvage	aglio orsino	ajo de oso
~ marjoram; oregano	Oregano	origan	origano	orégano
~ thyme	Feldthymian	serpolet	serpillo	serpol
woodruff	Waldmeister	aspérule	asperula; stellina odorosa	aspérula

[1] or pistachio nut

Alcoholic drinks

Alcoholic drinks English	Alkoholische Getränke German	Boissons alcooliques French	Bevande alcoliche Italian	Bebidas alcohólicas Spanish
amaretto (almond-flavoured liqueur)	Amaretto (Mandellikör)	amaretto (liqueur à l'amande amère)	amaretto	amaretto (licor de almendras)
anisette	Anisette (Anislikör)	anisette	anisetta	anisete; anís
aperitif	Aperitif	apéritif	aperitivo	aperitivo
beer	Bier	bière	birra	cerveza
bitter; dark beer; brown ale; stout	dunkles Bier	~ brune	~ scura	~ negra
bordeaux; claret	Bordeaux	bordeaux	bordeaux	burdeos
bottled beer	Flaschenbier	bière en bouteille	birra in bottiglia	cerveza embotellada
~ wine	Flaschenwein	vin en bouteille	vino in bottiglia	vino embotellado
brandy; schnapps	Schnaps; Weinbrand; Branntwein	eau-de-vie	acquavite; brandy	aguardiente; brandy
brown ale; dark beer; bitter; stout	dunkles Bier	bière brune	birra scura	cerveza negra
burgundy	Burgunder	bourgogne	borgogna	borgoña
calvados (apple brandy)	Calvados (Apfelschnaps)	calvados	calvados (acquavite di mele)	calvados (aguardiente de manzana)
canned beer	Dosenbier	bière en boîte	birra in lattina	cerveza en lata
cassis (liqueur made from blackcurrants)	Cassis (Likör aus schwarzen Johannisbeeren)	cassis (liqueur de cassis)	cassis (liquore a base di ribes nero)	casis (licor de grosella negra)
champagne	Champagner	champagne	champagne	champán; champaña
cider[1]	Apfelwein; Cidre	cidre	sidro	sidra
claret; bordeaux	Bordeaux	bordeaux	bordeaux	burdeos
cocktail	Cocktail	cocktail	cocktail	cóctel; combinado
cognac; french brandy	Cognac	cognac	cognac	coñac
cup (chilled drink of wine and flavourings)	Bowle (kaltes Getränk aus Wein und Früchten)	cup (boisson froide à base de vin et de fruits)	bowle (bevanda fredda di vino bianco e frutta)	bowle (bebida fría de vino blanco y fruta)

---

[1] Am. hard cider

Alcoholic drinks

Alcoholic drinks English	Alkoholische Getränke German	Boissons alcooliques French	Bevande alcoliche Italian	Bebidas alcohólicas Spanish
dark beer; brown ale; bitter; stout	dunkles Bier	bière brune	birra scura	cerveza negra
dessert wine	Dessertwein	vin de dessert	vino da dessert	vino de postre
draught beer; draft beer	Bier vom Fass; Fassbier	bière à la pression	birra alla spina	cerveza de barril
foreign beer	ausländisches Bier	~ étrangère	~ estera	~ de importación
fortified wine	Likörwein	vin de liqueur	vino liquoroso	vino generoso
french brandy; cognac	Cognac	cognac	cognac	coñac
gaelic coffee (hot coffee with Irish whisky and cream); irish coffee	Irishcoffee (heißer Kaffee mit Whisky und Schlagsahne)	café irlandais (café bouillant avec whisky et crème fraîche)	irish coffee (caffè bollente con whisky irlandese e panna)	café irlandés (café hirviendo con whisky y crema de nata)
gentian	Enzianschnaps	gentiane	genziana	genciana
german beer	deutsches Bier	bière allemande	birra tedesca	cerveza alemana
gin	Gin	gin	gin	ginebra
grappa; marc[1]	Trester[2]	marc	grappa	aguardiente de orujo
green wine; new wine; young wine	Primeur; neuer Wein	vin jeune; ~ nouveau; primeur	vino novello	vino nuevo
hock; rhine wine	Rheinwein	~ du Rhin	~ del Reno	~ del Rin
house wine; wine in carafe	Schoppenwein; offener Wein	~ en carafe; ~ ouvert	~ in caraffa; ~ sciolto; ~ sfuso	~ de la cuba; ~ de la casa
irish coffee; gaelic coffee (hot coffee with Irish whisky and cream)	Irishcoffee (heißer Kaffee mit Whisky und Schlagsahne)	café irlandais (café bouillant avec whisky et crème fraîche)	irish coffee (caffè bollente con whisky irlandese e panna)	café irlandés (café hirviendo con whisky y crema de nata)
kir (white wine and cassis)	Kir (Johannisbeerlikör und Weißwein)	kir (vin blanc et cassis)	kir (liquore di ribes nero e vino bianco)	kir (licor de grosella negra y vino blanco)
~ royal (champagne and cassis)	~ royal (Champagner und Johannisbeerlikör)	~ royal (champagne et cassis)	~ royal (champagne e liquore di ribes nero)	~ royal (champán y licor de grosella negra)
kirsch; kirschwasser	Kirschwasser	kirsch	kirsch	kirsch
kümmel	Kümmel	kummel	kümmel	kúmmel

---

1) or marc brandy - 2) oder Tresterbranntwein

Alcoholic drinks

Alcoholic drinks English	Alkoholische Getränke German	Boissons alcooliques French	Bevande alcoliche Italian	Bebidas alcohólicas Spanish
lager; pale ale; light beer	helles Bier	bière blonde	birra chiara	cerveza rubia
lemon liqueur	Zitronenlikör	liqueur au citron	limoncello	licor de limón
light beer; lager; pale ale	helles Bier	bière blonde	birra chiara	cerveza rubia
~ beer	Leichtbier[1]	~ légère	~ leggera	~ ligera
liqueur	Likör	liqueur	liquore	licor
local wine	Landwein	vin du pays	vino nostrano	vino del país
Madeira	Madeira	Madère	Madera	Madera; Madeira
Malaga	Malaga	Malaga	Malaga	Málaga
malmsey; malvoisie	Malvasier	malvoisie	malvasia	malvasía
maraschino (liqueur from sour cherries)	Maraschino (Likör aus der Sauerkirsche)	marasquin (liqueur de griottes)	maraschino (liquore di marasche)	marrasquino (licor de guindas)
marc[2]; grappa	Trester[3]	marc	grappa	aguardiente de orujo
moselle	Moselwein	vin de Moselle	vino della Mosella	mosela
mulberry Kir	Kir mit Maulbeeren	kir à la mûre	kir alle more	kir de mora
mulled wine	Glühwein	vin chaud	vin brûlé; vino caldo	vino caliente
Munich beer	Münchner Bier	bière de Munich	birra di Monaco	cerveza de Munich
muscatel; muscat	Muskateller	muscat	moscato	moscatel
must	Most	moût	mosto	mosto
new wine; green wine; young wine	Primeur; neuer Wein	vin jeune; ~ nouveau; primeur	vino novello	vino nuevo
non-alcoholic beer	alkoholfreies Bier	bière sans alcool	birra analcolica	cerveza sin alcohol
pale ale; lager; light beer	helles Bier	~ blonde	~ chiara	~ rubia
peach cup	Pfirsichbowle	cup aux pêches	bowle di pesca	bowle de melocotón
plum brandy	Zwetgenschnaps	quetsche	acquavite di prugna	aguardiente de ciruelas
port	Portwein	porto	porto	oporto
punch	Punsch	punch	punch; ponce	ponche
red wine	Rotwein	vin rouge	vino rosso; ~ nero	vino tinto
rhine wine; hock	Rheinwein	~ du Rhin	~ del Reno	~ del Rin

1) alkoholreduziertes Bier - 2) or marc brandy - 3) oder Tresterbranntwein

Alcoholic drinks

Alcoholic drinks English	Alkoholische Getränke German	Boissons alcooliques French	Bevande alcoliche Italian	Bebidas alcohólicas Spanish
rosé	Rosé[1]	rosé	rosé; rosato	vino rosado
rum	Rum	rhum	rum; rhum	ron
schnapps; brandy	Schnaps; Weinbrand; Branntwein	eau-de-vie	acquavite; brandy	aguardiente; brandy
sgroppino (frothy lemon sorbetto with liqueur)	Sgroppino (Zitronensorbet mit Likör)	sgroppino (sorbet au citron avec liqueur)	sgroppino (sorbetto al limone con liquore)	sgroppino (sorbete de limón y licor)
shandy[2]	Alsterwasser (Bier mit Limonade); Radler[3]	panaché; demi panaché	birra con limonata	clara (cerveza y gaseosa)
sherry	Sherry	xérès	sherry	jerez
sparkling wine	Sekt; Schaumwein	vin mousseux	spumante	vino espumoso; cava
stout; dark beer; brown ale; bitter	dunkles Bier	bière brune	birra scura	cerveza negra
straw wine	Strohwein	vin de paille	passito; vinsanto	vino generoso
sweet wine	Süßwein	~ doux	vino dolce	~ dulce
table wine	Tischwein	~ de table	~ da pasto	~ de mesa; ~ de pasto
vermouth	Wermut	vermouth	vermut	vermut
vodka	Wodka	vodka	vodka	vodka
walnut liqueur	Nusslikör	brou de noix	nocino	licor de nueces
whisky; whiskey	Whisky	whisky	whisky	whisky
~ and soda	~ mit Soda	~ et soda	~ con soda	~ con soda
white wine	Weißwein	vin blanc	vino bianco	vino blanco
wine	Wein	vin	vino	vino
~ in carafe; house wine	Schoppenwein; offener Wein	~ en carafe; ~ ouvert	~ in caraffa; ~ sciolto; ~ sfuso	~ de la cuba; ~ de la casa
woodruff cup	Maibowle; Waldmeisterbowle	cup à l'aspérule	bowle di asperula	bowle de aspérula
young wine; new wine; green wine	Primeur; neuer Wein	vin jeune; ~ nouveau; primeur	vino novello	vino nuevo

1) auch Roséwein - 2) Am. shandygaff - 3) auch Radlermaß

Non-alcoholic drinks

Non-alcoholic drinks[1)] English	**Alkoholfreie Getränke** German	**Boissons sans alcool** French	**Bevande analcoliche** Italian	**Bebidas sin alcohol** Spanish
aerated lemonade	Limonade[2)]	limonade gazeuse	gassosa; gazzosa	gaseosa
apple juice; sweet cider	Apfelsaft	jus de pommes	succo di mela	zumo de manzana
banana milk shake	Bananen-Milkshake	milk-shake à la banane	frullato alla banana	batido de plátano
barley coffee	Malzkaffee	café d'orge	caffè d'orzo	café de malta
black coffee	schwarzer Kaffee	~ noir; ~ nature	~ nero	~ solo
~ tea	~ Tee	thé noir	té nero	té negro
blackcurrant syrup	~ Johannisbeersaft	sirop de cassis	sciroppo di ribes nero	jarabe de grosellas negras
bottled sodas	Limonaden	sodas; boissons gazeuses	bibite gassate	limonadas efervescentes
buttermilk	Buttermilch	babeurre	latticello	leche de mantequilla; suero
caffeine-free coffee[3)]	koffeinfreier Kaffee	café décaféiné	caffè decaffeinato	café descafeinado
camomile tea	Kamillentee	tisane de camomille	infuso di camomilla	té de manzanilla
cappuccino	Cappuccino	cappuccino	cappuccino	capuchino
carrot juice	Karottensaft	jus de carotte	succo di carota	zumo de zanahoria
cocoa	Kakao	cacao	cacao	cacao
coffee	Kaffee	café	caffè	café
~ with brandy	~ mit Schnaps	~ arrosé	~ corretto	carajillo
~ with cream[4)]	~ mit Sahne	~ crème	~ con panna	café con nata
~ with milk[4)]	~ mit Milch; Milchkaffee	~ au lait; ~ crème	~ e latte; caffellatte	~ con leche
condensed milk	Kondensmilch	lait concentré	latte condensato	leche condensada
drink	Getränk	boisson	bevanda	bebida
elderberry syrup	Holundersirup	sirop de sureau	sciroppo di sambuco	jarabe de saúco
~ tea	Holundertee	tisane de sureau	tè di sambuco	té de saúco
espresso	Espresso	express; café express	espresso	exprés; café exprés
fruit juice	Fruchtsaft	jus de fruits	succo di frutta	zumo de fruta
grape juice	Traubensaft	~ de raisin	~ d'uva	~ de uvas
grapefruit juice	Grapefruitsaft	~ de pamplemousse	~ di pompelmo	~ de pomelo
green tea	grüner Tee	thé vert	té verde	té verde

---

1) or soft drinks - 2) auch Brause oder Brauselimonade - 3) or decaffeinated coffee - 4) or white coffee

Non-alcoholic drinks

Non-alcoholic drinks English	Alkoholfreie Getränke German	Boissons sans alcool French	Bevande analcoliche Italian	Bebidas sin alcohol Spanish
grenadine (pomegranate syrup)	Grenadine (Granatapfelsirup)	grenadine (sirop de grenade)	granatina (sciroppo di melagrana)	granadina (jarabe de granada)
herb tea	Kräutertee	thé aux herbes; tisane	tè di erbe; tisana; infuso	infusión; tisana
hot chocolate	Schokolade	chocolat	cioccolata	chocolate
ice cubes	Eiswürfel	glaçons	cubetti di ghiaccio	cubitos de hielo
iced tea	Eistee	thé glacé	tè freddo	té helado
lemon juice, freshly squeezed; ~ squash	frisch gepresster Zitronensaft	citron pressé	spremuta di limone	zumo de limón natural
lemonade	Zitronenlimonade; Limonade	citronnade	limonata	limonada
lime tea; linden tea	Lindenblütentee	tisane de tilleul	infuso di tiglio	infusión de tila
milk	Milch	lait	latte	leche
~ shake	Milchshake	milk-shake	frullato; frappé	batido
mineral water	Mineralwasser	eau minérale	acqua minerale	agua mineral
mint tea	Pfefferminztee	thé à la menthe	tè di menta	té de menta
natural mineral water	Mineralwasser ohne Kohlensäure	eau plate[1]	acqua minerale liscia; ~ minerale naturale	agua mineral sin gas
orange juice	Orangensaft	jus d'orange	succo d'arancia	zumo de naranja
~ juice, freshly squeezed; ~ squash	frisch gepresster Orangensaft	orange pressée	spremuta d'arancia	~ de naranja natural
orangeade	Orangenlimonade	orangeade	aranciata	naranjada
pasteurized milk	pasteurisierte Milch	lait pasteurisé	latte pastorizzato	leche pasteurizada
peach tea	Pfirsichtee	thé à la pêche	tè alla pesca	té de melocotón
percolated coffee[2]	Filterkaffee	café filtre	caffè filtro	café filtro
raspberry syrup	Himbeersirup	sirop de framboise	sciroppo di lampone	jarabe de frambuesas
redcurrant syrup[3]	roter Johannisbeersaft[4]	~ de groseilles	~ di ribes	~ de grosellas
rose-hip tea	Hagebuttentee	thé d'églantine	infuso di rosa canina	infusión de escaramujo
sea buckthorn syrup	Sanddornsaft	sirop d'argousier	sciroppo di olivello spinoso	jarabe de espino falso
seltzer	Selterswasser	eau de seltz; ~ gazeuse	selz; seltz	agua de Seltz

[1] ou eau minérale plate - [2] Am. drip coffee - [3] or currant syrup - [4] oder Johannisbeersaft

Non-alcoholic drinks

Non-alcoholic drinks English	Alkoholfreie Getränke German	Boissons sans alcool French	Bevande analcoliche Italian	Bebidas sin alcohol Spanish
skimmed milk	Magermilch	lait écrémé	latte scremato	leche desnatada
soda[1]	Sodawasser	soda	soda	soda
sour cherry syrup	Weichselsirup	sirop de griottes	sciroppo di amarena	jarabe de guindas
sparkling mineral water	Mineralwasser mit Kohlensäure	eau gazeuse[2]	acqua minerale gassata	agua mineral con gas
strawberry milk shake	Erdbeershake	milk-shake à la fraise	frullato alla fragola	batido de fresa
sweet cider; apple juice	Apfelsaft	jus de pommes	succo di mela	zumo de manzana
syrup[3]	Sirup	sirop	sciroppo	jarabe
tamarind lemonade	Tamarindenlimonade	limonade de tamarin	tamarindo	limonada de tamarindo
tea	Tee	thé	té; the	té
~ with lemon	~ mit Zitrone	~ au citron	~ al limone	~ con limón
~ with milk	~ mit Milch	~ au lait	~ al latte	~ con leche
tomato juice	Tomatensaft	jus de tomate	succo di pomodoro	jugo de tomate
vegetable juice	Gemüsesaft	~ de légumes	~ di verdura	zumo de verdura
water	Wasser	eau	acqua	agua
whole milk	Vollmilch	lait entier	latte intero	leche entera

---

1) or soda-water - 2) ou eau minérale gazeuse - 3) Am. sirup

Breakfast

Breakfast English	**Frühstück** German	**Petit déjeuner** French	**Prima colazione** Italian	**Desayuno** Spanish
acacia honey	Akazienhonig	miel d'acacia	miele d'acacia	miel de acacia
apricot jam	Aprikosenkonfitüre	confiture d'abricots	marmellata d'albicocche	mermelada de albaricoques
bacon	Bacon; Frühstücksspeck	bacon; lard fumé	bacon; pancetta affumicata	bacón; beicon; tocino ahumado
~ and eggs	Eier mit Bacon	œufs au bacon	uova al bacon	huevos con bacón
biscuits[1]	Kekse; Biskuits	gâteaux secs; biscuits	biscotti	galletas; bizcochos
black bread; brown bread	Schwarzbrot	pain noir	pane nero	pan moreno; ~ negro
~ coffee	schwarzer Kaffee	café noir; ~ nature	caffè nero	café solo
bread	Brot	pain	pane	pan
brioche (light slightly sweet bread); bun	Brioche (kleiner, runder Hefekuchen, feines Hefebrötchen, kleines Hefegebäck)	brioche (viennoiserie, à pâte levée)	brioche (piccolo dolce di pasta lievitata)	brioche (bollo de masa con levadura, ligeramente dulce)
brown bread; black bread	Schwarzbrot	pain noir	pane nero	pan moreno; ~ negro
~ sugar	brauner Zucker	sucre roux	zucchero di canna	azúcar moreno
butter	Butter	beurre	burro	mantequilla
caffeine-free coffee[2]	koffeinfreier Kaffee	café décaféiné	caffè decaffeinato	café descafeinado
cappuccino	Cappuccino	cappuccino	cappuccino	capuchino
cereals	Getreideflocken	céréales	fiocchi di cereali	cereales
~ with cream	~ mit Sahne	~ à la crème	~ di cereali con panna	~ con nata
Chantilly; whipped cream	Schlagsahne	crème Chantilly[3]	panna montata	nata batida; ~ montada; chantillí
cherry jam	Kirschkonfitüre	confiture de cerises	marmellata di ciliege	mermelada de cerezas
cocoa	Kakao	cacao	cacao	cacao
coffee	Kaffee	café	caffè	café
~ with cream[4]	~ mit Sahne	~ crème	~ con panna	~ con nata
~ with milk[4]	~ mit Milch; Milchkaffee	~ au lait; ~ crème	~ e latte; caffelatte	~ con leche

---

1) Am. cookies - 2) or decaffeinated coffee - 3) ou crème fouettée - 4) or white coffee

Breakfast

Breakfast English	Frühstück German	Petit déjeuner French	Prima colazione Italian	Desayuno Spanish
continental breakfast (coffee, hot milk, rolls and butter)	Milchkaffee komplett	café au lait complet	colazione continentale; caffelatte completo	café completo
cowberry jam[1]	Preiselbeerkonfitüre	marmelade d'airelles	marmellata di mirtilli rossi	mermelada de arándanos rojos
cream	Sahne; Rahm	crème; ~ fraîche	panna; crema	nata; crema
crispbread[2] (Swedish wholemeal crackers)	Knäckebrot (knusprige Scheiben Vollkornbrot)	knäckebrot (galettes de farine non blutée)	knäckebrot (gallette sottili di farina integrale)	knäckebrot (especie de pan integral sueco)
croissant; crescent[3]	Croissant; Hörnchen; Kipfel	croissant	cornetto; croissant	medialuna; croissant; cuerno
cube sugar; lump sugar	Würfelzucker	sucre en morceaux	zucchero in quadretti	azúcar en terrones; ~ de cortadillo
eggs	Eier	œufs	uova	huevos
~ cooked to order	~ nach Wunsch	~ au choix	~ a piacere	~ a elección; ~ a gusto
espresso	Espresso	express; café express	espresso	exprés; café exprés
French roll; roll	Brötchen; Semmel	petit pain	panino	panecillo; bollo; mollete
fried eggs[4]	Spiegeleier; Setzeier	œufs sur le plat; ~ poêlés; ~ au plat; ~ au miroir	uova al tegamino; ~ al piatto; ~ al burro	huevos al plato; ~ estrellados
fruit juice	Fruchtsaft	jus de fruits	succo di frutta	zumo de fruta
~ salad	Obstsalat	salade de fruits; macédoine; fruits rafraîchis	macedonia di frutta; insalata di frutta	ensalada de frutas; macedonia de frutas
~, stewed (compote)	Obstkompott	compote de fruits	frutta cotta	compota
~ yogurt	Fruchtjoghurt	yaourt aux fruits	yogurt alla frutta	yogur de fruta
Graham bread[5]	Grahambrot	pain Graham	pane Graham	pan Graham
grape juice	Traubensaft	jus de raisin	succo d'uva	zumo de uvas
grapefruit, iced	eisgekühlte Grapefruit	grapefruit frappé	pompelmo ghiacciato	pomelo helado
~ juice	Grapefruitsaft	jus de pamplemousse	succo di pompelmo	zumo de pomelo
ham	Schinken	jambon	prosciutto	jamón

---

1) also cranberry jam - 2) Am. rye crisps - 3) or crescent roll - 4) Am. sunny-side up eggs - 5) Am. whole wheat bread

Breakfast

Breakfast English	**Frühstück** German	**Petit déjeuner** French	**Prima colazione** Italian	**Desayuno** Spanish
ham and eggs (fried or scrambled)	Eier mit Schinken (Spiegeleier oder Rühreier)	œufs au jambon (sur le plat ou brouillés)	uova al prosciutto (al tegame o strapazzate)	huevos con jamón (al plato o revueltos)
~, grilled	gegrillter Schinken	jambon grillé	prosciutto alla griglia	jamón a la parrilla
~ omelette	Omelett mit Schinken	omelette au jambon	omelette al prosciutto	tortilla de jamón
hard-boiled eggs	hart gekochte Eier	œufs durs	uova sode	huevos duros
honey	Honig	miel	miele	miel
hot chocolate	Schokolade	chocolat	cioccolata	chocolate
jam; preserve	Konfitüre	confiture	confettura	confitura
lemon juice, freshly squeezed; ~ squash	frisch gepresster Zitronensaft	citron pressé	spremuta di limone	zumo de limón natural
~ marmalade	Zitronenmarmelade	marmelade de citron	marmellata di limone	mermelada de limón
low-fat yogurt	Magerjoghurt	yaourt maigre	yogurt magro	yogur magro
lump sugar; cube sugar	Würfelzucker	sucre en morceaux	zucchero in quadretti	azúcar en terrones; ~ de cortadillo
marmalade	Marmelade	marmelade	marmellata	mermelada
medium-boiled eggs	Fünfminuten-Eier; wachsweiche Eier	œufs mollets	uova bazzotte	huevos mollets; ~ encerados; ~ blandos
milk	Milch	lait	latte	leche
~ roll	Milchbrötchen	petit pain au lait	panino al latte	bollo de leche; mollete
mountain honey	Gebirgshonig	miel de montagne	miele di montagna	miel de montaña
muesli (flakes of cereals with nuts and dried fruit)	Müsli (Getreideflocken mit Obst und Nüssen)	muesli (mélange de céréales et de fruits secs)	müsli[1] (miscela di cereali, noci e frutta secca)	muesli (copos de cereales con fruta seca y nueces)
muffin	Muffin (Kleingebäck)	muffin (petit pain doux)	muffin (focaccina dolce)	muffin (panecillo dulce)
natural yogurt; plain yogurt	Naturjoghurt	yaourt nature	yogurt naturale	yogur natural
omelette; omelet	Omelett	omelette	omelette	tortilla
orange juice	Orangensaft	jus d'orange	succo d'arancia	zumo de naranja
~ juice, freshly squeezed; ~ squash	frisch gepresster Orangensaft	orange pressée	spremuta d'arancia	~ de naranja natural

---

[1] o muesli

Breakfast

Breakfast	**Frühstück**	**Petit déjeuner**	**Prima colazione**	**Desayuno**
English	German	French	Italian	Spanish
orange marmalade	Orangenmarmelade	marmelade d'oranges	marmellata di arance	mermelada de naranjas
pasteurized milk	pasteurisierte Milch	lait pasteurisé	latte pastorizzato	leche pasteurizada
pastry	Gebäck	pâtisserie; petit gâteau	pasta	pasta
peach jam	Pfirsichkonfitüre	confiture de pêches	marmellata di pesche	mermelada de melocotón
percolated coffee[1]	Filterkaffee	café filtre	caffè filtro	café filtro
plain omelette	Omelett natur	omelette nature	omelette al naturale; ~ semplice	tortilla francesa; ~ sencilla; ~ al natural
~ yogurt; natural yogurt	Naturjoghurt	yaourt nature	yogurt naturale	yogur natural
plum jam	Pflaumenkonfitüre	confiture de prunes	marmellata di prugne	mermelada de ciruelas
poached eggs	pochierte Eier; verlorene Eier	œufs pochés	uova affogate; ~ in camicia	huevos escalfados
porridge[2]	Porridge (Haferbrei)	porridge	porridge (farinata d'avena)	porridge (copos de avena)
preserve; jam	Konfitüre	confiture	confettura	confitura
raspberry jam	Himbeerkonfitüre	~ de framboises	marmellata di lamponi	mermelada de frambuesas
redcurrant jam	Johannisbeerkonfitüre	~ de groseilles	~ di ribes	~ de grosellas
roll; French roll	Brötchen; Semmel	petit pain	panino	panecillo; bollo; mollete
rusks[3]; zwieback	Zwieback	biscottes	fette biscottate; pane biscottato	biscotes
rye-bread	Roggenbrot	pain de seigle	pane di segale	pan de centeno
scrambled eggs	Rühreier	œufs brouillés	uova strapazzate	huevos revueltos
skimmed milk	Magermilch	lait écrémé	latte scremato	leche desnatada
soft-boiled eggs	Dreiminuten-Eier; weich gekochte Eier	œufs à la coque	uova alla coque; ~ al guscio	huevos pasados por agua[4]
strawberry jam	Erdbeerkonfitüre	confiture de fraises	marmellata di fragole	mermelada de fresas
sugar	Zucker	sucre	zucchero	azúcar
tea	Tee	thé	tè; the	té
~, rolls, jam and butter	~ komplett	~ complet	~ completo	~ completo
~ with lemon	~ mit Zitrone	~ au citron	~ al limone	~ con limón

---

1) Am. drip coffee - 2) Am. oatmeal - 3) or biscuit rusks - 4) o huevos en cáscara

Breakfast

Breakfast English	**Frühstück** German	**Petit déjeuner** French	**Prima colazione** Italian	**Desayuno** Spanish
tea with milk	Tee mit Milch	thé au lait	tè al latte	té con leche
~ with rum	~ mit Rum	~ au rhum	~ al rum	~ con ron
toast	Röstbrot; Scheibe Toast	toast; tranche de pain grillé	toast; fetta di pane tostato	tostada
~, buttered	Toast mit Butter	~ beurré	fetta di pane tostato con burro	toast con mantequilla
tomato juice	Tomatensaft	jus de tomate	succo di pomodoro	jugo de tomate
vegetable juice	Gemüsesaft	~ de légumes	~ di verdura	zumo de verdura
whipped cream; Chantilly	Schlagsahne	crème Chantilly[1]	panna montata	nata batida; ~ montada; chantillí
white bread; wheat bread	Weißbrot	pain blanc	pane bianco	pan blanco
wholemeal bread	Vollkornbrot; Schrotbrot	~ cornplet	~ integrale	~ completo; ~ integral
yogurt[2]	Jogurt[3]	yaourt; yogourt	yogurt[4]	yogur
zwieback; rusks[5]	Zwieback	biscottes	fette biscottate; pane biscottato	biscotes

---

1) ou crème fouettée - 2) or yoghurt - 3) oder Joghurt - 4) o iogurt, yoghurt - 5) or biscuit rusks

Culinary and service terms

Terminology English	Fachausdrücke German	Terminologie French	Terminologia Italian	Terminología Spanish
à la carte meal	Mahlzeit nach der Karte	repas à la carte	pasto alla carta	comida a la carta
according to amount	je nach Menge	selon quantité	secondo quantità	según cantidad
~ to size	~ nach Größe	~ grosseur	~ grandezza	~ tamaño
acid; sour	sauer	aigre; acide; sur	acido	ácido; agrio
afternoon tea; teatime	Jause *f*	goûter *m*; five o'clock	merenda *f*	merienda *f*; café *m* (de las cinco)
appetite	Appetit *m*	appétit *m*	appetito *m*	apetito *m*
aroma; flavouring	Aroma *n*	arôme *m*	aroma *m*	aroma *m*
aromatic	aromatisch	aromatique	aromatico	aromático
~ vinegar	Kräuteressig	vinaigre aromatique	aceto aromatico	vinagre aromático
as much as you like	so viel man will	à discrétion; ~ volonté	a volontà	a voluntad; ~ discreción
ash-tray	Aschenbecher *m*	cendrier *m*	portacenere *m*; posacenere *m*	cenicero *m*
aspic	Aspik *m*	aspic *m*	aspic *m*	gelatina *f*
assorted; mixed	gemischt	mélangé; mêlé; assorti; varié	assortito; misto	mixto; variado; surtido
at choice	nach Wahl; ~ Wunsch	au choix	a scelta; ~ piacere	a elección
~ fixed price	zu festem Preis	à prix fixe	~ prezzo fisso	~ precio fijo
~ once; immediately	sofort	tout de suite	subito	en seguida
~ pleasure	nach Belieben	à discrétion; ~ volonté	a volontà	a voluntad
~ room temperature; chambré	temperiert; chambriert	~ température ambiante; chambré	~ temperatura ambiente	~ temperatura ambiente
attendance; service	Bedienung *f*	service *m*	servizio *m*	servicio *m*
au gratin; baked	gratiniert; überbacken	au gratin; gratiné	al gratin; gratinato	al gratén; gratinado
bacon	Bacon; Frühstücksspeck	bacon; lard fumé	bacon; pancetta affumicata	bacón; beicon; tocino ahumado
~ fat; lard	Speck *m*	lard *m*	lardo *m*	tocino *m*
bad	schlecht	mauvais	cattivo	malo

Culinary and service terms

Terminology English	Fachausdrücke German	Terminologie French	Terminologia Italian	Terminología Spanish
bain-marie	Bainmarie *n*; Wasserbad	bain-marie *m*	bagnomaria *m*	baño María *m*
bake; gratin	Gratin *n*	gratin *m*	gratin *m*	gratén *m*
baked; au gratin	gratiniert; überbacken	au gratin; gratiné	al gratin; gratinato	al gratén; gratinado
baked; oven-roasted; oven-cooked	gebacken; aus dem Ofen; im Ofen gebacken	~ four[1]	~ forno	~ horno
balsamic vinegar	Balsamessig *m*	vinaigre *m* balsamique	aceto *m* balsamico	vinagre *m* balsámico
banquet	Bankett *n*	banquet *m*	banchetto *m*	banquete *m*
barley	Gerste *f*	orge *f*	orzo *m*	cebada *f*
batter; dough	Backteig *m*	pâte à frire; ~ à beignets	pastella *f*	pasta de freír; ~ *f* de buñuelos
beignet; fritter	Beignet *m*	beignet *m*; fritot *m*	frittella	buñuelo
beverage; drink	Getränk *n*	boisson *f*	bevanda *f*	bebida *f*
bicarbonate of soda	Natron *n*	bicarbonate *m* de soude	bicarbonato *m* di sodio	bicarbonato *m* de sosa
big; large	dick	gros (*f* grosse)	grosso	grueso
bill[2]	Rechnung *f*	addition *f*	conto *m*	cuenta *f*
~ of fare; menu	Speisekarte *f*	carte *f* des mets; menu	lista *f* delle vivande	carta de platos[3]; menú
biscuit dough; sponge	Biskuitteig *m*	pâte à biscuit[4]	pan di Spagna; pasta margherita	bizcocho
bitter	bitter	amer (*f* amère)	amaro	amargo
boiled	gesotten	bouilli	lessato; bollito	hervido; cocido
bone	Knochen *m*	os *m*	osso *m*	hueso *m*
bottle	Flasche *f*	bouteille *f*	bottiglia *f*	botella *f*
~ opener	Flaschenöffner *m*	ouvre-bouteilles[5] *m*	apribottiglie; levacapsule *m*	abridor *m*
bouillon cube; stock cube; meat cube	Suppenwürfel	tablette de bouillon	dado *m* per brodo	cubito de caldo[6]
bouquet	Bouquet[7] *n*	bouquet *m*	bouquet *m*	bouquet; buqué
~ garni; bunch of herbs	Kräutersträußchen *n*; Kräuterbündel *n*	~ garni	mazzetto di odori	ramillete *m*; manojo de hierbas[8]

---

1) aussi rôti au four - 2) Am. check - 3) o lista de platos - 4) ou génoise - 5) ou décapsuleur *m* - 6) o pastilla de caldo - 7) auch Bukett - 8) o manojito de hierbas

Culinary and service terms

Terminology English	**Fachausdrücke** German	**Terminologie** French	**Terminologia** Italian	**Terminología** Spanish
braised; pot-roasted	geschmort; braisiert	braisé; en daube	brasato; stufato	estofado; braseado
bread-basket	Brotkorb *m*	corbeille *f* à pain	cestino *m* del pane	cestilla *f* del pan
breadcrumbs	Paniermehl *n*; Semmelbrösel *pl*	chapelure *f*	pangrattato *m*	pan rallado; pangrattato *m*
breaded; crumbed	paniert	pané	impanato; panato	empanado; rebozado
breakfast	Frühstück *n*	petit déjeuner *m*	prima colazione *f*	desayuno *m*
~ buffet	Frühstücksbuffet	~ déjeuner au buffet	~ colazione al buffet	buffet de desayuno
brine; pickle; souse	Salzlake; Pökel *m*	saumure *f*	salamoia *f*	salmuera *f*; adobo *m*
brochette; kebab; skewer	Spießchen *n*	brochette *f*	spiedino *m*	brocheta *f*; broqueta *f*
broiled; grilled	gegrillt; vom Grill; ~ Rost; gebraten (auf dem Rost)	grillé; au gril	alla griglia; ai ferri; in gratella	a la parrilla; emparrillado
brown rice	Naturreis	riz complet; ~ brun	riso integrale	arroz con cáscara
~ sugar	brauner Zucker	sucre roux	zucchero di canna	azúcar moreno
buckwheat	Buchweizen *m*	sarrasin; blé *m* noir	grano *m* saraceno	trigo sarraceno; alforfón *m*
buffet	Buffet[1] *n*	buffet *m*	buffet *m*	bufé; buffet[2] *m*
bulgur (cracked wheat)	Bulgur *m* (Weizengrütze *f*)	boulgour *m* (blé *m* concassé)	bulghur *m* (grano *m* spezzato)	boulgour *m* (trigo *m* molido)
bunch of herbs; bouquet garni	Kräutersträußchen *n*; Kräuterbündel *n*	bouquet garni	mazzetto di odori	ramillete *m*; manojo de hierbas[3]
burnt	verbrannt	brûlé	bruciato	quemado
business lunch	Arbeitsessen; Business-Lunch *m*	déjeuner d'affaires	colazione di lavoro	comida de negocios
butter	Butter *f*	beurre *m*	burro *m*	mantequilla
buttermilk	Buttermilch *f*	babeurre *m*	latticello	leche de mantequilla; suero
cafeteria; self-service	Selbstbedienungs-Restaurant	restaurant libre-service	self-service	restaurante autoservicio
cake; patty; meatball	Frikadelle; Bulette	boulette; fricadelle *f*	polpetta	albóndiga
can-opener; tin-opener	Dosenöffner *m*	ouvre-boîte *m*	apriscatole *m*	abrelatas *m*

---

1) oder Büfett - 2) o bufet(e) - 3) o manojito de hierbas

Culinary and service terms

Terminology English	Fachausdrücke German	Terminologie French	Terminologia Italian	Terminología Spanish
candied citron peel	Zitronat n	cédrat confit	cedro candito	cidra confitada
candlelight dinner	Diner bei Kerzenlicht	dîner aux chandelles	pranzo a lume di candela	cena con velas
cane sugar[1]	Rohrzucker m	sucre de canne	zucchero di canna	azúcar de caña
canned; tinned	Dosen-...	en boîte; ~ conserve	in scatola	en lata; ~ conserva
carafe	Karaffe f	carafe f	caraffa f	garrafa f; jarra f
caramel (burnt sugar)	Karamell[2] m	caramel (sucre fondu)	caramello m	caramelo (azúcar tostado)
caramelized[3]	karamellisiert	caramelisé	caramellato	acaramelado; caramelizado
carefully prepared; soigné	soigniert; gepflegt	soigné	soigné; curato	esmerado
casserole; stewpan	Kasserolle f; Schmortopf m	cocotte f; casserole f	casseruola f	cacerola f; cazo m
castor sugar	Grießzucker m	sucre semoule; ~ en poudre	zucchero semolato	azúcar granulado
cellar	Keller m	cave f	cantina f	bodega f
cereals pl	Getreide n	céréales f pl	cereali m pl	cereales m pl
chafing-dish; hotplate	Wärmeplatte f	chauffe-plats m	scaldapiatti m	calientaplatos m
chair	Stuhl m	chaise f	sedia f	silla f
chambré; at room temperature	temperiert; chambriert	à température ambiante; chambré	a temperatura ambiente	a temperatura ambiente
champagne-cooler	Sektkühler m	seau m à champagne	secchiello m da champagne	cubo m del champaña
change; small change	Kleingeld n; Wechselgeld n	monnaie f; petit monnaie f	spiccioli m pl	dinero m suelto; calderilla f
change; remainder	Rest m (von Geld)	reste m; restant m	resto m	vuelta f; resto m
Chantilly; whipped cream	Schlagsahne f	crème Chantilly[4]	panna montata	nata batida; ~ montada; chantillí
charbroiled	vom Holzkohlengrill	au feu de bois	alla brace	a la brasa
charge; price; rate	Preis m	prix m	prezzo m	precio m
cheese trolley	Käsewagen	chariot de fromages	carrello dei formaggi	carrito de quesos
chef's ...	... des Chefs	... du chef	... dello chef	... del chef
chicken-frill; paper-frill	Kotelettmanschette f	manchette f; papillote f	papillote	papillote
chief cook; chef; head-cook	Küchenchef m; Chef	chef m (de cuisine)	capocuoco m; chef m	jefe de cocina m; chef m
children's menu	Kindermenü	menu pour enfants	menu per bambini	menú para niños

1) also demerara sugar - 2) auch Karamellzucker - 3) also caramelised - 4) ou crème fouettée

Culinary and service terms

Terminology English	**Fachausdrücke** German	**Terminologie** French	**Terminologia** Italian	**Terminología** Spanish
chilled; iced	eisgekühlt	glacé; frappé (Getränke)	ghiacciato; gelato	helado
chocolate	Schokolade f	chocolat m	cioccolato m	chocolate m
choice; selection	Auswahl	assortiment	assortimento	surtido
choice	auserlesen	choisi	scelto	selecto
chop; cutlet	Kotelett n; Rippchen n	côte f; côtelette f	costoletta f; costina f; braciola f	chuleta f; costilla f
chopped; minced	gehackt	haché	tritato	picado
choux pastry	Brandteig m	pâte f à choux	pasta f da bignè	pasta f lionesa
christmas Eve dinner	Weihnachtsdiner	réveillon de Noël	cenone di Natale	cena de Nochebuena
~ menu	Weihnachtsmenü n	menu m de Noël	menu m di Natale	menú m de Navidad
cider vinegar	Apfelessig m	vinaigre m de cidre	aceto m di mele	vinagre m de sidra
cigar	Zigarre f	cigare m	sigaro m	puro m; cigarro m
cigarette	Zigarette f	cigarette f	sigaretta f	cigarrillo m
civet; game stew[1]; salmi	Wildragout n; Salmi n; Civet n	ragoût de gibier; salmis m; civet	stufato di selvaggina; salmì m; civet	estofado de caza[2]; salmis; civet
clean	rein; sauber	propre	pulito	limpio
cloak-room	Garderobe f	vestiaire m	guardaroba m	guardarropa m
coarse salt	grobes Salz	gros sel	sale grosso	sal gruesa
coated	überzogen	nappé; arrosé	cosparso	bañado; napado; rociado
cocoa	Kakao m	cacao	cacao	cacao
coffee-pot	Kaffeekanne f	cafetière f	caffettiera f	cafetera f
coffee spoon	Kaffeelöffel m	petite cuiller; cuiller f à café	cucchiaino m	cucharilla f; cucharita f
cold	kalt	froid	freddo	frío
~ buffet	kaltes Buffet n	buffet m froid	buffet m freddo	buffet m frío
~ dish	~ Gericht	plat froid	piatto freddo	plato frío
compote; stewed fruit	Kompott n	compote f	frutta cotta; composta	compota f
confit	Confit (Eingemachtes)	confit m	confit	confit

---

[1] also ragout of game - [2] o ragú de caza

Culinary and service terms

Terminology English	Fachausdrücke German	Terminologie French	Terminologia Italian	Terminología Spanish
continental breakfast (coffee, hot milk, rolls and butter)	Milchkaffee komplett	café au lait complet	colazione continentale; caffelatte completo	café completo
cook (male)	Koch *m*	cuisinier *m*	cuoco *m*	cocinero *m*
~ (female)	Köchin *f*	cuisinière *f*	cuoca *f*	cocinera *f*
cooked	gekocht	cuit	cotto	cocido; hervido
cooking	Kochen *n*	cuisson *f*	cottura *f*	cocción *f*
~ time: … minutes	Kochzeit: … Minuten	~ … minutes	~ … minuti	~ … minutos
coral (ovary of a lobster)	Corail *n* (Muschelrogen *m*)	corail	corallo (uova di crostacei)	coral *m* (huevas de marisco)
cork	Korken *m*	bouchon *m*	tappo *m*; turacciolo *m*	corcho *m*; tapón *m*
corkscrew	Korkenzieher *m*	tire-bouchon *m*	cavatappi *m*	sacacorchos *m*; tirabuzón *m*
corn oil	Maisöl	huile de maïs	olio di mais	aceite de maíz
corner table	Tisch in der Ecke	table d'angle; ~ dans le coin	tavolo d'angolo	mesa de rinconera
cornflour[1]	Stärkemehl *n*	fécule *f*	fecola	fécula
cottage cheese; curd cheese	Quark *m*	fromage blanc	ricotta *f*	requesón *m*; queso fresco
course	Gang *m*	plat *m*; service *m*	portata *f*; piatto *m*	plato *m*
court-bouillon (fishstock)	Fischsud *m*	court-bouillon *m*	court-bouillon	caldo corto
cover; lid	Deckel *m*	couvercle	coperchio	cobertera
cover	Gedeck *n*	couvert *m*	coperto *m*	cubierto *m*
cream	Sahne *f*, Rahm *m*	crème *f*, ~ *f* fraîche	panna *f*; crema *f*	nata *f*; crema *f*
creamed; in cream	in Sahne	à la crème	alla panna; ~ crema	a la crema; con crema; ~ nata
credit card	Kreditkarte *f*	carte de crédit	carta di credito	tarjeta de crédito
crêpe; pancake	Crêpe *f*	crêpe *f*	crespella *f*; crêpe	crepe *f*
crisp	knusprig	croustillant; croquant	croccante	crujiente
croquette (fried ball of minced food)	Krokette *f*	croquette *f*	crocchetta *f*	croqueta *f*

---

[1] Am. cornstarch

Culinary and service terms

Terminology English	**Fachausdrücke** German	**Terminologie** French	**Terminologia** Italian	**Terminología** Spanish
cruet-stand	Öl- und Essigständer *m*; Menage *f*	huilier *m*; ménagère *f*	oliera *f*	vinagreras *f pl*
crumbed; breaded	paniert	pané	impanato; panato	empanado; rebozado
cube sugar; lump sugar	Würfelzucker	sucre en morceaux	zucchero in quadretti	azúcar en terrones; ~ de cortadillo
cup	Tasse *f*	tasse *f*	tazza *f*	taza *f*
curd cheese; cottage cheese	Quark *m*	fromage blanc	ricotta *f*	requesón *m*; queso fresco
curdled milk	Dickmilch	lait caillé	latte cagliato	leche cuajada
cured; salt; pickled	gepökelt	salé; saumuré	salato; in salamoia	salado; salpreso
curried; in curry	mit Curry	au curry	al curry	al curry; con curry
custard filling; pastry cream	Konditorcreme	crème pâtissière	crema pasticcera	crema pastelera
customer	Kunde *m*	client *m*	cliente *m*	cliente *m*
cutlery	Besteck *n*	couvert *m* (cuiller, fourchette, couteau)	posate *f pl*	cubierto *m* (cuchara, tenedor, cuchillo)
cutlet; chop	Kotelett *n*; Rippchen *n*	côte *f*, côtelette *f*	costoletta *f*; costina *f*; braciola *f*	chuleta *f*; costilla *f*
day's bill of fare; set menu	Tageskarte *f*	carte *f* du jour	lista *f* del giorno	carta *f* del día
deep-fried; fried; french-fried	in Fett gebacken; frittiert	frit	fritto	frito
deep-frozen; frozen	tiefgefroren; tiefgekühlt	surgelé	surgelato; congelato	congelado
delicious; exquisite	köstlich	délicieux (*f* délicieuse)	squisito	delicioso
dessert; sweet (course)	Dessert *n*; Nachtisch *m*	dessert *m*	dessert *m*	postre *m*
~ plate	Dessertteller	assiette à dessert	piatto da dessert	plato de postre
diet	Diät *f*	régime *m*	dieta *f*	régimen *m*; dieta *f*
dietary cuisine	Diätkost	cuisine de régime	cucina dietetica	cocina de régimen
digestible; easily digested; of easy digestion	leicht verdaulich	facile à digérer; de facile digestion	di facile digestione	de fácil digestión
digestion	Verdauung *f*	digestion *f*	digestione *f*	digestión *f*

Culinary and service terms

Terminology English	Fachausdrücke German	Terminologie French	Terminologia Italian	Terminología Spanish
dining room	Speisesaal *m*	salle *f* à manger	sala *f* da pranzo	comedor *m*
dinner	Abendessen *n*; Diner *n*	dîner *m*	cena *f*; pranzo *m*	cena *f*
~ is served at …	es wird um … Uhr gespeist	on dîne à … heures	si pranza alle …	se come a las …
dip; dipping sauce	Dip *m* (dicke Sauce)	dip *m*; assaisonnement *m*	salsa *f*	salsa *f*
dish	Gericht *n*; Speise *f*, Platte *f*	plat *m*; mets *m*	piatto *m*; pietanza *f*	plato *m*; guiso *m*
~ of the day; today special[1]	Tagesgericht *n*	~ *m* du jour	~ *m* del giorno	~ *m* del día
~ to order[2]	Gericht auf Bestellung	~ sur commande	~ da farsi	~ a pedido
domestic; local	einheimisch; hiesig	local; du pays	nostrano; locale	local; de la región; del país
double	doppelt	double	doppio	doble
dough; batter	Backteig *m*	pâte à frire; ~ à beignets	pastella *f*	pasta de freír; ~ *f* de buñuelos
dough; paste; pastry	Teig *m*	pâte *f*	pasta *f*	pasta *f*, masa
dozen; a dozen	Dutzend; pro Dutzend	douzaine *f*; la douzaine	dozzina *f*; la dozzina	docena *f*; la docena
dressing; salad dressing	Dressing *n*; Salatsauce *f*	sauce (pour salades)	condimento (per insalata)	salsa (para ensaladas)
dressing; stuffing; filling; farce	Füllung *f*, Farce *f*	farce *f*	ripieno *m*; farcia *f*	relleno *m*
dried mushrooms	Trockenpilze	champignons séchés	funghi secchi	setas secas
drink; beverage	Getränk *n*	boisson *f*	bevanda *f*	bebida *f*
drinking-straw; straw	Strohhalm *m*; Trinkhalm *m*	paille *f*, chalumeau *m*	cannuccia *f*	paja *f*, pajita *f*
drinks (not) included	Getränke (nicht) inbegriffen	boissons (non) comprises; ~ en sus	bevande (non) comprese	bebidas (no) incluidas
dry	trocken	sec (*f* sèche)	secco	seco
dumpling; quenelle	Kloß; Klößchen	boulette; quenelle *f*	gnocco; gnocchetto	albóndiga; albondiguilla
dumpling; knödel	Knödel *m*	boulette *f*, knödel *f*	gnocco; canederlo *m*	albóndiga *f*
dumplings; quenelles	Nockerln	noques; quenelles	gnocchetti	albondiguillas
each; per person; ~ head	pro Person	par personne; ~ tête	a persona, ~ testa	por persona
each	~ Stück	la pièce	al pezzo	~ pieza; la pieza

---

[1] or today speciality - [2] also dish prepared to order

Culinary and service terms

Terminology English	**Fachausdrücke** German	**Terminologie** French	**Terminologia** Italian	**Terminología** Spanish
easily digested; digestible; of easy digestion	leicht verdaulich	facile à digérer; de facile digestion	di facile digestione	de fácil digestión
Easter menu	Ostermenü *n*	menu *m* de Pâques	menu *m* di Pasqua	menú *m* de Pascua
edible	essbar	comestible	commestibile	comestible
egg-cup	Eierbecher *m*	coquetier *m*	portauovo *m*	huevera *f*
egg white; white of egg	Eiweiß *n*	blanc *m* d'œuf	chiara *f* d'uovo; albume *m*	clara *f* de huevo
egg-yolk; yolk of egg	Eigelb *n*	jaune *m* d'œuf	rosso *m* d'uovo; tuorlo *m*	yema *f* (de huevo)
en papillote (in paper casing)	en Papillote (in Butterpapier oder Alufolie)	en papillote	al cartoccio	en papillote (asado en un papel)
engaged; occupied	besetzt	occupé; pris	occupato	ocupado
~ table; occupied table	besetzter Tisch	table occupée	tavolo occupato	mesa ocupada
entire; whole	ganz (ungeteilt)	entier; tout	intero; tutto	entero; todo
escalope	Schnitzel *n*	escalope *f*	scaloppa; scaloppina *f*	escalope *m*; escalopa *f*
excellent; first-class; very good	ausgezeichnet	excellent	eccellente; ottimo	excelente
exotic	exotisch	exotique	esotico	exótico
~ dish	exotisches Gericht	plat exotique	piatto esotico	plato exótico
exquisite; delicious	köstlich	délicieux (*f* délicieuse)	squisito	delicioso
extra charge	Zuschlag *m*	supplément *m*	supplemento *m*	suplemento *m*
farce; stuffing; filling; dressing	Füllung *f*; Farce *f*	farce *f*	ripieno *m*; farcia *f*	relleno *m*
fat	Fett *n*	graisse *f*	grasso *m*	grasa *f*
fatty; fat	fett	gras (*f* grasse)	grasso	graso
filled; stuffed	gefüllt	farci	ripieno; farcito	relleno
filling; stuffing; dressing; farce	Füllung *f*; Farce *f*	farce *f*	ripieno *m*; farcia *f*	relleno *m*
finger-bowl; finger-glass	Fingerschale *f*	rince-doigts *m*	lavadita; sciacquadita *m*	lavadedos *m*

Culinary and service terms

Terminology English	Fachausdrücke German	Terminologie French	Terminologia Italian	Terminología Spanish
first-class; excellent; very good	ausgezeichnet	excellent	eccellente; ottimo	excelente
first course	erster Gang	premier plat	primo piatto	primer plato
fish-bone	Gräte *f*	arête *f*	lisca; spina di pesce	espina *f*
fish dish	Fischgericht *n*	plat *m* de poisson	piatto *m* di pesce	plato *m* de pescado
fish-kettle	Fischkessel *m*	poissonnière *f*	pesciera *f*; pesciaiola *f*	besuguera *f*
fish knife and fork	Fischbesteck *n*	couvert *m* à poisson	posate *f* da pesce	cubierto *m* de pescado
~ menu	Fischmenü	menu de poisson	menu di pesce	menú de pescado
~ ragout; matelote	Fischragout *n*; Matelote *f*	matelote *f*	stufato di pesce	estofado de pescado
~ specialities	Fischspezialitäten *f*	spécialités *f* de poisson	specialità *f* di pesce	especialidades *f* de pescado
~ steak	Fischsteak *n*; Fischschnitte *f*	darne *f*	trancio *m* di pesce	tajada *f* de pescado
five-course menu	Fünf-Gänge-Menü	menu à cinq plats	menu di cinque portate	menú de cinco platos
fixed price meal	Mahlzeit zu festem Preis	repas à prix fixe	pasto a prezzo fisso	comida a precio fijo
flaky pastry; puff pastry	Blätterteig *m*	pâte feuilletée	pasta *f* sfoglia	hojaldre *m*; pasta de hojaldre
flambé; flaming	flambiert	flambé	alla fiamma; flambé	flameado
flat; tasteless; insipid	geschmacklos; fade	fade; sans goût	insipido	insípido; soso
flatfish	Plattfisch	poisson plat	pesce piatto	pez de cuerpo aplanado
flavour; taste	Geschmack *m*	goût *m*; saveur *f*	gusto *m*; sapore *m*	gusto *m*; sabor *m*
flavouring; aroma	Aroma *n*	arôme *m*	aroma *m*	aroma *m*
fleurons (small puff pastry crescents)	Fleurons *m* (Blätterteig-Halbmonde)	fleurons *m*	sfogliatine *f* (a forma di mezzaluna)	fleurons *m* (hojaldre en forma de media luna)
flour	Mehl *n*	farine *f*	farina *f*	harina *f*
fork	Gabel *f*	fourchette *f*	forchetta *f*	tenedor *m*
free-range duck	Freilandente	canard de ferme	anatra di cortile	pato de granja
free table; vacant table	freier Tisch	table libre	tavolo libero	mesa libre
freezer	Gefrierfach *n*; Tiefkühlfach *n*	freezer	congelatore; freezer	congelador *m*
French cuisine	französische Küche	cuisine française	cucina francese	cocina francesa

Culinary and service terms

Terminology English	**Fachausdrücke** German	**Terminologie** French	**Terminologia** Italian	**Terminología** Spanish
French dressing	Vinaigrette f	vinaigrette f	vinaigrette f	vinagreta f
fresh	frisch	frais (f fraîche)	fresco	fresco
freshwater fish	Süßwasserfisch	poisson d'eau douce	pesce d'acqua dolce	pescado de agua dulce
fricassee	Frikassee n	fricassée f, blanquette f	fricassea f	fricasé m; blanqueta
fried ...	Frittüre f	friture f	frittura f	fritura f, fritada f, frito m
fried; deep-fried; french-fried	in Fett gebacken; frittiert	frit	fritto	frito
fritter; beignet	Beignet m	beignet m; fritot m	frittella	buñuelo
frosting; icing[1]	Glasur f; Glace f	glace f	glassa f; ghiaccia f	baño m (de azúcar); glasa f
frozen; deep-frozen	tiefgefroren; tiefgekühlt	surgelé	surgelato; congelato	congelado
fruit basket	Früchtekorb m	corbeille f à fruits	crestino m da frutta	cestilla f de frutas
fruit-dish; fruit bowl	Obstschale f	coupe f à fruits; fruitier m	fruttiera f	frutero m
fruit yogurt	Fruchtjoghurt	yaourt aux fruits	yogurt alla frutta	yogur de fruta
frying-pan[2]	Pfanne f; Bratpfanne f	poêle f	padella f	sartén f
full	voll	plein	pieno	lleno
gala dinner	Galadiner	dîner de gala	pranzo di gala	cena de gala
galantine	Galantine f	galantine f	galantina f	galantina f
game stew[3]; salmi; civet	Wildragout n; Salmi n; Civet n	ragoût de gibier; salmis m; civet	stufato di selvaggina; salmì m; civet	estofado de caza[4]; salmis; civet
garnish[5]; vegetables pl	Beilage f	garniture f	contorno m; guarnizione f	guarnición f
gastronome; gourmet	Feinschmecker m	gourmet m	buongustaio m	gourmet m; gastrónomo m
gelatin[6]	Gelatine f	gélatine f	gelatina; colla di pesce	gelatina f; cola de pescado
giant; jumbo	Riesen-...	géant	gigante	gigante
glass	Glas n	verre m	bicchiere m	vaso m
glazed (Gebäck: iced, frosted)	glasiert[7]	glacé	glassato	glaseado
golden syrup[8]; treacle	Melasse; Zuckersirup	mélasse f	melassa f	melaza f
good	gut	bon (f bonne)	buono	bueno

---

1) or sugar-icing - 2) Am. skillet - 3) also ragout of game - 4) o ragú de caza - 5) also side dish - 6) or gelatine - 7) auch glaciert - 8) Am. molasses

Culinary and service terms

Terminology English	Fachausdrücke German	Terminologie French	Terminologia Italian	Terminología Spanish
goose fat; ~ grease	Gänseschmalz n	graisse d'oie	grasso d'oca	mantequilla de ganso
goulash	Gulasch m	goulache; goulasch m	gulasch m	gulasch
gourmet; gastronome	Feinschmecker m	gourmet m	buongustaio m	gourmet m; gastrónomo m
grated	gerieben	râpé	grattugiato; grattato	rallado
gratin; bake	Gratin n	gratin m	gratin m	gratén m
gratin; soufflé	Auflauf m	gratin; soufflé m	gratin; soufflé m	gratén m; soufflé; suflé m
gratuity; tip	Trinkgeld n	pourboire m	mancia f	propina f
gravy; brown gravy	Bratensauce f	jus m	sugo m di carne	jugo m de carne
~ boat; sauce boat	Soßenschüssel f; Sauciere f	saucière f	salsiera f	salsera f
green spelt	Grünkern m	épeautre vert	farro verde	farro verde
grilled; broiled	gegrillt; vom Grill; ~ Rost; gebraten (auf dem Rost)	grillé; au gril	alla griglia; ai ferri; in gratella	a la parrilla; emparrillado
guest	Gast m	hôte m	ospite m	huésped m
half	halb	demi	mezzo	medio
~ a litre	halbes Liter	demi-litre	~ litro	~ litro
half-bottle[1]	halbe Flasche	demi-bouteille	mezza bottiglia	media botella
half-dozen	halbes Dutzend	demi-douzaine	~ dozzina	~ docena
half-portion	halbe Portion	demi-portion	~ porzione	~ ración; ~ porción
hard	hart	dur	duro	duro
harissa (chili sauce)	Harissa (Chilisauce)	harissa (sauce au piment rouge)	harissa (salsa di peperoncino)	harissa (salsa de guindilla)
head-cook; chief cook; chef	Küchenchef m; Chef	chef m (de cuisine)	capocuoco m; chef m	jefe de cocina m; chef m
headwaiter; maître d'hôtel	Maître m; Oberkellner m	maître m (d'hotel)	maître m; direttore m; capocameriere m	maître m; jefe m de comedor; primer camarero m
heavy; indigestible	schwer verdaulich; unverdaulich	indigeste	indigesto	indigesto; dificil de digerir
help yourself!	bedienen Sie sich	servez-vous	si serva	sírvase Vd.

---

[1] 0.6 pints

Culinary and service terms

Terminology English	Fachausdrücke German	Terminologie French	Terminologia Italian	Terminología Spanish
helping; serving; portion	Portion f	portion f	porzione f	ración f; porción f
herbs	Kräuter	herbes f	erbe f	hierbas f
here is (pl here are)	hier ist (pl hier sind)	voici	ecco; ~ qui	he aquí
high chair	Kinderstuhl	chaise d'enfant[1]	seggiolone (per bambini)	silla de niño
home-made (home-baked)	hausgemacht	maison	casereccio	casero
home-smoked	hausgeräuchert	fumé maison	affumicato in casa	ahumado en casa
honey	Honig m	miel m	miele m	miel f
hot	heiß	chaud	caldo; molto caldo; caldissimo	caliente
hot; spicy; sharp	pikant; scharf	épicé; piquant	piccante	picante
~ dish	warmes Gericht	plat chaud	piatto caldo	plato caliente
~ pot; single-dish meal; hotchpotch	Eintopf; Eintopfgericht	~ unique; potée	~ unico	~ único; puchero
hotplate; chafing-dish	Wärmeplatte f	chauffe-plats m	scaldapiatti m	calientaplatos m
hour	Stunde f	heure f	ora f	hora f
ice	Eis n	glace f	ghiaccio m	hielo m
~ bucket; ~ pail	Eiskübel m	seau m à glace	secchiello m del ghiaccio	cubo m para hielo
~ cube	Eiswürfel m	glaçons m	cubetti di ghiaccio	cubitos de hielo
iced; chilled	eisgekühlt	glacé; frappé (Getränke)	ghiacciato; gelato	helado
icing[2]; frosting	Glasur f; Glace f	glace f	glassa f, ghiaccia f	baño m (de azúcar); glasa f
~ sugar[3]	Puderzucker; Staubzucker	sucre glace	zucchero a velo	azúcar glas; ~ de flour
if you please; please	bitte	s'il vous plaît	prego; per favore	por favor
immediately; at once	sofort	tout de suite	subito	en seguida
in cream; creamed	in Sahne	à la crème	alla panna; ~ crema	a la crema; con crema; ~ nata
~ jelly; jellied	~ Gelee	en gelée; à la gelée	in gelatina	en gelatina
~ salt crust	~ Salzkruste	au sel; en croûte de sel	al sale; in crosta di sale	a la sal

---

1) ou chaise haute - 2) or sugar-icing - 3) Am. confectioners' sugar

Culinary and service terms

Terminology English	**Fachausdrücke** German	**Terminologie** French	**Terminologia** Italian	**Terminología** Spanish
indigestible; heavy	schwer verdaulich; unverdaulich	indigeste	indigesto	indigesto; difícil de digerir
ingredients	Zutaten f	ingrédients m	ingredienti m	ingredientes m
insipid; tasteless; flat	geschmacklos; fade	fade; sans goût	insipido	insípido; soso
instant; moment	Augenblick m	instant m	momento m; istante m	momento m; instante m
international cuisine	internationale Küche	cuisine internationale	cucina internazionale	cocina internacional
jam; preserve	Konfitüre	confiture f	confettura	confitura
jellied; in jelly	in Gelee	en gelée; à la gelée	in gelatina	en gelatina
jelly	Gelee m o. n; Sülze f	gelée f	gelatina f	gelatina f
joint; roast	Braten m	rôti m	arrosto m	asado
jug; pitcher	Krug m	cruche f	brocca f	jarra f; cántaro m
juice	Saft m	jus m	sugo m; succo m (di frutta)	jugo m; zumo m (de fruta)
juicy; succulent	saftig	juteux (f juteuse)	sugoso[1]	jugoso; suculento
jumbo; giant	Riesen-…	géant	gigante	gigante
kebab; brochette; skewer	Spießchen n	brochette f	spiedino m	brocheta f; broqueta f
kitchen	Küche f	cuisine f	cucina f	cocina f
knife	Messer n	couteau m	coltello m	cuchillo m
knödel; dumpling	Knödel m	boulette f; knödel f	gnocco; canederlo m	albóndiga f
lard	Schweineschmalz m; Schmalz m	saindoux m	strutto m	mantequilla f de cerdo
lard; bacon fat	Speck m	lard m	lardo m	tocino m
larded	gespickt	piqué; lardé	lardellato	mechado; lardeado
large; big	dick	gros (f grosse)	grosso	grueso
lavatory[2]; toilets	Toiletten f pl	toilettes f pl; lavabos m pl	toilette f; gabinetto m; bagno m	servicios pl; retrete m; lavabo m
layer	Schicht f	couche f	strato m	capa f
lean	mager	maigre	magro	magro
lemon peel; ~ zest	Zitronenschale f	zeste m de citron	buccia f di limone	cáscara de limón

---

1) o succoso - 2) Am. restroom, ladies' room, men's room

Culinary and service terms

Terminology English	Fachausdrücke German	Terminologie French	Terminologia Italian	Terminología Spanish
lenten dish; meatless dish	Fastenspeise *f*; Fastenkost *f*	plat *m* maigre	piatto *m* di magro	plato *m* de vigilia[1]
lid; cover	Deckel *m*	couvercle	coperchio	cobertera
light	leicht	léger	leggero	ligero
lights; matches	Zündhölzer *n pl*; Streichhölzer *n pl*	allumettes *f pl*	fiammiferi *m pl*	cerillas *f pl*; fósforos *m pl*
liqueur glass; small glass	Likörglas *n*	petit verre; verre à liqueur	bicchierino *m*	copita *f*
liquid	flüssig	liquide	liquido	líquido
litre[2] (bottle of 1 3/4 pints)	Liter *m* u. *n*	litre *m*	litro *m*	litro *m*
little; small	klein	petit	piccolo	pequeño
local; domestic	einheimisch; hiesig	local; du pays	nostrano; locale	local; de la región; del país
~ dish; regional dish	typisches Gericht; Gericht *n* der Region	plat typique; ~ *m* local; mets *m* local	piatto *m* tipico	plato *m* típico; ~ *m* local
low-calorie	kalorienarm	à basses calories; allégé	ipocalorico	bajo en calorías
~ dish	kalorienarmes Gericht	plat allégé	piatto ipocalorico	plato bajo en calorías
low-fat yogurt	Magerjoghurt	yaourt maigre	yogurt magro	yogur desnatado
lukewarm; warm; tepid	lauwarm	tiède	tiepido	tibio; templado
lump sugar; cube sugar	Würfelzucker	sucre en morceaux	zucchero in quadretti	azúcar en terrones; ~ de cortadillo
lunch; luncheon	Mittagessen *n*	déjeuner *m*	pranzo *m*; colazione *f*	almuerzo *m*; comida *f*
main course; ~ dish	Hauptgericht *n*	plat *m* principal	piatto *m* forte	plato *m* principal[3]
~ course and vegetables	Tagesgericht mit Beilagen	~ du jour garni	~ del giorno guarnito	~ del día con guarnición
maître d'hôtel; headwaiter	Maître *m*; Oberkellner *m*	maître *m* (d'hotel)	maître *m*; direttore *m*; capocameriere *m*	maître *m*; jefe *m* de comedor; primer camarero *m*
maple syrup	Ahornsirup *m*	sirop d'érable	sciroppo d'acero	jarabe de arce
margarine[4]	Margarine *f*	margarine *f*	margarina *f*	margarina *f*
marinade; pickle; souse	Marinade *f*; Beize *f*	marinade *f*	marinata	marinada *f*; adobo; escabeche *m*

---

1) o plato de viernes - 2) Am. liter - 3) o plato fuerte - 4) Am. oleomargarine

Culinary and service terms

Terminology English	Fachausdrücke German	Terminologie French	Terminologia Italian	Terminología Spanish
marinated; soused; pickled	mariniert; gebeizt	mariné; en marinade	marinato	marinado; en escabeche; adobado
marine fish; sea fish	Seefisch	poisson de mer	pesce di mare	pescado de mar
marmalade	Marmelade	marmelade *f*	marmellata	mermelada
marzipan	Marzipan *n*	massepain *m*	marzapane *m*	mazapán *m*
matches; lights	Zündhölzer *n pl*; Streichhölzer *n pl*	allumettes *f pl*	fiammiferi *m pl*	cerillas *f pl*; fósforos *m pl*
matelote; fish ragout	Fischragout *n*; Matelote *f*	matelote *f*	stufato di pesce	estofado de pescado
meal	Mahlzeit *f*	repas *m*	pasto *m*	comida *f*
meat cube; stock cube; bouillon cube	Suppenwürfel	tablette de bouillon	dado *m* per brodo	cubito de caldo[1]
~ dish	Fleischgericht *n*	plat de viande	piatto di carne	plato de carne
meatball; cake; patty	Frikadelle; Bulette	boulette; fricadelle *f*	polpetta	albóndiga
meatless dish; lenten dish	Fastenspeise *f*; Fastenkost *f*	plat *m* maigre	piatto *m* di magro	plato *m* de vigilia[2]
médaillon[3]; noisette	Medaillon *n*	médaillon *m*	medaglione *m*	medallón *m*
mediterranean cuisine	mediterrane Küche	cuisine méditerranéenne	cucina mediterranea	cocina mediterránea
melted	zerlassen	fondu	fuso	derretido; fundido
menu (dishes served)	Menü *n*	menu *m*	menu *m*; menù *m*	menú *m*; minuta *f*
menu; bill of fare	Speisekarte *f*	carte *f* des mets; menu	lista *f* delle vivande	carta de platos[4]; menú
milk-jug	Milchkännchen *n*	pot *m* à lait	bricco *m* del latte	jarrita *f* de leche
millet	Hirse	millet *m*	miglio	mijo
minced; chopped	gehackt	haché	tritato	picado
~ meat	Hackfleisch	hachis de viande	carne macinata	carne picada
mixed; assorted	gemischt	mélangé; mêlé; assorti; varié	assortito; misto	mixto; variado; surtido
moment; instant	Augenblick *m*	instant *m*	momento *m*; istante *m*	momento *m*; instante *m*
mould; pudding	Flan *m*	flan *m*	sformato *m*; flan *m*	flan *m*; budín *m*
mould[5]	Form *f*; Backform *f*	moule *m*; forme *f*	stampo *m*; forma *f*	molde *m*

---

1) o pastilla de caldo - 2) o plato de viernes - 3) also medallion - 4) o lista de platos - 5) form which gives food a shape

Culinary and service terms

Terminology English	**Fachausdrücke** German	**Terminologie** French	**Terminologia** Italian	**Terminología** Spanish
mousse; whip	Schaum; Schaumcreme	mousse *f*	spuma *f*; mousse *f*	espuma *f*; mousse
mustard	Senf *m*	moutarde *f*	senape[1] *f*; mostarda *f*	mostaza *f*
~ fruit	Senffrüchte	fruits confits à la moutarde	mostarda di frutta	fruta confitada en mostaza
mustard-pot	Senftopf *m*	moutardier *m*	mostardiera *f*	mostacera *f*
napkin; serviette	Serviette *f*	serviette *f*	tovagliolo *m*; salvietta *f*	servilleta *f*
natural yogurt; plain yogurt	Naturjoghurt	yaourt nature	yogurt naturale	yogur natural
New Year's Eve dinner	Neujahrsdiner	réveillon de la Saint-Sylvestre	cenone di San Silvestro	cena de Nochevieja
noisette; médaillon[2]	Medaillon *n*	médaillon *m*	medaglione *m*	medallón *m*
number	Nummer *f*	numéro *m*	numero *m*	número *m*
nutcrackers *pl*	Nussknacker *m*	casse-noix *m*; casse-noisette *m*	schiaccianoci *m*	cascanueces *m*
oat flakes	Haferflocken	flocons d'avoine	fiocchi d'avena	copos de avena
oatmeal	Hafermehl *n*	farine d'avoine	farina *f* d'avena	harina *f* de avena
occupied; engaged	besetzt	occupé; pris	occupato	ocupado
~ table; engaged table	besetzter Tisch	table occupée	tavolo occupato	mesa ocupada
odour; smell	Geruch *m*	odeur *f*	odore *m*	olor *m*
of easy digestion; easily digested; digestible	leicht verdaulich	facile à digérer; de facile digestion	di facile digestione	de fácil digestión
oil	Öl *n*	huile *f*	olio *m*	aceite *m*
olive oil	Olivenöl	~ d'olive	~ d'oliva	~ de oliva
on request[3]	auf Bestellung	sur commande	su ordinazione	por encargo; a pedido
~ request	~ Wunsch	~ demande	a richiesta	a petición
~ reservation	~ Vormerkung	~ réservation	su prenotazione	bajo reserva
~ the spit; spit-roasted	vom Spieß	à la broche	allo spiedo	al asador
order	Bestellung *f*	commande *f*	ordinazione *f*; comanda *f*	pedido *m*; encargo *m*
organic	biologisch	biologique	biologico	biológico
our special ...	nach Art des Hauses	... maison	... della casa	... de la casa

1) o senapa - 2) also medallion - 3) also to order

Culinary and service terms

Terminology English	Fachausdrücke German	Terminologie French	Terminologia Italian	Terminología Spanish
our special dish	Spezialität des Hauses	plat maison	piatto della casa	especialidad de la casa
out of season	außer Saison	hors de saison	fuori stagione	fuera de temporada
outdoor restaurant[1]	Restaurant im Freien	restaurant en plein air	ristorante all'aperto	restaurante al aire libre
oven	Ofen *m*; Backofen *m*	four *m*	forno *m*	horno *m*
oven-roasted; baked; oven-cooked	gebacken; aus dem Ofen; im Ofen gebacken	au four[2]	al forno	al horno
overripe	überreif	trop mûr	troppo maturo	muy maduro
pan-fried; sauté; sautéed	gebraten (in der Pfanne oder in Butter); geröstet (in der Pfanne); sautiert	poêlé; sauté	sauté[3]; saltato; rosolato; fritto nel burro	salteado; rehogado
pancake; crêpe	Crêpe *f*	crêpe *f*	crespella *f*; crêpe	crepe *f*
pancetta; streaky bacon	durchwachsener Speck	lard maigre; ~ de poitrine	pancetta	tocino entreverado
paper-frill; chicken-frill	Kotelettmanschette *f*	manchette *f*; papillote *f*	papillote	papillote
paper napkin	Papierserviette *f*	serviette *f* en papier	tovagliolo *m* di carta	servilleta de papel
paste; pastry; dough	Teig *m*	pâte *f*	pasta *f*	pasta *f*; masa
pastry cream; custard filling	Konditorcreme	crème pâtissière	crema pasticcera	crema pastelera
pat of butter[4]	Butterröllchen *n*	coquille de beurre	ricciolo *m* di burro	bolilla de mantequilla
pâté; pie	Pastete	pâté en croûte	pâté in crosta	pastel; paté *m*
pâté; terrine	Terrine; Pastete ohne Teigumhüllung	terrine; pâté en terrine	terrina	paté; terrina
patron; regular customer	Stammgast *m*	habitué; client régulier	cliente *m* abituale	cliente *m* habitual
patty; cake; meatball	Frikadelle; Bulette	boulette; fricadelle *f*	polpetta	albóndiga
peel; rind	Schale *f* (von Obst); Rinde *f*	pelure *f* (de fruit); écorce *f*	buccia *f*; scorza *f*	piel *f* (de fruta); cáscara *f*
~ (lemon); zest	~ *f* (von Zitrusfrüchten)	zeste *m*	buccia *f*; scorza *f* (di agrumi)	corteza *f*; cáscara *f* (de limón o naranja)
pepper mill	Pfeffermühle *f*	moulin *m* à poivre	macinapepe; macinino	molinillo de pimienta
~ pot[5]; ~ caster	Pfefferstreuer *m*	poivrier *m*; poivrière *f*	pepaiola *f*	pimentero *m*
per glass	pro Glas	le verre	al bicchiere	por vaso

---

1) also open-air restaurant - 2) aussi rôti au four - 3) undeklinierbar - 4) also roll of butter - 5) Am. pepper shaker

Culinary and service terms

Terminology English	**Fachausdrücke** German	**Terminologie** French	**Terminologia** Italian	**Terminología** Spanish
per person; ~ head; each	pro Person	par personne; ~ tête	a persona; ~ testa	por persona
pickle; marinade; souse	Marinade f; Beize f	marinade f	marinata	marinada f; adobo; escabeche m
pickle; brine; souse	Salzlake; Pökel m	saumure f	salamoia f	salmuera f; adobo m
pickled; salt; cured	gepökelt	salé; saumuré	salato; in salamoia	salado; salpreso
pickled; marinated; soused	mariniert; gebeizt	mariné; en marinade	marinato	marinado; en escabeche; adobado
pie; pâté	Pastete	pâté en croûte	pâté in crosta	pastel; paté m
piece	Stück n	pièce f; morceau m	pezzo m	pieza f; pedazo m; trozo m
pinch	Prise f	pincée f; prise f	presa f; pizzico m	pizca; pellizca
pitcher; jug	Krug m	cruche f	brocca f	jarra f; cántaro m
plain chocolate[1]	Zartbitter-Schokolade	chocolat noir; ~ amer	cioccolato fondente; ~ amaro	chocolate amargo; ~ negro
~ cooking[2]	bürgerliche Küche	cuisine bourgeoise	cucina casalinga	cocina casera
~ yogurt; natural yogurt	Naturjoghurt	yaourt nature	yogurt naturale	yogur natural
plate; platter	Platte f	plat m	piatto m (di portata)	fuente f; plato m
plate[3]	Teller m	assiette f	piatto m	plato m
please; if you please	bitte	s'il vous plaît	prego; per favore	por favor
~ ask for the wine-list	verlangen Sie die Weinkarte	veuillez consulter notre carte des vins	chiedete la lista dei vini	pida Vd. la carta de vinos
portion; helping; serving	Portion f	portion f	porzione f	ración f; porción f
pot	Topf m; Kochtopf m	marmite f	pentola f	olla f; marmita; cazuela; puchero m
pot-roasted; braised	geschmort; braisiert	braisé; en daube	brasato; stufato	estofado; braseado
preparation	Zubereitung	préparation	preparazione	preparación
prepared at table	am Tisch zubereitet	préparé à la table	preparato al tavolo	preparado en la mesa
preserve; jam	Konfitüre	confiture f	confettura	confitura
price; charge; rate	Preis m	prix m	prezzo m	precio m

1) or dark chocolate - 2) also good plain cooking - 3) Am. plate or dish

Culinary and service terms

Terminology English	**Fachausdrücke** German	**Terminologie** French	**Terminologia** Italian	**Terminología** Spanish
pudding	Pudding *m*	pouding; pudding	budino *m*	pudín; budín *m*; flan *m*
puff pastry; flaky pastry	Blätterteig *m*	pâte feuilletée	pasta *f* sfoglia	hojaldre *m*; pasta de hojaldre
purée	Püree *n*	purée *f*	purè *m*; purea *f*; passato *m*	puré *m*
quarter	Viertel *n*	quart *m*	quarto *m*	cuarto *m*
~ bottle[1]	Viertelliterflasche *f*	bouteille d'un quart	bottiglia da un quarto	botella de un cuarto
~ of a chicken	Viertel Huhn	quart de poulet	quarto di pollo	cuarto de pollo
quenelle; dumpling	Kloß; Klößchen	boulette; quenelle *f*	gnocco; gnocchetto	albóndiga; albondiguilla
quenelles; dumplings	Nockerln	noques; quenelles	gnocchetti	albondiguillas
quiche flan	Quiche *f*	quiche *f*	quiche *f*	quiche; torta *f*
ragout; stew	Ragout *n*	sauté *m*; ragoût *m*	stufato *m*; spezzatino *m*	ragú *m*; ragout *m*; guisado *m*
raisins	Rosinen	raisins secs	uvetta; uva passa	pasas; uvas pasas
rare; underdone	halb durch; englisch; blutig (Steak)	saignant	al sangue	poco hecho
raspberry vinegar	Himbeeressig	vinaigre de framboises	aceto di lamponi	vinagre de frambuesa
rate; price; charge	Preis *m*	prix *m*	prezzo *m*	precio *m*
raw	roh	cru	crudo	crudo
ready	fertig	prêt	pronto	listo
~ dishes	fertige Gerichte	plats tout prêts	piatti pronti	platos listos
recipe	Rezept *n*	recette *f*	ricetta *f*	receta *f*
refrigerator	Kühlschrank *m*	réfrigérateur; frigidaire	frigorifero *m*	nevera *f*; frigorífico *m*; refrigerador *m*
regional cuisine	regionale Küche	cuisine régionale	cucina regionale	cocina regional
~ dish; local dish	typisches Gericht; Gericht *n* der Region	plat typique; ~ *m* local; mets *m* local	piatto *m* tipico	plato *m* típico; ~ *m* local
~ specialities	regionale Spezialitäten	spécialités régionales	specialità regionali	especialidades regionales
regular customer; patron	Stammgast *m*	habitué; client régulier	cliente *m* abituale	cliente *m* habitual

---

[1] 0.3 pints

Culinary and service terms

Terminology English	**Fachausdrücke** German	**Terminologie** French	**Terminologia** Italian	**Terminología** Spanish
remainder; change	Rest *m* (von Geld)	reste *m*; restant *m*	resto *m*	vuelta *f*; resto *m*
reserved	reserviert	réservé	riservato; prenotato	reservado
~ table	reservierter Tisch	table réservée	tavolo riservato	mesa reservada
restaurant	Restaurant *n*; Gasthaus *n*	restaurant *m*	ristorante *m*; trattoria *f*	restaurante *m*; fonda *f*
~, vegetarian	vegetarisches Restaurant	~ *m* végétarien	~ vegetariano	~ vegetariano
rind; peel	Schale *f* (von Obst); Rinde *f*	pelure *f* (de fruit); écorce *f*	buccia *f*; scorza *f*	piel *f* (de fruta); cáscara *f*
ring	Rand *m*; Ring *m*	bordure *f*; couronne *f*; turban	corona *f*; anello *m*	corona *f*
ripe	reif	mûr	maturo	maduro
roast; joint	Braten *m*	rôti *m*	arrosto *m*	asado
roast; roasted	gebraten	rôti	arrostito; arrosto	asado
roll; roulade	Röllchen *n*; Roulade *f*	paupiette *f*	involtino *m*	rollo; rollito; popieta
rolling cart; trolley; wagon	Wagen *m*; Servierwagen *m*	chariot *m*; voiture *f*	carrello *m*	carrito[1] *m*
room service	Zimmerservice *m*	service à l'étage	servizio *m* in camera	servicio *m* en habitación
roux (flour browned in fat)	Mehlschwitze *f*; Einbrenne *f*	roux *m* (farine roussie dans du beurre)	roux; salsa *f* rossa (farina rosolata nel burro)	salsa *f* rubia (harina tostada en mantequilla)
royal icing	Zuckerguss *m*	glace *f* royale	glassa reale	baño de azúcar; glasa *f* real
rye	Roggen *m*	seigle *m*	segale *f*	centeno *m*
salad bowl	Salatschüssel *f*	saladier *m*	insalatiera *f*	ensaladera *f*
~ buffet	Salatbuffet	salades au buffet	buffet di insalate	buffet de ensaladas
~ dressing; dressing	Dressing *n*; Salatsauce *f*	sauce (pour salades)	condimento (per insalata)	salsa (para ensaladas)
salmi; game stew[2]; civet	Wildragout *n*; Salmi *n*; Civet *n*	ragoût de gibier; salmis *m*; civet	stufato di selvaggina; salmì *m*; civet	estofado de caza[3]; salmis; civet
salt	Salz *n*	sel *m*	sale *m*	sal *f*
salt; pickled; cured	gepökelt	salé; saumuré	salato; in salamoia	salado; salpreso
salt-cellar[4]; salt-sifter	Salzstreuer *m*	salière *f*	saliera *f*	salero *m*
salty	salzig	salé	salato	salado
sauce boat; gravy boat	Soßenschüssel *f*; Sauciere *f*	saucière *f*	salsiera *f*	salsera *f*

1) o carrito de servicio - 2) also ragout of game - 3) o ragú de caza - 4) Am. saltshaker

Culinary and service terms

Terminology English	**Fachausdrücke** German	**Terminologie** French	**Terminologia** Italian	**Terminología** Spanish
saucer	Untertasse *f*	soucoupe *f*	piattino *m*	platillo *m*
sauerkraut	Sauerkraut *n*	choucroute *f*	crauti *pl*	chucrut *m*
sauté; sautéed; pan-fried	gebraten (in der Pfanne oder in Butter); geröstet (in der Pfanne); sautiert	poêlé; sauté	sauté[1]; saltato; rosolato; fritto nel burro	salteado; rehogado
savoury; tasty	schmackhaft	savoureux (*f* savoureuse)	saporito; gustoso	sabroso; apetitoso
sea fish; marine fish	Seefisch	poisson de mer	pesce di mare	pescado de mar
~ salt	Meersalz	sel marin	sale marino	sal marina
seasonal dishes	saisonale Gerichte	plats de saison	piatti stagionali	platos de temporada
seasoning	Würze *f*	assaisonnement *m*	condimento *m*	condimento *m*
second course	zweiter Gang	deuxième plat	secondo piatto	segundo plato
seed oil	Samenöl	huile végétale	olio di semi	aceite de semillas
selection; choice	Auswahl	assortiment	assortimento	surtido
self-service; cafeteria	Selbstbedienungs-Restaurant	restaurant libre-service	self-service	restaurante autoservicio
semolina	Grieß *m*	semoule *f*	semolino	sémola
service; attendance	Bedienung *f*	service *m*	servizio *m*	servicio *m*
~ (not) included; tip (not) included	~ (nicht) inbegriffen; Trinkgeld (nicht) inbegriffen	~ (non) compris; pourboire (non) compris	~ (non) compreso; mancia (non) inclusa	~ (no) incluido
~ table	Serviertisch *m*	table *f* de service	tavolo *m* di servizio	mesa *f* de servicio; aparador *m*
serviette; napkin	Serviette *f*	serviette *f*	tovagliolo *m*; salvietta *f*	servilleta *f*
serving; helping; portion	Portion *f*	portion *f*	porzione *f*	ración *f*; porción *f*
set menu; day's bill of fare	Tageskarte *f*	carte *f* du jour	lista *f* del giorno	carta *f* del día
sharp; hot; spicy	pikant; scharf	épicé; piquant	piccante	picante
~ (knife)	scharf (Messer)	coupant; tranchant	tagliente; affilato	afilado; cortante
sherry vinegar	Sherryessig	vinaigre de xérès	aceto di sherry	vinagre de jerez

---

[1] undeklinierbar

Culinary and service terms

Terminology English	Fachausdrücke German	Terminologie French	Terminologia Italian	Terminología Spanish
short pastry	Mürbeteig *m*	pâte sablée; ~ sucrée	pasta frolla *f*	pasta *f* quebrada dulce; pastaflora *f*
shortcrust pastry; short pastry	Pastetenteig; Mürbeteig	~ brisée; ~ à foncer	~ brisée	~ quebrada
sieve	Sieb *n*; Mehlsieb *n*	tamis *m*	setaccio *m*	tamiz *m*
single-dish meal; hot pot; hotchpotch	Eintopf; Eintopfgericht	plat unique; potée	piatto unico	plato único; puchero
siphon; siphon-bottle	Siphon *m*	siphon *m*	sifone *m*	sifón *m*
skewer; brochette; kebab	Spießchen *n*	brochette *f*	spiedino *m*	brocheta *f*; broqueta *f*
slice	Scheibe *f*; Schnitte *f*	tranche *f*	fetta *f*; trancia *f*; trancio *m*	lonja; rebanada *f* (Brot); tajada *f*
small; little	klein	petit	piccolo	pequeño
~ change; change	Kleingeld *n*; Wechselgeld *n*	monnaie *f*; petit monnaie *f*	spiccioli *m pl*	dinero *m* suelto; calderilla *f*
~ glass; liqueur glass	Likörglas *n*	petit verre; verre à liqueur	bicchierino *m*	copita *f*
smell; odour	Geruch *m*	odeur *f*	odore *m*	olor *m*
smoked	geräuchert	fumé	affumicato	ahumado
smothered; stewed	gedünstet	étuvé; en ragoût	stufato; in umido	estofado; guisado
snack	Imbiss *m*	casse-croûte[1] *m*; en-cas *m*	spuntino *m*	refrigerio *m*; tentempié *m*; colación *f*
snack-bar	Imbissstube; Snackbar	snack; snack-bar; cafétéria	tavola calda	cafetería
soft	weich	mou (*f* molle)	molle	blando
soft; tender	zart	tendre	tenero	tierno
soigné; carefully prepared	soigniert; gepflegt	soigné	soigné; curato	esmerado
sommelier; wine butler	Weinkellner *m*; Sommelier	sommelier *m*	sommelier	sumiller; sommelier
soufflé; gratin	Auflauf *m*	gratin; soufflé *m*	gratin; soufflé *m*	gratén; soufflé; suflé *m*
soufflé	Soufflé *n*	soufflé *m*	soufflé *m*	soufflé; suflé *m*
soup-plate	Suppenteller *m*	assiette *f* creuse	piatto *m* fondo	plato sopero; ~ hondo
soup-tureen; tureen	Suppenschüssel *f*	soupière *f*	zuppiera *f*	sopera *f*

---

[1] ou légère collation

Culinary and service terms

Terminology English	Fachausdrücke German	Terminologie French	Terminologia Italian	Terminología Spanish
sour; acid	sauer	aigre; acide; sur	acido	ácido; agrio
~ cream; soured cream	Sauerrahm *m*	crème aigre	panna acida	nata agria; crema agria
souse; marinade; pickle	Marinade *f*, Beize *f*	marinade *f*	marinata	marinada *f*, adobo; escabeche *m*
souse; brine; pickle	Salzlake; Pökel *m*	saumure *f*	salamoia *f*	salmuera *f*, adobo *m*
soused; marinated; pickled	mariniert; gebeizt	mariné; en marinade	marinato	marinado; en escabeche; adobado
speciality; special	Spezialität *f*	spécialité *f*	specialità *f*	especialidad *f*
spelt	Dinkel	épeautre *m*	farro	espelta; farro
spicy; hot; sharp	pikant; scharf	épicé; piquant	piccante	picante
spit-roasted; on the spit	vom Spieß	à la broche	allo spiedo	al asador
sponge; biscuit dough	Biskuitteig *m*	pâte à biscuit[1]	pan di Spagna; pasta margherita	bizcocho
spoon	Löffel *m*	cuiller *f*, cuillère *f*	cucchiaio *m*	cuchara *f*
starters from the trolley	Vorspeisen vom Wagen	chariot des hors-d'œuvre	antipasti dal carrello	carrito de entremeses
steamed	gedämpft	à la vapeur	al vapore	al vapor
stew; ragout	Ragout *n*	sauté *m*; ragoût *m*	stufato *m*; spezzatino *m*	ragú *m*; ragout *m*; guisado
stewed; smothered	gedünstet	étuvé; en ragoût	stufato; in umido	estofado; guisado
~ fruit; compote	Kompott *n*	compote *f*	frutta cotta; composta	compota *f*
stewpan; casserole	Kasserolle *f*, Schmortopf *m*	cocotte *f*, casserole *f*	casseruola *f*	cacerola *f*, cazo *m*
stock cube; bouillon cube; meat cube	Suppenwürfel	tablette de bouillon	dado *m* per brodo	cubito de caldo[2]
strainer	Sieb *n*; Teesieb; Seiher *m*	passoire *f*	colino *m*	colador *m*
straw; drinking-straw	Strohhalm *m*; Trinkhalm *m*	paille *f*, chalumeau *m*	cannuccia *f*	paja *f*, pajita *f*
streaky bacon; pancetta	durchwachsener Speck	lard maigre; ~ de poitrine	pancetta	tocino entreverado
stuffed; filled	gefüllt	farci	ripieno; farcito	relleno

---

1) ou génoise - 2) o pastilla de caldo

Culinary and service terms

Terminology English	Fachausdrücke German	Terminologie French	Terminologia Italian	Terminología Spanish
stuffing; filling; dressing; farce	Füllung f; Farce f	farce f	ripieno m; farcia f	relleno m
succulent; juicy	saftig	juteux (f juteuse)	sugoso[1]	jugoso; suculento
suet	Nierenfett n	graisse f de rognon	grasso m di rognone	grasa f de riñones
sugar	Zucker m	sucre m	zucchero m	azúcar m
sugar-bowl; sugar-basin	Zuckerdose f	sucrier m	zuccheriera f	azucarero m
sugar-candy	Kandiszucker	sucre candi	zucchero candito	azúcar cande; ~ candi
sugar-tongs	Zuckerzange f	pinces f à sucre	mollette f per lo zucchero	tenacillas f para azúcar
sugared	gezuckert	sucré	zuccherato	azucarado
suggested dishes	empfohlene Gerichte	plats recommandés	piatti consigliati	platos recomendados
sunflower oil	Sonnenblumenöl	huile de tournesol	olio di girasole	aceite de girasol
sweet (course); dessert	Dessert n; Nachtisch m	dessert m	dessert m	postre m
sweet	süß	doux (f douce)	dolce	dulce
sweet; ~ dish; dessert	Süßspeise f	entremets m	dolce m	dulce m
sweet-and-sour	süßsauer	à l'aigre-doux	in agrodolce	en agridulce
sweetened	gesüßt	édulcoré	edulcorato	edulcorado
sweets from the trolley	Nachspeisen vom Wagen	chariot des desserts	dolci dal carrello	carrito de postres
syrup	Sirup m	sirop m	sciroppo m	jarabe m; sirope m
table	Tisch m	table f	tavolo m; tavola f	mesa f
~ by the window	~ am Fenster	~ près de la fenêtre	~ vicino alla finestra	~ cerca de la ventana
~ for ... persons	~ für ... Personen	~ pour ... couverts	~ per ... persone	~ para ... personas
~, occupied; engaged table	besetzter Tisch	~ occupée	~ occupato	~ ocupada
tablecloth	Tischtuch n	nappe f	tovaglia f	mantel m
tables on the terrace	Tische auf der Terrasse	tables en terrasse	tavoli in terrazza	mesas en la terraza
taste; flavour	Geschmack m	goût m; saveur f	gusto m; sapore m	gusto m; sabor m
tasteless; insipid; flat	geschmacklos; fade	fade; sans goût	insipido	insípido; soso
tasting menu	Degustationsmenü	menu dégustation	menu degustazione	menú de degustación
tasty; savoury	schmackhaft	savoureux (f savoureuse)	saporito; gustoso	sabroso; apetitoso

---

[1] o succoso

Culinary and service terms

Terminology English	**Fachausdrücke** German	**Terminologie** French	**Terminologia** Italian	**Terminología** Spanish
tea spoon	Teelöffel *m*	petite cuiller; cuiller *f* à thé	cucchiaino *m*	cucharilla *f*; cucharita *f*
teapot	Teekanne *f*	théière *f*	teiera *f*	tetera *f*
teatime; afternoon tea	Jause *f*	goûter *m*; five o'clock	merenda *f*	merienda *f*, café *m* (de las cinco)
telephone	Telefon *n*	téléphone *m*	telefono *m*	teléfono *m*
tender; soft	zart	tendre	tenero	tierno
tepid; lukewarm; warm	lauwarm	tiède	tiepido	tibio; templado
terrine; pâté	Terrine; Pastete ohne Teigumhüllung	terrine; pâté en terrine	terrina	paté; terrina
thank you!	danke!	merci!	grazie!	gracias
~ you very much!	~ bestens!; besten Dank!	~ beaucoup!	~ tante!	muchas gracias
the chef suggests	der Chef empfiehlt; unser Küchenchef empfiehlt	le chef vous recommande	lo chef consiglia	el chef recomienda
thick	dickflüssig	épais (*f* épaisse)	denso	espeso; denso
thin	dünn	mince	sottile	delgado
three-course menu	Drei-Gänge-Menü	menu à trois plats	menu di tre portate	menú de tres platos
timbale	Timbale *f* (Auflauf)	timbale *f*	timballo *m*	timbal *m* (pastel relleno)
tin-opener; can-opener	Dosenöffner *m*	ouvre-boîte *m*	apriscatole *m*	abrelatas *m*
tinned; canned	Dosen-...	en boîte; ~ conserve	in scatola	en lata; ~ conserva
tip; gratuity	Trinkgeld *n*	pourboire *m*	mancia *f*	propina *f*
~ (not) included; service (not) included	Bedienung (nicht) inbegriffen; Trinkgeld (nicht) inbegriffen	service (non) compris; pourboire (non) compris	servizio (non) compreso; mancia (non) inclusa	servicio (no) incluido
to abstain from meat	kein Fleisch essen	faire maigre	mangiare di magro	comer de vigilia
to add	hinzufügen	ajouter	aggiungere	añadir; agregar
to bake	backen (im Ofen)	cuire au four	cuocere in forno	cocer al horno; hornear
to be enough	genügen	suffire	bastare	bastar
to be mistaken	sich irren	se tromper	sbagliare	equivocarse

Culinary and service terms

Terminology English	Fachausdrücke German	Terminologie French	Terminologia Italian	Terminología Spanish
to beat; to whip; beaten; whipped	schlagen; geschlagen	fouetter; fouetté	sbattere; sbattuto	batir; batido
to bind; to thicken	legieren (Sauce, Suppe); binden	lier	legare; addensare	ligar; espesar
to blanch	blanchieren	blanchir	scottare	blanquear
to blend; to mix	mischen	mélanger; mêler	mescolare	mezclar
to bone; boned; boneless	entbeinen; ausbeinen; entbeint	désosser; désossé	disossare; disossato	deshuesar[1]; deshuesado
to book; to reserve	vormerken; reservieren	réserver; retenir	prenotare; riservare	reservar
to braise; to stew	schmoren	braiser	brasare; stufare	estofar; brasear
to bring	bringen	apporter	portare	traer
to broil; to grill	grillen[2]	griller	grigliare	emparrillar
to brown slightly	anbraten	gaire revenir	soffriggere	sofreír; rehogar
to call	rufen	appeler	chiamare	llamar
to carve	zerlegen; tranchieren	découper	trinciare	trinchar
to choose; to select	wählen	choisir	scegliere	escoger; elegir
to clear[3]	abräumen; wegräumen	desservir	sparecchiare	quitar la mesa
to coat	nappieren	napper	cospargere; nappare	napar; bañar
to cook	kochen	cuire	cuocere	cocer; hervir; cocinar; guisar
to cool	abkühlen	refroidir	raffreddare	enfriar[4]
to cover	zudecken	couvrir	coprire	cubrir
to cut	schneiden	couper	tagliare	cortar
to deep-fry; to fry	backen (in der Pfanne); frittieren	frire	friggere	freír
to desire; to wish	wünschen	désirer	desiderare	desear
to dine; to have dinner	zu Abend essen	dîner	cenare; pranzare	cenar; comer
to displease	bedauern	regretter	dispiacere	sentir; desagradar
to dredge; to sprinkle	bestreuen	saupoudrer	cospargere	espolvorear

1) o desosar - 2) auch grillieren - 3) or to clear away - 4) o poner a enfriar

Culinary and service terms

Terminology English	**Fachausdrücke** German	**Terminologie** French	**Terminologia** Italian	**Terminología** Spanish
to dress the salad	den Salat anmachen	assaisonner la salade	condire l'insalata	aderezar la ensalada[1]
to drink	trinken	boire	bere	beber
to eat	essen; speisen	manger	mangiare	comer
to eat à la carte	à la carte essen	~ à la carte	~ alla carta	~ a la carta
to farce; to stuff	füllen; farcieren	farcir	farcire	rellenar
to fill[2]	füllen	remplir	riempire	rellenar
to flour	mit Mehl bestreuen	enfariner	infarinare	enharinar
to fry; to deep-fry	backen (in der Pfanne); frittieren	frire	friggere	freír
to garnish; garnished	garnieren; garniert; mit Beilage	garnir; garni	guarnire; guarnito; con contorno	guarnecer; guarnecido
to grill; to broil	grillen[3]	griller	grigliare	emparrillar
to grind; ground	mahlen; gemahlen	moudre; moulu	macinare; macinato	moler; molido
to have breakfast[4]	frühstücken	déjeuner	far colazione	desayunar
to have dinner; to dine	zu Abend essen	dîner	cenare; pranzare	cenar; comer
to have lunch; to lunch	~ Mittag essen	déjeuner	pranzare	almorzar
to heat up; to warm up; to reheat	aufwärmen	réchauffer	riscaldare	recalentar
to lay; to put	legen	mettre	mettere	poner; meter
to lay the table	den Tisch decken	~ le couvert; dresser la table	apparecchiare la tavola	~ la mesa
to lunch; to have lunch	zu Mittag essen	déjeuner	pranzare	almorzar
to melt	zerlassen	fondre	fondere	derretir; fundir
to mix; to blend	mischen	mélanger; mêler	mescolare	mezclar
to open	öffnen	ouvrir	aprire	abrir
to order	bestellen	commander	ordinare	pedir; encargar; ordenar
to peel	schälen	éplucher	sbucciare	pelar; mondar
to pepper	pfeffern	poivrer	pepare	sazonar con pimienta

1) o aliñar la ensalada - 2) or to fill up - 3) auch grillieren - 4) also to breakfast

Culinary and service terms

Terminology English	**Fachausdrücke** German	**Terminologie** French	**Terminologia** Italian	**Terminología** Spanish
to pit; to stone	entkernen	énoyauter	snocciolare	deshuesar
to poach	pochieren	pocher	sobbollire; bollire per il pepe	escalfar; hervir; cocer
to pour[1]	einschenken	verser	versare (da bere)	echar (de beber)
to prefer	vorziehen	préférer	preferire	preferir
to prepare	zubereiten	préparer	preparare	preparar
to put; to lay	legen	mettre	mettere	poner; meter
to put in warm	warm stellen	~ au chaud	~ in caldo	~ a calentar
to recommend; to suggest	empfehlen	conseiller; recommander	consigliare	recomendar; aconsejar
to reduce	einkochen; eindicken	réduire	ridurre; condensare	reducir
to reheat; to warm up; to heat up	aufwärmen	réchauffer	riscaldare	recalentar
to replace; to substitute	ersetzen	remplacer	sostituire	sustituir; remplazar
to reserve; to book	vormerken; reservieren	réserver; retenir	prenotare; riservare	reservar
to roast	braten	rôtir	arrostire	asar
to salt; salted	salzen; gesalzen	saler; salé	salare; salato	salar; salado
to season; to spice	würzen	assaisonner	condire; aromatizzare	condimentar; sazonar
to select; to choose	wählen	choisir	scegliere	escoger; elegir
to serve	auftragen; bedienen; servieren	servir	servire	servir
to shape; to turn	tournieren	tourner	dar forma	tornear
to show	zeigen	montrer	monstrare	mostrar
to sift; to sieve	sieben	tamiser	setacciare; passare al setaccio	tamizar
to spice; to season	würzen	assaisonner	condire; aromatizzare	condimentar; sazonar
to spread	bestreichen	tartiner	spalmare	untar
to sprinkle; to dredge	bestreuen	saupoudrer	cospargere	espolvorear
to squeeze	auspressen; pressen	presser	spremere	exprimir
to stew	dünsten	étuver; braiser	stufare	estofar

---

[1] also to pour out

Culinary and service terms

Terminology English	**Fachausdrücke** German	**Terminologie** French	**Terminologia** Italian	**Terminología** Spanish
to stew; to braise	schmoren	braiser	brasare; stufare	estofar; brasear
to stone; to pit	entkernen	énoyauter	snocciolare	deshuesar
to stuff; to farce	füllen; farcieren	farcir	farcire	rellenar
to substitute; to replace	ersetzen	remplacer	sostituire	sustituir; remplazar
to sugar	zuckern	sucrer	zuccherare	azucarar
to suggest; to recommend	empfehlen	conseiller; recommander	consigliare	recomendar; aconsejar
to sweeten	süßen	édulcorer	dolcificare	edulcorar; dulcificar
to taste	kosten; probieren; versuchen; schmecken	goûter (Getränke: déguster)	assaggiare	degustar[1]; probar
to the left	links	à gauche	a sinistra	a la izquierda
to the right	rechts	~ droite	~ destra	~ la derecha
to thicken; to bind	legieren (Sauce, Suppe); binden	lier	legare; addensare	ligar; espesar
to thin out	verdünnen	allonger	allungare	diluir
to turn; to shape	tournieren	tourner	dar forma	tornear
to turn out; to unmould	stürzen (aus der Form)	démouler	sformare	desmoldar
to turn sour	sauer werden	tourner à l'aigre	diventar acido; inacidire	agriarse; cuajarse (leche)
to uncork	entkorken	déboucher	stappare; sturare	destapar; descorchar
to unmould; to turn out	stürzen (aus der Form)	démouler	sformare	desmoldar
to warm up; to heat up; to reheat	aufwärmen	réchauffer	riscaldare	recalentar
to whip; to beat; beaten; whipped	schlagen; geschlagen	fouetter; fouetté	sbattere; sbattuto	batir; batido
to wish; to desire	wünschen	désirer	desiderare	desear
to write	schreiben	écrire	scrivere	escribir
today special[2]; dish of the day	Tagesgericht *n*	plat *m* du jour	piatto *m* del giorno	plato *m* del día

---

1) o gustar - 2) or today speciality

Culinary and service terms

Terminology English	Fachausdrücke German	Terminologie French	Terminologia Italian	Terminología Spanish
toilets; lavatory[1]	Toiletten *f pl*	toilettes *f pl*; lavabos *m pl*	toilette *f*; gabinetto *m*; bagno *m*	servicios *pl*; retrete *m*; lavabo *m*
tomato paste; ~ purée	Tomatenmark *n*	concentré *m* de tomates	concentrato di pomodoro	concentrado de tomate; conserva *f* de tomate
too; ~ much	zu; ~ viel	trop	troppo	demasiado
toothpicks	Zahnstocher *m*	cure-dents *m*	stuzzicadenti *m*	palillos *m*; mondadientes *m*
tough	zäh	coriace	duro; tiglioso	duro
tourist menu	Touristenmenü	menu touristique	menu turistico	menú turístico
traditional cuisine	traditionelle Küche	cuisine traditionnelle	cucina tradizionale	cocina tradicional
tray	Tablett *n*	plateau *m*	vassoio *m*	bandeja *f*
treacle; golden syrup[2]	Melasse; Zuckersirup	mélasse *f*	melassa *f*	melaza *f*
trolley; wagon; rolling cart	Wagen *m*; Servierwagen *m*	chariot *m*; voiture *f*	carrello *m*	carrito[3] *m*
truffled	getrüffelt	truffé	tartufato; con tartufi	trufado
tumbler; water glass	Wasserglas *n*	verre *m* à eau	bicchiere *m* da acqua	vaso *m* para agua
tureen; soup-tureen	Suppenschüssel *f*	soupière *f*	zuppiera *f*	sopera *f*
underdone; rare	halb durch; englisch; blutig (Steak)	saignant	al sangue	poco hecho
unripe	unreif	non mûr	non maturo; acerbo	no maduro
unsalted	salzlos	sans sel	~ salato	sin sal
vacant table; free table	freier Tisch	table libre	tavolo libero	mesa libre
vanilla pod; ~ bean	Vanilleschote *f*	gousse *f* de vanille	stecca di vaniglia	vaina de vainilla
~ sugar	Vanillezucker	sucre vanillé	zucchero vanigliato	azúcar vainillado
vegetable fat	Pflanzenfett *n*	graisse *f* végétale	grasso *m* vegetale	grasa *f* vegetal
vegetables *pl*	Gemüse *n*	légumes *m pl*	verdura *f*	verduras
~ in season	Beilagen je nach Jahreszeit	garniture de saison	contorno di stagione	guarnición del tiempo
vegetarian	vegetarisch	végétarien	vegetariano	vegetariano
~ cuisine	vegetarische Küche	cuisine végétarienne	cucina vegetariana	cocina vegetariana
~ restaurant	vegetarisches Restaurant	restaurant *m* végétarien	ristorante vegetariano	restaurante vegetariano

1) Am. restroom, ladies' room, men's room - 2) Am. molasses - 3) o carrito de servicio

Culinary and service terms

Terminology English	**Fachausdrücke** German	**Terminologie** French	**Terminologia** Italian	**Terminología** Spanish
very good; excellent; first-class	ausgezeichnet	excellent	eccellente; ottimo	excelente
vine leaves	Weinblätter	feuilles de vigne	foglie di vite	hojas de vid
vinegar	Essig *m*	vinaigre *m*	aceto *m*	vinagre *m*
vintage year; ~ date	Jahrgang; Weinjahr	millésime *m*; année *f*	annata *f*	añada; año *m*
virgin olive oil	reines Olivenöl	huile d'olive vierge	olio vergine d'oliva	aceite de oliva virgen
wagon; trolley; rolling cart	Wagen *m*; Servierwagen *m*	chariot *m*; voiture *f*	carrello *m*	carrito[1] *m*
waiter	Ober *m*; Kellner *m*	garçon *m*	cameriere *m*	camarero[2] *m*
waiting time: ... minutes	Zubereitungszeit: ... Minuten	... minutes d'attente	... minuti d'attesa	... minutos de esperea
waitress	Kellnerin *f*	serveuse *f*	cameriera *f*	camarera *f*
warm; lukewarm; tepid	lauwarm	tiède	tiepido	tibio; templado
warm	warm	chaud	caldo	caliente
water glass; tumbler	Wasserglas *n*	verre *m* à eau	bicchiere *m* da acqua	vaso *m* para agua
well done	gut durchgebraten	bien cuit	ben cotto	bien hecho
wheat	Weizen *m*	blé *m*; froment *m*	grano *m*; frumento *m*	trigo *m*
~ flour	Weizenmehl	farine de froment	farina di frumento	harina de trigo
whip; mousse	Schaum; Schaumcreme	mousse *f*	spuma *f*; mousse *f*	espuma *f*; mousse
whipped cream; Chantilly	Schlagsahne *f*	crème Chantilly[3]	panna montata	nata batida; ~ montada; chantillí
white chocolate	weiße Schokolade	chocolat blanc	cioccolato bianco	chocolate blanco
~ of egg; egg white	Eiweiß *n*	blanc *m* d'œuf	chiara *f* d'uovo; albume *m*	clara *f* de huevo
whole; entire	ganz (ungeteilt)	entier; tout	intero; tutto	entero; todo
wholemeal flour	Vollkornmehl	farine complète	farina integrale	harina integral
~ pasta	Vollkornnudeln	pâtes au blé complet[4]	pasta integrale	pasta integral
~ spaghetti	Vollkornspaghetti	spaghettis au blé complet	spaghetti integrali	espaguetis integrales
wild	wild	sauvage	selvatico	silvestre; salvaje
~ rice	Wildreis	riz sauvage	riso selvaggio	arroz salvaje

1) o carrito de servicio - 2) Am. mozo *m* - 3) ou crème fouettée - 4) ou pâtes intégrales

Culinary and service terms

Terminology English	**Fachausdrücke** German	**Terminologie** French	**Terminologia** Italian	**Terminología** Spanish
wine butler; sommelier	Weinkellner *m*; Sommelier	sommelier *m*	sommelier	sumiller; sommelier
wine-cradle	Weinflaschen-Korb *m*	panier verseur	cestino *m* versavino	cesta para botellas
wine glass	Weinglas *n*	verre *m* à vin	bicchiere *m* da vino	vaso *m* para vino; copa *f* para vino
wine-list	Weinkarte *f*	carte *f* des vins	lista *f* dei vini	carta *f* de vinos
with aromatic spices	mit Aromen	aux aromates	agli aromi	con especias
~ herbs	~ Kräutern	~ herbes; ~ fines herbes	alle erbe	a las hierbas
~ vegetables	~ Beilagen	garni	con contorno	con guarnición
wood-burning oven	Holzofen	four à bois	forno a legna	horno de leña
yeast	Hefe	levain; levure *f*	lievito *m*	levadura *f*
~ dough; ~ pastry	Hefeteig *m*	pâte levée	pasta *f* lievitata	masa de levadura
yogurt[1]	Jogurt[2] *m* u. *n*	yaourt; yogourt	yogurt[3]	yogur
yolk of egg; egg-yolk	Eigelb *n*	jaune *m* d'œuf	rosso *m* d'uovo; tuorlo *m*	yema *f* (de huevo)
zest; peel (lemon)	Schale *f* (von Zitrusfrüchten)	zeste *m*	buccia *f*; scorza *f* (di agrumi)	corteza *f*; cáscara *f* (de limón o naranja)

---

1) or yoghurt - 2) oder Joghurt - 3) o iogurt, yoghurt

Glossary and historical comments

Alsacienne, à l'	dish garnished with sauerkraut
Amphitryon	a munificent host
Anglaise, à l'	vegetables cooked in salt water; fish coated in egg-and-breadcrumb and then sautéd or deep-fried
Argenteuil	dish garnished with asparagus (town, northwest of Paris, renowned for its asparagus fields)
Bacchus	Roman god of wine
béarnaise, à la	dish served with sauce béarnaise (from Béarn, a former French province)
Béchamel, Louis de	Marquis de Béchamel, steward of Louis XIV. He is supposed to have invented the béchamel sauce.
beignet	from the Celtic bigne (tumor, swelling)
Bellevue, en	dish of fish or poultry in jelly, richly garnished
Bercy	suburb of Paris
Bernhardt, Sarah	celebrated French actress (1844–1923)
bigarade	bitter kind of orange
Bismarck, Otto	Fürst von Bismarck, first chancellor of The German Empire (1815–1898)
Bourguignonne, à la	dish cooked in red wine, usually garnished with small onions and button mushrooms
Bretonne, à la	dish garnished with white beans, whole or mashed
Brillat-Savarin, Anthelme	French lawyer, politician, and writer, author of the celebrated work "Physiologie du goût" (1755–1826)
Brunoise	vegetables cut into small cubes
canapés	small (toasted) slices of bread topped with a savoury
cantaloup	a variety of melon. The name derives from Cantalupo, near Rome.

Glossary and historical comments

Cardinal	dish of marine fish garnished with lobster
Carême, Marie-Antoine	famous French chef, author of many works on gastronomy (Le Maître d'hôtel français, Le cruisinieur parisien, etc.; 1784–1833)
Chantilly, à la	dish with sweetened or flavoured whipped cream (from Chantilly, near Paris, celebrated for its château and racecourse)
Chateaubriand, François-René	French diplomat and author, born in Saint-Malo (1768–1848)
chaud-froid	dish of cold cooked meat, poultry, fish or game served in jelly
civet	hare or game stew cooked with red wine and the animal's blood
Clamart	dish garnished with peas (a southwest suburb of Paris)
Colbert, Jean-Baptiste	French statesman, minister of finance to King Louis XIV (1619–1683)
Conti	dish with mashed lentils (Princes de Conti, a junior branch of the House of Condé)
Cordon bleu	the "blue ribbon" worn by the Knights-grand-cross of the Holy Ghost; applied by extension to a first-class cook
court-bouillon	stock flavoured with wine (or vinegar) and spices, used in fish dishes
crapaudine, en	pigeon or chicken shaped like a toad and grilled; from the French "crapaud" (toad)
Crécy	dish garnished with carrots (Crécy-en-Ponthieu, town in the French Somme department)
curry	hot Indian mixture of ground spices containing turmeric, cardamom, coriander, ginger, cumin, etc; also a dish flavoured with this
Diana	Roman goddess of hunting, the Greek Artemis

Glossary and historical comments

du Barry	dish garnished with cauliflower (Comtesse du Barry, mistress of the French king Louis XV, condemned by the Revolutionary Tribunal of Paris and guillotined; 1743–1793)
Dubois, Urbain François	French cook, author of several books on the culinary art (1818–1901)
Dugléré, Adolphe	celebrated French chef of the Café Anglais in Paris (1805–1884)
duxelles	sautéd chopped mushrooms used as a stuffing or a garnish
entrée	dish served before the joint
entremets	sweet dish
Esau	in the Old Testament, son of Isaac and Rebekah. He sold his birthright to his brother Jacob for a lentil dish.
Escoffier, Auguste	French chef, known as "the king of chefs and the chef of kings", author of the famous "Le guide culinaire", translated into all languages (1847–1935)
Flamande, à la	dish garnished with cabbage (from Flanders, an ancient countship)
fleurons	puffs of pastry-work for use as a garnish
florentine, à la	dish garnished with spinach
forestière, à la	dish with wild mushrooms, chiefly chanterelles and morels
gastronomy	the art and science of good eating and drinking, including the preparation and service of food
gourmet	a connaisseur of fine wine and food
Grimod de la Reynière	French gourmet, author of the "Almanach des gourmands" (1758–1837)
Helder	Dutch port, naval battle between an Anglo-French and a Dutch fleet in 1673
Holstein	– Friedrich Holstein, German diplomat (1837–1909) – German region, now part of Schleswig-Holstein

Glossary and historical comments

Hongroise, à la	dish flavoured with paprika
Indienne, à l'	dish flavoured with curry and usually served with rice
jardinière, à la	dish garnished with various vegetables
Joinville	François d'Orléans, Prince de Joinville, third son of Louis-Philippe, king of the French (1818–1900)
Judic, à la	dish garnished with braised lettuce (Anna Judic, French comedienne; 1850–1911)
Julienne, en	vegetables (or truffles and other foodstuff) cut into thin strips
Lady Curzon	wife of Lord Curzon, Great Britain's viceroy of India (1859–1925)
Londonderry	Charles William Vane, Marquis of Londonderry, English statesman (1778–1854)
Lucullus	Roman general, famous for the luxury of his banquets (106–57 B.C.)
Lyonnaise, à la	dish with sautéd onions (from Lyon, capital of the French Rhône department)
Macaire, Robert	character in the play "L'Auberge des Adrets", made popular by the French actor Frédérick Lemaître (1800–1876)
Macédoine	mixture of fruit or vegetables cut up small (from Macedonia, multiracial area of the Balkan Peninsula)
Maintenon	Françoise d'Aubigné, Marquise de Maintenon, secretly married to Louis XIV of France (1635–1719)
malossol	delicate, slightly salted caviar; from the Russion "malosolny" (slightly salted)
Maltaise, à la	dish containing blood oranges
Marengo	village in northern Italy, where Napoleon Bonaparte defeated the Austrians (June 14, 1800)
Maryland	Middle Atlantic state of the U.S.
Masséna, André	duc de Rivoli, prince d'Essling, a leading French general (1758–1817)

Glossary and historical comments

Melba	Dame Nellie Melba, stage name of Helen Armstrong Mitchell, Australian operatic soprano, born near Melbourne (1861–1931)
Meyerbeer, Giacomo	German opera composer, born in Berlin (1791–1864)
Mirabeau, Honoré-Gabriel	French politician, one of the greatest orators of the National Assembly (1749–1791)
Mireille	opera by Charles Gounod, based on the Provençal poem by mistral
Mirepoix	mixture of sautéd chopped carrots, onions, celery, and bacon, used in sauces etc. (Duc de Mirepoix, Marshal of France; 1699–1757)
Montmorency	dish containing cherries (– town in the French Seine-et-Oise department, renowned for its cherries – distinguished French family)
Mornay	dish covered with Mornay sauce (a cheese-flavoured white sauce) and gratinated
Mulligatawny	East Indian soup highly seasoned with curry; from Tamil "milagu-tannir" (pepper-water)
Nantua, à la	dish garnished with crayfish (town in the French Ain department)
Natives	top-quality oysters reared in British waters
Navarin	French stew of mutton and vegetables (from Navarino, a Greek port, where the Anglo-French defeated the Turco-Egyptian fleet in 1827)
Nesselrode	dish with mashed chestnuts (Count von Nesselrode, Russian diplomat; 1780–1862)
Newburgh	city on the Hudson River, southeastern New York, U.S.
Niçoise, à la	dish with tomatoes, garlic, olives, and anchovies (from Nice, a French town on the Mediterranean coast)
Normande, à la	dish with cream, cider, calvados, apples, etc (from Normandy, a former province of northern France)

Glossary and historical comments

Orlov	noble Russian family
Paillard	well-known restaurant in Paris
Parmentier	dish with potatoes (Antoine Augustin Parmentier, French agronomist, developed the growing of potatoes in France; 1737–1813)
Périgourdine, à la	dish served with a truffle sauce (from Périgord, a district in the southwest of France, well-known for its truffles)
Piémontaise, à la	dish garnished with risotto (from Piemonte, a region in northern Italy)
Polonaise, à la	boiled vegetables coated with fried breadcrumbs
Pont Neuf	second-oldest bridge across the Seine River in Paris
Portugaise, à la	dish containing tomatoes
Printanière, à la	dish garnished with mixed vegetables
Provençale, à la	dish with olive oil, tomato and garlic (from Provence, a former province in the southeast of France)
Rachel, Elisa	French tragedienne (1820–1858)
ravigote	from the French "ravigoter" (to strengthen)
Richelieu	Louis-François-Armand, duc de Richelieu, Marshal of France and grand-nephew of cardinal de Richelieu (1696–1788)
Rossini	dish garnished with truffles, foie gras, and Madeira sauce (Italian operatic composer and gourmet, celebrated for his comic operas; 1792–1868)
Rothschild	name of a famous European banking dinasty, founded by Mayer Anselm Rothschild, born in Frankfurt am Main in 1743

Glossary and historical comments

Saint-Germain	dish with mashed peas
Saint-Honoré	Parisian gateau, named after the baker's patron saint
Saint-Hubert	dish consisting of game (name of the hunter's patron saint)
Sandwich	named after John Mantagu, Earl of Sandwich, said to have eaten sandwiches when he once spent 24 hours at the gaming-table (1718–1792)
savoury	savoury dish served at the beginning or end of dinner
Sévigné	Marie de Rabutin-Chantal, Marquise de Sévigné, famous for her letters to her daughter Mme de Grignan (1626–1696)
Soubise, à la	dish with mashed onions (Charles de Rohan, prince de Soubise, Marshal of France; 1715–1787)
Strasbourgeoise, à la	dish garnished with sauerkraut and goose-liver
Stroganov	a wealthy Russian merchant family
tabasco	very pungent sauce made from hot red peppers (Tabasco, name of a river and state of Mexico)
Thermidor	the eleventh month of the French revolutionary calendar (from July 19 to August 17); from Greek "thermos" (heat) and "doron" (gift)
Turbigo	town of Lombardy in Italy where the French defeated the Austrians in 1800 and 1859
Vichy, à la	dish garnished with carrots (Spa in the department of Allier in France)
Villeroi, à la	dish coated with sauce Villeroi, then breaded and deep-fried (François de Neufville, duc de Villeroi, Marshal of France; 1644–1730)
Waldorf(-Astoria)	name of a prestigeful hotel in New York, built in 1931

Dishes prepared at the guest's table

Flambé cookery

Nowadays a good chef is supposed to be able to prepare dishes on the chafing-dish. Therefore, there is an increased demand for such recipes.

Classic cookery books do not usually contain any recipes of this kind. Inly maîtres and their assistants are expert in the field, and so we have asked them to contribute some recipes to the book. The following dishes have been chosen because they can be prepared easily and quickly. In this culinary art there are of course no limits to one's creativity and imagination.

USEFUL HINTS

Spirits to be used for flambé dishes must have a high alcoholic content. Should the spirit contain too little alcohol, pure alcohol or a stronger spirit must be added. Some maîtres concoct their own special mixtures.

If you hold the pan in a slanting position and accompany the flame with the spoon filled with spirit, it will flare up more easily.

Sweets should be surrounded by lumps of sugar, which absorb the alcohol and function as wiks to feed the flames.

It is a good idea to sprinkle castor sugar – from as high as possible – over crêpes or omelettes while they are still flambé. The sugar will burn with a slight crackle.

If you do not have much time at your disposal, prepare only desserts. They are served at the end of the meal thus allowing you to work without time pressure.

FOR THE "MISE EN PLACE"

salt, pepper, paprika
icing, castor and lump sugar
spirits
tomato ketchup, Worcester sauce and other sauces
peeled tomatoes
cream
lemons and oranges
a small lemon-squeezer

Other ingredients, such as mustard, curry, etc. according to the dishes to be prepared.

Dishes prepared at the guest's table

Fish

BASS VESUVIUS

Clean the fish, remove the bones and grill (prepare in the kitchen). To make the sauce put some knobs of butter in the chafing-dish pan, add some Worcester sauce, fennel seeds and lemon juice.

Put the grilled fish in the sauce, pour cognac over it and ignite. Serve as soon as the flame dies down.

TROUT IN CHABLIS*

Place some butter in the pan and the lightly floured fish fillets.

When the fillets are browned, remove them, and add cubes of tomatoes, basil leaves, salt and pepper to the sauce.

Let the sauce boil, lay the fillets in it again and pour Chablis over them.

TROUT FOUR SEASONS

Finely chop half a bayleaf, a little parsley, some garlic and onion, one celery leaf and the green of a fennel. Add nutmeg and pepper. Bring a brown or lake-trout to the boil in the appropriate amount of water. Remove the fish before it is completely cooked, put it on a covered plate.

Melt some butter in an (oval) pan, add a little cream and the chopped herbs, stirring all the time. Salt to taste.

Now lay the trout in the sauce, cover the pan and simmer gently.

When it is done, put the fish on a hot dish, pour the sauce over it and serve with green peas and boiled potatoes.

SPINY LOBSTERS BELLE EPOQUE

Chop finely one shallot and some parsley, put them into the pan and add butter and oil. As soon as they are browned, add tomato sauce and a glass of dry white wine. Stir well.

Remove the tails from small lobsters (150–200 g) and put them into the pan. Add salt and pepper, turn the heat up and simmer, stirring all the time.

When they are cooked, add brandy and ignite. Serve at once sprinkled with chopped parsley of chervil.

DEVILED SCAMPI

Melt some butter in the pan and add a finely chopped onion.

As soon as it begins to brown, add previously boiled and halved scampi. Sprinkle with salt, pepper and curry. Let them brown slightly.

Pour brandy into the pan, and set light to it.

Serve with quarters of lemon and fresh parsley.

---

* fillets of sole are prepared similarly: replace tomatoes with lemon juice

Dishes prepared at the guest's table

Meat

CALF'S KIDNEYS NAPOLEON

Melt butter in the pan, turn the heat up high and fry the thickly sliced kidneys. Add cognac and ignite. When the flame dies down, put the kidneys on a dish and keep them warm.

Add a spoonful of finely chopped, browned onion, broth and a dash of Worcester sauce to the sauce in the pan, bring it to the boil, then add a little cream.

Leave the sauce on the heat until it is thick then pour it over the kidneys.

CALF'S LIVER AMBASSADOR

Melt butter in the pan and add the tinly sliced liver. Brown it, turning the heat up.

When it is nearly done, pour cognac over it and ignite. Remove the liver and keep it warm on a dish.

Add broth and finely chopped onion to the gravy, boil it up, then stir in a spoonful of sour cream.

Pour the sauce over the liver.

MEDALLION OF VEAL DOMINIC

Put butter, rosemary, and a medallion of veal covered with a slice of ham in the pan. As soon as it begins to fry, remove the rosemary and add salt and pepper.

When it is done, pour on cognac. Finally add mushrooms and a sour cream sauce.

FILLET OF VEAL BELLE POMPADOUR

Melt butter in the pan, put the fillet slices in and brown over a high flame. When they are browned on both sides, pour in a generous amount of cognac and ignite. Remove the meat and keep it warm.

Add broth, let it boil, then add a spoonful of cream, stirring lightly, so that it thickens.

Just before serving, add a pinch of curry and then pour the sauce onto the slices of fillet.

FILLET STEAK VORONOV

Brown a knob of butter in the pan and lay the fairly thickly cut fillet steaks in it. Remove when they are browned and keep warm on a dish.

Add a few teaspoonfuls of mustard (of differend kinds if available) and cook for 2 or 3 minutes.

Put the steaks back into the pan, letting them absorb the sauce. Pour a liberal amount of brandy into the pan and serve.

Dishes prepared at the guest's table

FILLET STEAK SPLENDID

Heat some butter and a tablespoon of olive oil in a covered stewpan. Place the salted and lightly floured fillet steak in it. When it is browned, put it to one side.

Now prepare the sauce with the following ingredients: ½ glass of dry white wine; bayleaf, sage and rosemary; Worcester sauce; nutmeg and pepper.

Pour the wine into the saucepan, then add all the other ingredients, stirring well. When the sauce begins to thicken, add cream and some black olives.

Put the fillet steak back into the pan, cover and let it simmer. Finally check the seasoning and add salt if necessary.

Serve the steak on a slice of fried bread, coat with the sauce and garnish with the olives.

BEEF FILLET EN BOÎTE

Heat the stewpan and melt a knob of butter and a little oil. Do not put the fillet into the pan before it is really hot to prevent the juice of the meat from seeping.

Meanwhile in another pan prepare a mustard sauce using French mustard, a little Worcester sauce, nutmeg, salt, pepper, and a few drops of oil.

When the fillet is almost done add the sauce, turn the meat, prick it with a fork to allow the sauce to penetrate into the centre. Finally add cognac.

Serve directly from the stewpan, holding it close to the guest to enable him to enjoy the appetizing aroma.

Béarnaise sauce (or mustard) can be served with this dish, separately.

TOURNEDOS CATHERINA THE GREAT

Pour vodka on a cooked tenderloin steak, light it, cover and set aside.

Fry onions and parsley in butter. Add salt, pepper, curry, English mustard, Worcester sauce, and a little broth. When the sauce has thickened, pour it over the tournedos.

MARCO POLO SKEWERS

Thread on the skewers pieces of calf's liver and kidney alternated with pieces of bacon-fat and sage leaves. Put butter, salt, pepper, nutmeg and the skewers into the pan.

When they are done, pour whisky over them, ignite and serve flambé.

QUEEN SKEWERS

Prepare as for Marco Polo skewers, but use pre-cooked chicken and veal instead of liver and kidney.

CHICKEN MEPHISTOPHELES

Carve a roast chicken and keep it warm on a hotplate.

Melt some butter in the pan. Add a spoonful of French mustard and half a small tin of pâté de foie gras. Add 1 or 2 glasses of white wine and season with pepper, oregano, cayenne, curry and other spices to your liking.

Put the pieces of chicken into this sauce, pour on whisky and set light to it.

Lastly, add some cream and serve immediately.

Dishes prepared at the guest's table

FONDUE BOURGUIGNONNE

Fill a copper fondue-pot with olive oil and put it on the fondue stand. Cut a beef fillet into small cubes (approx. 150 g per person) and prepare the fondue forks or skewers.

Each guest skewers a meat cube, dips it into the boiling oil and fries it to his liking.

Mixed pickles, chips, and various sauces, such as ketchup, Worcester sauce, mayonnaise, tartare and béarnaise sauce may be served with the fondue.

CHINESE FONDUE

Proceed as with fondue bourguignonne, but use chicken broth instead of olive oil.

BACCHUS FONDUE

Cut veal fillets into small pieces (150 g per person). Heat a litre of white wine (do not let it boil) and add a whole onion, a bayleaf and a clove.

The same sauces as for Fondue bourguignonne can be served as side dishes.

Sweets

BANANAS FLAMBÉ

Prepare the bananas beforehand as follows: cut them lengthwise into two halves, flour them, dip in a beaten egg and then once more in flour. Brown them in butter and place them side by side in the pan.

In the dining-room put the pan onto the stand. Sprinkle the bananas generously with icing sugar, pour some kirsch ober them and ignite.

Keep spooning the kirsch over the bananas until the flame goes out.

BANANAS FLAMBÉ ELIZABETH

Heat castor sugar in the pan and when it just begins to caramelize add some knobs of butter, the juice of an orange and a glass of Grand Marnier (or another liqueur).

Put the halved bananas into the sauce and cook for 3 or 4 minutes. Now add a glass of cognac and ignite.

PEACHES FLAMBÉ VENUS

Melt some butter in the pan. Before it browns, put in halved or quartered tinned peaches.

Let them brown slightly, pour a glass of liqueur over them and ignite. Before the alcohol has completely evaporated, put out the flame with the lid of the pan. Remove the peaches and keep them warm.

Add the syrup to the remaining sauce, then some cream until the mixture becomes thick. Pour it over the peaches and serve.

Dishes prepared at the guest's table

GOURMET'S PEAR

Put halved pears and some butter mixed with sugar into the pan. Heat it well, then pour cognac over them, ignite and let the flame burn. Remove the pears and put them on a dish.

Pour a hot chocolate sauce into the rest of the sauce, mix well and add a littel cognac, if you like.

Coat the pears with this sauce and decorate with whipped cream.

PINEAPPLE HAWAIIAN PARADSE

Melt butter in the pan, then add a few lumps of sugar which have been previously rubbed with an orange peel. When the sugar has almost melted, add the tinned pineapple slices and brown slightly on both sides.

Pour on rum and ignite. Add the pineapple syrup and cook for another 3 or 4 minutes. Put 1 or 2 slices of pineapple onto each plate, garnish with a plum in the middle of each slice, pour the sauce over them and serve.

RUM OMELETTE CORDON BLEU

Heat the pan well, then put in a pre-cooked omelette, fold it in half, sprinkle generously with castor sugar and with a hot iron put a design on it for decorative effect.

When the pan is sufficiently hot, pour some rum in and ignite. Spoon the rum over the omelette several times. Serve it on a warm plate.

CRÊPES SUZETTE (I)

Prepare the following cream in advance: mix butter, icing sugar, Curaçao and the grated peel of an orange or tangerine.

In the dining-room put part of this mixture into the pan. As soon as it begins to boil, add the previously cooked pancakes, one at a time, and let them absorb the flavour. With a spoon and a fork fold each pancake in four and line them up on the edge of the pan.

Spoon the sauce over the pancakes and move them all to the middle of the pan.

Pour an orange liqueur (such as Grand Marnier or Curaçao) plus some other kind of the guest's choice over the pancakes, slant the pan and ignite. Sprinkle the burning pancakes with castor sugar, letting it shower over the pancakes for effect. It will crackle slightly as it burns. Allow 3 pancakes per person.

CRÊPES SUZETTE (II)

Let castor sugar caramelize slowly. Add some butter and a little orange juice, stirring continuosly.

Then rub lumps of sugar with orange peel and put them into the pan.

Sprinkle them with orange liqueur and kirsch and crush the lumps with a fork. Cook the sauce till it thickens.

Finally put in the pancakes, one at a time, and proceed as in the above recipe.

Glossary of drinks

Americano: aperitif consisting of equal quantities of bitters and Italian vermouth, diluted with soda

Angostura: the bark of a Venezuelan tree from which a bittertonic is extracted, often used in cocktails

Applejack: American for apple brandy

Armagnac: top-quality brandy, similar to cognac, from Armagnac, a region in the Gers department

Arrack: a spirit which is very similar to rum, distilled from rice. Imported from Java (Batavia arrack) and India.

Bacardi: white rum produced in Cuba

Bénédictine: find herbal liqueur made in the Benedictine monastery in Fécamp in Normandy. The abbreviation D.O.M. stands for "Deo Optimo Maximo".

Bourbon: American whisky chiefly distilled from corn (from Bourbon County in Kentucky)

Brandy: an alcoholic beverage distilled from wine or fermented fruit juice.

Calvados: apple brandy produced in Calvados in France

Cobbler: drink of wine or liqueur, sugar, lemon, pounded ice, and whatever fruit is in season

Cocktail: alcoholic drink made of various spirits mixed in a shaker with pounded ice

Cognac: high-quality French brandy produced in the Cognac area (Charente department). The choice variety is known as "fine champagne".

Cointreau: orange-flavoured French liqueur, similar to Curaçao; in cocktails it can be replaced by Triple sec.

Crème: liqueur with a high sugar content and a low alcohol content.

Curaçao: liqueur flavoured with the peel of bitter oranges, produced in the island of Curaçao in the Antilles

Dubonnet: French aperitif

Fizz: a refreshing drink, a mixture of a strong liqueur, sugar, lemon juice, and soda water. Gin fizz is the most famous of its kind.

Flip: drink made of a dessert wide (or a strong liqueur), sugar and a fresh egg-yolk mixed in the shaker

Gin (London gin): English colourless spirit flavoured with juniper berries

Grand Marnier: excellent French liqueur made from cognac and oranges

Grenadine: pomegranate syrup, bright red in colour

Highball: iced drink of spirits diluted with soda water

Kirsch: cherry brandy. Swiss and Black Forest kirsch are the most famous varieties.

Long drink: cold alcoholic drink diluted with soda and served in a tall glass

Ouzo: a Greek spirit flavoured with aniseed

Orange bitters: liquor used as a flavouring in cocktails

Pastis: French aperitif flavoured with aniseed

Pernod: French aperitif with aniseed and vermouth which is drunk diluted with water

Port: strong, sweet, fortified wine made in Oporto, city in Portugal

Rum: strong liquor distilled from sugar-cane; best-known varieties: Jamaica rum (dark-brown) and Cuban rum (light yellow)

Sake: national Japanese alcoholic drink distilled from rice, warmed before serving

Sambuca: Italian liqueur flavoured with aniseed, a typical local drink from Civitavecchia and Viterbo.

Sherry: a Spanish fortified wine (from the Spanish town of Jerez)

Syrup: thick sweet liquid made by dissolving sugar in boiling water

Soft drink: a non-alcoholic drink

Glossary of drinks

Sour: drink of spirits with lemon- or lime-juice and sugar
Straight whisky: American for neat whisky
Tequila: national Mexican liquor with a very high alcohol content made from an agave plant.
Triple sec: a sweet liqueur with an orange aroma, similar to Curaçao and Cointreau
Tumbler: drinking-glass without a handle or foot
Vermouth: strong sweet wine flavoured with wormwood; from the German Wermut (wormwood, absinth)
Vodka: a Russian or Polish spirit distilled from rye, wheat, barley, etc. The name is a diminuitive of the Russian voda (water)
Whisky: a spirit distilled from various grains and including the Scotch made from malted barley with a characteristic smoky flavour, the Irish distilled from fermented malt and subject to three distillations, the Canadian distilled from rye and barley and the American whisky made either from rye (rye whisky) or corn (bourbon)
Zest: orange or lemon peel used as a flavouring

Cocktails*

Gin-Cocktails

Martini dry
Gin	⁴⁄₅
French vermouth	¹⁄₅

Serve with an olive or lemon peel.
(Take whisky instead of gin
and you get a Manhattan).

Alexandra
Gin	¹⁄₃
Crème de cacao	¹⁄₃
Fresh cream	¹⁄₃

(Take brandy instead of gin
and you get an Alexander).

Bronx
Gin	³⁄₆
French vermouth	¹⁄₆
Italian vermouth	¹⁄₆
Orange juice	¹⁄₆

(Can be served with orange or lemon peel).

Dubonnet
Gin	¹⁄₂
Dubonnet	¹⁄₂

Serve with lemon peel.

Negroni
Gin	¹⁄₃
Italian vermouth	¹⁄₃
Bitters	¹⁄₃

Orange blossom
Gin	²⁄₃
Orange juice	¹⁄₃

(You can add a dash of grenadine).

Paradise
Gin	³⁄₆
Apricot brandy	¹⁄₆
Orange juice	²⁄₆

White lady
Gin	²⁄₄
Triple sec (or Cointreau)	¹⁄₄
Lemon juice	¹⁄₄

(Take brandy instead of gin
and you get a Sidecar).

Brandy-Cocktails

Sidecar
Brandy	²⁄₄
Triple sec (or Cointreau)	¹⁄₄
Lemon juice	¹⁄₄

(Take gin instead of brandy
and you get a White Lady).

Alexander
Brandy	¹⁄₃
Crème de cacao	¹⁄₃
Fresh cream	¹⁄₃

(Take gin instead of brandy
and you get an Alexandra).

Stinger
Brandy	²⁄₃
Crème de mente	¹⁄₃

Brandy cocktail
Brandy	1 glass
Angostura	2 dashes
Sugar syrup	1 teaspoolful

(Grenadine, curaçao or triple sec
are usable instead of sugar syrup).

---

* For dry cocktails use a larger quantity of the main spirit and add French instead of Italian vermouth.

Cocktails*

Rum-Coctails

Daiquiri
Cuban rum	5/6
Lemon juice	1/6
Sugar syrup (or grenadine)	1 teaspoonful

Bacardi
Bacardi rum	3/6
Lemon juice	1/6
Grenadine	1 teaspoonrul
Gin	2/6

Presidente
Bacardi rum	3/4
French vermouth	1/4
Grenadine	1/2 teaspoonful

Rum cocktail
Bacardi rum	1 glass
Angostura	1 dash
Sugar syrup	1/2 teaspoonful

Whisky-Cocktails

Manhattan
Canadian whisky	2/3
Italian vermouth	1/3
Angostura	1 dash

Serve with an olive.

Old-fashioned
Bourbon (or rye whisky)	1 glass
Angostura	2 dashes
Sugar	1 teaspoonful

Squeeze lemon peel on it
and garnish with a slice of orange.
(Take gin instead of whisky
and you get an Old-fashioned gin cocktail).

Rob Roy
Scotch whisky	2/3
Italian vermouth	1/3
Angostura	1 dash

Serve with a cherry.

Whisky cocktail
American whisky	1 glass
Angostura	2 dashes
Sugar syrup	1 teaspoonful

(Grenadine or curaçao are usable instead of sugar syrup).

Vodka-Cocktails

Bloody Mary
Vodka	1/2 glass
Tomato juice	1 1/2 glass
Lemon juice	1 teaspoonful

Serve in a tumbler with salt and paprika.

Vodka sour
Vodka	1 glass
Juice of half a lemon	
Sugar syrup	1 teaspoonful

(If you want a gin sour, a brandy sour or a whisky sour take these other spirits instead of vodka).

---

* For dry cocktails use a larger quantity of the main spirit and add French instead of Italian vermouth.